D1229082

Dedicated with love to my mom,
who always believed in me

CONTENTS

PREFACE

Anybody's Guide to Total Fitness, 12th edition, is a definitive blend of cutting-edge scientific research and reliable practical applications for creating an optimal health, fitness and wellness lifestyle. The 12th edition incorporates the recent U.S. Department of Health and Human Services Updated Physical Activity Guidelines as well as the revised American College of Cardiology and American Heart Association blood pressure guidelines. The text offers personalized instruction on how to customize exercise programs for high intensity interval training (HIIT), indoor cycling, aerobic kickboxing, circuit training, boot camp programs, and aquatic workouts. Plus, the 12th edition advances the original science-based Peripheral Heart Action (PHA) training method and 2 PHA workouts. As well, this new edition includes 12 great HIIT workouts and the highly effective biomotor functional power exercises. *Anybody's Guide to Total Fitness,* 12th edition, has a brand-new, over-the-top weight management section launching the 'inch by inch, it's a cinch' small changes approach to weight management success. It includes an all-inclusive summary on the lifestyle characteristics and habits of thousands of the real life biggest losers from the National Weight Control registry.

Specific advice on yoga, Pilates, and mind-body fitness is also provided. Readers will learn about several contemporary health issues including self-concept, substance abuse, responsible drinking, tobacco use, stress maintenance, technostress, creative problem solving, and time management. The 12th edition simplifies modern-day evidence on fitness trackers, cortisol and body weight, hydration for exercise, muscle soreness, metabolism, good sugars versus bad sugars, fat burner supplements, nutrient timing and energy balance. What really elevates *Anybody's Guide to Total Fitness,* 12th edition, is the over 125 biomechanically correct fitness photos. A full platform of flexibility, strength, core, stability ball, and targeted exercises are presented and explained. In addition, the 12th edition provides a newly written and modernistic question and answer section on health, weight management and exercise. An expanded, all-inclusive list of internet sources on fitness, health, wellness, aging, disease, fitness organizations provides great resources for additional readings and research. The online profile guide that accompanies the text is a behavioral modification planner and assessment supplement that promotes positive, self-directed goal attainment. Both inspirationally and practically, *Anybody's Guide to Total Fitness* 12th edition is your source for long-term health and fitness success.

ACKNOWLEDGMENTS

I would like to express my deep appreciation and gratitude to my original editorial advisory board of Dr. Carol L. Christensen, Dr. Craig J. Cisar, Dr. Gail G. Evans, Dr. Susan Kutner, Lori Leeds, R.P.T., Dr. Thomas A. MacLean, Dr. Susan Pate, Dr. Robert Pearl, Dr. Jay D. Pruzansky, Dr. Norman T. Reynolds, Richard V. Schroeder, M.S., and Dr. Phillip A. Sienna. Their advice, expertise, and thoughtful review of this book were invaluable.

I sincerely thank the following people who have made generous contributions to this project and deserve special acknowledgment: Emmanuel Athans, Molly Burke, Mert and Tanya Carpenter, Kim Drummond, Janice Earle, Carrie Ekins, Eric Finch, Dixie Fisher, Sue Forster-Cox, Marla Graves, Jerry Gonsalves, Jean Harding, Louise Herndon, Michael Le Doux, Shirley H. M. Reekie, Pauline Reimer, Joe Samuels, Wendy Russum, Dolores Sargent, Amy Scofield, Carol Stewart, Ph.D., Debbie Sporleder, Carol Sullivan, Pamela Staver, and Teri Wexted.

I would also like to thank the following special people who have been a source of inspiration and have guided me in countless ways: Covert Bailey, Dr. Barton Byers, Dr. Laurence Berkowitz, Ed and Shirley Burke, Don Callahan, Roy Cerrito, Dr. Barbara Conry, Yvonne Cotton, Peter and Kathie Davis, Justine Dineen, Anita Del Grande, Jerry Dollard, Ronda Gates, Dr. Telemachos A. Greanias, Dr. William F. Gustafson, Ellen Herbst, Dr. Vivian H. Heyward, Dr. Clair W. Jennett, DeAun Kizer, Bob Kravitz, Joyce Malone, Dr. Bruce Ogilvie, Lawrence R. Petulla, Marty Urand, and Lawrence Biscontini.

For their enthusiastic support, I am grateful to my friends at the Los Gatos Athletic Club, the faculty and staff of the Department of Kinesiology at San Jose State University, everyone at Aerobics Plus and the faculty and staff in Exercise Science at the University of New Mexico.

I am also deeply indebted to my friend Chuck Drummond for providing such wise counsel and friendship.

To Dr. Susan Pate, my original editor and lifetime friend, I thank you in a thousand different ways.

To Jill Pankey, my original graphic designer, I thank you for your artistic imagination, creative expression, and for the many hours of hard work you devoted to this original book.

In the 11th edition we introduced photographs to the book. I thank my outstanding photographer, Jacob Covell, and my fabulous models: Tony Nuñez, Kurt Escobar, Trisha McLain, Ludmila Malakhov, Vivian Thu Nguyen, Cecille Thomas, Olivia Thomas, Nicholas Beltz, and Mitch Silva.

Most importantly, I thank the many student readers of *Anybody's Guide to Total Fitness* who have been an incredible source of enthusiasm for me.

ABOUT THE AUTHOR

Len Kravitz, Ph.D., is a professor, researcher, and program coordinator of Exercise Science at the University of New Mexico where he was won the "The Presidential Award of Distinction" (2017) and "Outstanding Teacher of the Year" award (2004). Len was honored with the 1999 Canadian Fitness Professional "International Presenter of the Year," the 2006 Canadian Fitness Professional "Specialty Presenter of the Year" award, the American Council on Exercise 2006 "Fitness Educator of the Year," and the 2010 Global Award for his contributions to the Aquatic Exercise Association. Dr. Kravitz has authored more than 300 peer-review articles on health and fitness for several national publications and has been featured on CNN News, Dateline, and CBS This Morning.

Len Kravitz is a versatile movement specialist with a broad range of skills, which include competitive gymnastics at the national and international levels and professional theater/

© Jacob Covell

mime performances on stage and video. He is the creator of *Anybody's Workout, Anybody's 3-in-1 Workout, Anybody's Step Workout,* and the *SuperAbs* exercise videos, which have been featured in national magazines and TV shows. Len is the author of *HIIT Your Limit* and co-author of *Essentials of Eccentric Exercise.* Dr. Kravitz's innovative technique and teaching style have made him a sought-after lecturer for fitness professionals around the United States, Canada, Australia, Europe, Taiwan, Brazil, Thailand, and Japan.

WELCOME TO A HEALTHY WAY OF LIFE

Living and enjoying life to its fullest is a wonderful goal. And you can have it! Fitness is a way of life that allows you to function and perform at your best. It's a harmonic balance of prescribed exercise, healthy eating habits, preventative health care, effective stress management, and a common-sense lifestyle. Your level of fitness helps determine the quality of your life. You are in control of how you look, feel, and live.

The following information is based on sound physiological principles and research. With a minimal investment of your time, you can follow these concepts and create a fitness plan that will help you obtain the most from your life.

I have presented a specific aerobics program for you. You may wish to supplement it with a running, swimming, or cycling program of your own.

Be patient, use your knowledge, set your goals, listen to your body, and commit yourself to a healthy way of life.

© Jacob Covell

SECTION 1
Starting Out

© Jacob Covell

What Exercise Will Do for You

Benefits of a well-balanced health and fitness program that most people experience from regular exercise include:

○ A healthy appearance
○ Good posture and alignment
○ Fluid, easy movement
○ Stronger joints and firmer muscles
○ Lowered risk for low-back pain
○ A decreased susceptibility to injury
○ Fewer aches and pains
○ Improved mental awareness, self-esteem, and self-confidence
○ Improved ability to relax
○ Better handling of stress
○ Help in preventing and coping with depression
○ More restful sleep
○ Increased job productivity
○ More energy and vitality
○ An increased ability to enjoy life

New Scientific Evidence Shows Exercise Combats Many Health Conditions

Recent scientific research affirms that regular physical activity and exercise may help combat the following health conditions: coronary heart disease, type 2 diabetes (including insulin resistance, pre-diabetes, and gestational diabetes), obesity, metabolic syndrome, peripheral artery disease, hypertension, stroke, congestive heart failure, endothelial dysfunction (diminished functioning of the inner lining of blood vessels), dyslipidemia (abnormal blood lipid levels), osteoporosis, osteoarthritis, balance problems, bone fracture (and falls), rheumatoid arthritis, colon cancer, breast cancer, endometrial cancer, polycystic ovary syndrome (woman's levels of the sex hormones estrogen and progesterone are out of balance), nonalcoholic fatty liver disease, diverticulitis (pouches form in the wall of the colon), constipation, gallbladder diseases, sarcopenia (loss of muscle with aging), deep vein thrombosis (blood clot that forms in a vein deep in the body), accelerated biological aging, premature death, low cardiorespiratory fitness, cognitive dysfunction, depression, anxiety and pain.

© Jacob Covell

Specific Benefits from Regular Resistance Training

Resistance exercise, independently, has been shown to be very effective for improving well-being and reducing the risk of several progressive health conditions as shown below.

- Increase in bone mineral density in specific sites that are trained
- Improvement of resting systolic and diastolic blood pressure when elevated
- Enhanced physical function in activities of daily living
- Heightened cognitive abilities
- Improvement of self-esteem and self-concept
- Slowing of sarcopenia and age-related factors in skeletal muscle
- Better management and control of depression
- Some research has shown improvements in blood lipid profile to include lower triglycerides (blood fats), higher HDL (the good) cholesterol and lower LDL (the bad) cholesterol
- Improvement in insulin sensitivity and glycemic control
- Increase in resting metabolic rate

> **Did You Know?**
>
> The American Diabetes Association recommends resistance exercise for all of the major muscle groups, 3 days/week, progressing to 3 sets of 8 to 10 repetitions each.
>
> *Based on Westcott, W. L. (2015). Build muscle, improve health: Benefits associated with resistance exercise. ACSM's Health & Fitness Journal, 19(4), 22–27.

© Jacob Covell

Stickin' to It!

Ten Steps to Succeed in an Exercise Program

One of the biggest challenges with any exercise program is sticking to it. Movement is natural, but exercise is a unique behavior that we all have to learn. As you start exercising, don't let early awkwardness or uneven skill development get you down—it happens to everyone. In fact, you will be amazed by how fast you learn and adapt to exercise effectively and capably. To help you become a steadfast exercise enthusiast, I devised the following ten steps on how to succeed in an exercise program. They are drawn from the scientific literature and my many years in the fitness industry.

1. **Set goals before you begin.** Having short-term and long-term goals makes a big difference. For fitness goal setting, think of your short-term goals as daily, weekly, or even monthly targets, and consider your long-term goals as semiannual and/or annual ones. My philosophical approach to starting an exercise program is the following phrase: inch by inch, it's a cinch. To apply this approach to yourself, break up your goals into some really manageable stages. Also, as you progress in your exercise program feel free to revisit and modify your goals at any time. You are ready.

> **Did You Know?**
>
> Working out during the day when you have the most energy often yields the best fitness results.

2. **Reward yourself as you attain some of your goals.** Keep track of your progress. As you achieve some of the goals you have written out, reward yourself with a well-meaning gift, such as a book, new outfit, movie, new app, show, or—better yet—some new exercise gear.

3. **Regularly self-evaluate how your exercise program (and lifestyle) is progressing.** To evaluate your progress, I suggest you write (or type) out a health, fitness, and lifestyle evaluation list (See Student Profile Guide) that includes things you are doing right (not smoking, eating well, not abusing substances, etc.) and things you need to improve (not consistently exercising, neglecting to deal with stress, sleeping inconsistently, etc.). Next, self-assess ways you can shift more entries to the "right side". For instance, learning some yoga breathing techniques may help you manage your stress and improve your sleep patterns. Self-evaluation is a great way to consistently self-improve.

4. **Find a workout partner.** Research on sticking to an exercise program indicates we are more likely to adhere to daily exercise routines when we exercise with another person or persons. It's best to partner with someone whose fitness level and goals are similar to yours. But, if that's not possible, a partner who gives you support for your exercise program (whom you also support) is better than no partner. Discuss what exercise activities or fitness classes you both enjoy, and commit to participating in them as workout partners.

5. **Schedule your workouts on your daily and monthly calendar.** With your workout partner, schedule your exercise sessions three to five days per week. Treat your workout time like a special meeting that can't be cancelled (except for emergencies), because doing so will help ensure you don't just blow it off for other obligations and tasks. I am frequently asked if it is better to exercise in the early morning, mid-morning, afternoon, or evening. My reply is always the same: select a time of day that has the best chance of helping you succeed. And if you discover the time you've chosen doesn't seem to work, feel empowered to try another time. Let's face it: you, like most people, are juggling multiple school-related and family-related activities daily. Once you determine a time or times that are best for your workouts, be selfish about preserving that time for your workouts. Dedicate this time block to yourself.

6. **Get in tune with your body by "body checking."** Body checking is a technique I have used for many years, and something you can do readily. Let me explain how it works. Always assess how your body

reacts during your workout and recovers after your workout. If the exercise session feels too hard, immediately slow down or lighten the intensity. If it feels too easy, go ahead and challenge yourself a little more. If you are unusually tired after your workouts, you are most likely doing too much or your diet is insufficient to fuel your workouts. Body checking is a way of listening to your bodily signals during and after exercise and then responding. I call it body checking because your body is incredibly intelligent, and during exercise it is sending you hundreds of signals. Listen to these messages and respond appropriately! If you are just starting a new exercise program, it is always best to progress gradually. Over the years I've always told students and clients I've trained that the first several workouts should feel too easy. Let your body adjust to the workouts and build strength and stamina. Most fitness injuries come from people doing too much, too soon, too fast, and too hard; don't get trapped in this downward spiral, as it may lead to your early "retirement" from exercise. Learning body checking shows a real dedication to respecting your exercising body.

7. **Wear comfortable clothing and proper shoes.** Your exercise clothing should permit you to move freely and allow your body to cool itself. Be aware that some exercise clothing fabrics have chemicals that may not be safe during exercise. Some of the more exercise friendly fabrics include bamboo pulp, cotton, cotton blends, nylon, polyester, and spandex. Proper attire is important for exercise enjoyment and success.

8. **Plan your exercise at least one to two hours after a meal.** By waiting to work out after eating a meal, you will prevent stomach cramping and pain. Eating too close to exercise may also make you too tired; you don't want your digestive system competing with your muscles for energy. Prior to a workout, always choose foods that your body finds easy to digest.

9. **Be ready for some exercise speed bumps.** Yes, we all have speed bumps when it comes to exercise— even people who have been training for years. Most of these come in the form of a missed workout or a lapsed goal. First and foremost, don't get angry with yourself if you miss a workout or backslide on one of your goals. In fact, the first step is to forgive yourself for the lapse. Next, try to focus on what caused the lapse and how you may better deal with it in the future. For instance, if you start missing your workouts, perhaps you are scheduling them at the wrong time. Or, if you are too tired to exercise, it may be that you need to have a light snack a couple hours before your workout. Speed bumps are challenging, but they won't undo all the progress you've made. When experiencing an exercise speed bump, reflect and focus on the best way(s) for getting back on track.

10. **Consider using a fitness tracker.** Our world is flourishing with fitness trackers, mobile apps, and other wearable devices that calculate our daily movements and exercise. Some of the newer fitness products are quite accurate in measuring calories, steps, heart rate, and other physiological data. Another factor some of the newer trackers measure is a physiological factor known as heart rate variability. This factor informs you about the variation between heartbeats. A healthy heart has healthy heartbeat variability. Heart rate variability monitoring may be able to detect a person experiencing too much stress, overtraining, or a compromised immune system. Also, these fitness trackers really do inspire people to move more. Don't, however, expect trackers to help you automatically lose weight. Weight management requires learning new strategies to modify behaviors. At this time, there are few randomized controlled studies focusing on the impact of wearable technology on health behavior change. However, some trackers do include goal setting, self-monitoring, and feedback content that closely matches recommendations for positive behavior change. Therefore, the future of this technology has broad implications for use in fitness, clinical, public health and rehabilitation settings. So, consider trying a few of them out and see how they work for you. Most importantly, stay positive and believe in yourself. You are in control.

Five Key Components of Fitness

Your body is a complex organism designed for action. Being physically fit means that the heart, blood vessels, lungs, and muscles function at optimal efficiency. Following are five key components of health-related physical fitness with which you need to be concerned.

1. **Cardiorespiratory Endurance/Aerobic Conditioning** is the ability of the body's heart, lungs, blood vessels, and major muscle groups to persist in continuous rhythmic exercise such as brisk walking, jogging, swimming, aerobics, rowing, cycling, step training, skating, and cross-country skiing. Regular aerobic conditioning may prevent or reduce the likelihood of cardiovascular disease. Cardiorespiratory endurance is a vital component of health-related fitness.

> **Did You Know?**
>
> By giving up smoking, doing regular exercise, and cutting excess weight you can elevate your HDL (good) cholesterol.

2. **Muscular Strength** is the ability of the muscles to exert maximal or near maximal force against resistance. Stronger muscles protect the joints that they surround and reduce the incidence of injury from physical activity.

   An increase in muscle mass will also boost the body's metabolism.

© Jacob Covell

© Jacob Covell

3. **Muscular Endurance** is the ability of skeletal muscle to exert force (not necessarily maximal) over an extended period of time. Strength, skill, performance, speed of movement, and power are closely associated with this component. Muscular endurance helps to prevent injuries and improve posture.

4. **Flexibility** is the range of motion of the muscles and joints of the body. It has to do with your skeletal muscles' natural and conditioned ability to extend beyond their normal resting length. Increased flexibility will enhance performance and reduce the incidence of injury.

© Jacob Covell

© Jacob Covell

5. **Body Composition** is the relationship of percentage of body fat to lean body weight (muscle, bone, water, vital organs). Being overfat, which usually starts in childhood, has a limiting effect on the other components of fitness. High body fat is associated with a number of health problems including heart disease, high blood pressure, stroke, diabetes, cancer, and back pain.

© Jacob Covell

On Your Mark, Get Set…Wait!

Cardiovascular disease (CVD) is a broad term including diseases of the heart and blood vessels, such as heart attack, coronary artery disease, congestive heart failure, and stroke. Because CVD is the number-one killer of both women and men globally, identifying risk factors is important toward avoiding health problems. Consult a health or fitness practitioner before embarking on a strenuous program of exercise to determine your CVD risk.

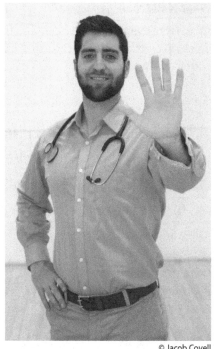

© Jacob Covell

RISK FACTOR	CRITERIA
Risk Factors	
Family history	Myocardial infarction or sudden death before 55 years of age in father or other male first-degree relative (i.e., brother or son) or before 65 years of age in mother or female first-degree relative (i.e., sister or daughter)
Cigarette smoking	Current cigarette smoker or those who quit within previous 6 months
High blood pressure	Systolic blood pressure 130–139 mmHg or diastolic blood pressure 80–89 mmHg (confirmed on two separate occasions) or taking antihypertensive medication
Hypercholesterolemia	Total serum cholesterol > 200 mg/dL, or high-density lipoprotein cholesterol < 40 mg/dL, or on lipid-lowering medication. If LDL-C is available, use > 130 mg/dL rather than total cholesterol.
Impaired fasting glucose	Fasting blood glucose of ≥ 110 mg/dL (confirmed on at least two separate occasions)
Obesity	Body Mass Index of ≥ 30 kg/m^2 or waist girth > 102 cm (40 inches) for men and > 88 cm (35 inches) for women or waist/hip ratio ≥ 0.95 for men and ≥ 0.86 for women
Sedentary lifestyle	Persons not participating in a regular exercise program or meeting the minimal physical activity recommendations from the U.S. Surgeon General's report (accumulating 30 minutes or more of moderate intensity [somewhat hard] physical activity on most days of the week)
Protective Factor	
High serum HDL-C	> 60 mg/dL of high density lipoprotein cholesterol

Metabolic Syndrome

What Is Metabolic Syndrome?

One out of every five Americans has metabolic syndrome. This is a cluster of health irregularities that raise a person's risk of heart disease, stroke and type 2 diabetes considerably. How do you know if you have metabolic syndrome?

A person has metabolic syndrome if they have at least three of the following:

1. Fasting blood sugar of at least 110 mg/dL
2. Systolic blood pressure 130–139 mmHg or diastolic blood pressure 80–89 mmHg
3. Triglycerides of at least 150 mg/dL
4. HDL (healthy) cholesterol of less than 50 mg/dL for women or less than 40 mg/dL for men
5. A waist circumference greater than 35 inches for women or greater than 40 inches for men

How Can You Prevent Metabolic Syndrome?

Daily aerobic exercise of at least 30 accumulated minutes at a moderate intensity is recommended. If you are overweight, weight loss is very beneficial. Eating a heart healthy diet is also encouraged. This includes eating less saturated fat in your diet. Also, limit your consumption of butter, cheese, whole milk and ice cream. Eat more foods rich in healthy protein such as chicken, seafood, eggs, nuts, lean beef and beans.

In addition, eat more fresh fruits and vegetables and include more whole grain fiber containing foods, which have less of an impact on blood glucose levels. Select more polyunsaturated fats such as vegetable oils, salad dressings, nuts and fish foods. Lastly, try to avoid refined carbohydrates such as cakes and cookies.

© Jacob Covell

Blood Pressure

Recently, at the American Heart Association annual meeting in Anaheim, CA, the American College of Cardiology and American Heart Association released their new high blood pressure (i.e., hypertension) guidelines (See at end of this section). The updated classifications now categorize hypertension stage one as resting systolic blood pressure of 130–139 mmHg or a resting diastolic blood pressure of 80–89 mmHg. This updated criteria raises the previous prevalence of adults with hypertension from a reported 32 percent to 46 percent in the United States. From a health perspective, for the last 100 years scientists have observed a strong association with high blood pressure and the risk of clinical health complications (i.e., high cholesterol, kidney disease, obesity) and death from stroke and heart disease. Research indicates that >50 percent of deaths from coronary heart disease and stroke occur among individuals with hypertension. The rationale for the new guidelines is based from a preponderance of studies showing a high association between elevated systolic and diastolic blood pressure to cardiovascular disease.

Tips to Help You Lower Your Blood Pressure (if above normal)

1. **Lose Extra Weight:** If overweight, for every 20 lbs. you lose there is a drop of about 5 to 20 points in your systolic blood pressure.
2. **Eat Less Saturated Fat in Your Diet:** Choose more vegetables, fruits and low-fat dairy foods in your diet.
3. **Exercise Daily:** Shoot for at least 30 minutes of moderate intensity exercise on most days of the week. This can be continuous or accumulated minutes (i.e., such as three 10-minute walks during the day).
4. **Reduce Sodium Intake:** Eat no more than 2,400 mg of sodium per day with an optimal goal of keeping sodium intake to about 1,500 mg.
5. **Limit Alcohol Consumption:** If you do drink, have no more than two drinks per day for men and one for women. Examples of one drink are a 12-ounce beer, 5 ounces of wine, or 1.5 ounces of 80-proof whiskey.

TAKE NOTE: If your blood pressure varies a lot, make sure it is being measured correctly. You should be seated quietly for at least five minutes in a chair, feet on the floor, with your arm supported at the height of your heart. At least two measurements should be taken. Some persons have what is referred to as "office hypertension" or "white coat hypertension" which is a rise in blood pressure due to nervousness from just being at a doctor's office. If this is you, take some extra minutes to relax before measurements.

Blood Pressure Guidelines

BP CATEGORY	SYSTOLIC BP		DIASTOLIC BP
Normal	< 120 mmHg	AND	< 80 mmHg
Elevated	120–139 mmHg	AND	< 80 mmHg
Hypertension (High Blood Pressure)			
Stage 1	130–139 mmHg	OR	80–89 mmHg
Stage 2	≥ 140 mmHg	OR	≥ 90 mmHg
Blood pressure (BP) is based on ≥2 careful readings on ≥2 occasions. Source: Whelton et al., 2017.			

Type 2 Diabetes

Aerobic Exercise and Resistance Training Are Best!

According to the World Health Organization, the global prevalence of diabetes is estimated to be 9% among adults aged 18 years of age. The U.S. Centers for Disease Control reports that more than 100 million Americans have prediabetes or diabetes and the majority of people with prediabetes are unaware they have it. Left untreated, 15–30% of people with pre-diabetes will develop diabetes within 5 years. Pre-diabetes can be reversed with regular exercise, weight loss (if overweight), a healthy diet (limiting sugar and saturated fats intake), and avoiding tobacco use. Aerobic training has been the traditional exercise intervention for improving metabolic profiles in persons with type 2 diabetes. Recently, resistance training has gained much attention for its value in improving glycemic control. Resistance exercise promotes glucose utilization by an increase in glucose transporters and more insulin receptors on the muscle cell. So, for optimal prediabetes and type 2 diabetes prevention and or management, definitely include aerobic and resistance training workouts throughout the week.

What Is the Hemoglobin A1c (HbA$_{1c}$) and eAG?

Hemoglobin, the oxygen carrying protein inside a red blood cell sometimes joins (or glycates) with the glucose in the bloodstream. The more glucose in the blood will result in more hemoglobin becoming glycated. Hemoglobin A$_{1c}$ (the 'A' stands for adult and the 1c is the component on hemoglobin the glucose binds) provides an average of blood sugar control over the past two to three months. It is used (along with daily monitoring) to make adjustments in a person's diabetes medicines and lifestyle. A$_{1c}$ is reported as a percent (i.e., 7%). The eAG, or 'estimated average glucose' is a unit similar to what one regularly reads in self-monitoring blood glucose. The eAG uses the same units (mg/dl) as a glucose meter. Similar to the A$_{1c}$, the eAG shows the average blood sugar has been over the previous two to three months.

The normal range for the hemoglobin A$_{1c}$ test, for persons without diabetes is between 4% and 5.6%. Hemoglobin A$_{1c}$ levels between 5.7% and 6.4% indicate an increased risk of diabetes referred to as prediabetes. A person with A$_{1c}$ of 6.5% or higher has diabetes. The goal for people with diabetes is a hemoglobin A$_{1c}$ less than 7%.

© Jacob Covell

How Fit Are You?

Here are some simple self-assessment tests to help determine or monitor your level of fitness. Periodically retest yourself to monitor your progress. STOP if you feel any nausea, discomfort, dizziness, or breathlessness. Perform the test on another day.

© Jacob Covell

© Jacob Covell

© Jacob Covell

© Jacob Covell

1.5-Mile Run Test

1. Establish a distance of 1.5 miles. This is six laps around most school tracks (which are usually one-quarter mile).

2. Use a stopwatch to time yourself.

3. Warm up with some easy jogging and gentle stretching before you start.

4. Cover the distance as fast as you can (running/walking). Cool down gradually at the conclusion with brisk walking for several minutes.

5. Record score and rating in the *Student Profile Guide*.

© Stepan Bormotov/Shutterstock.com

Rating the 1.5-Mile Run Time (Minutes)							
FITNESS CATEGORY		**AGE (YEARS)**					
		13–19	20–29	30–39	40–49	50–59	60+
I. Very poor	(men)	>15:31*	>16:01	>16:31	>17:31	>19:01	>20:01
	(women)	>18:31	>19:01	>19:31	>20:01	>20:31	>21:01
II. Poor	(men)	12:11–15:30	14:01–16:00	14:44–16:30	15:36–17:30	17:01–19:00	19:01–20:00
	(women)	16:55–18:30	18:31–19:00	19:01–19:30	19:01–20:00	20:01–20:30	21:00–21:31
III. Fair	(men)	10:49–12:10	12:01–14:00	12:31–14:45	13:01–15:35	14:31–17:00	16:16–19:00
	(women)	14:31–16:54	15:55–18:30	16:31–19:00	17:31–19:30	19:01–20:00	19:31–20:30
IV. Good	(men)	9:41–10:48	10:46–12:00	11:01–12:30	11:31–13:00	12:31–14:30	14:00–16:15
	(women)	12:30–14:30	13:31–15:54	14:31–16:30	15:56–17:30	16:31–19:00	17:31–19:30
V. Excellent	(men)	8:37–9:40	9:45–10:45	10:00–11:00	10:30–11:30	11:00–12:30	11:15–13:59
	(women)	11:50–12:29	12:30–13:30	13:00–14:30	13:45–15:55	14:30–16:30	16:30–17:30
VI. Superior	(men)	<8:37	<9:45	<10:00	<10:30	<11:00	<11:15
	(women)	<11:50	<12:30	<13:00	<13:45	<14:30	<16:30

< Means "less than"; > means "more than."

"Ratings Based on 1.5 Mile Run" from AEROBICS PROGRAM/ by Kenneth H. Cooper, copyright © 1982 by Kenneth H. Cooper. Used by permission of Bantam Books, an imprint of Random House, a division of Penguin Random House LLC. All rights reserved.

Rockport Fitness Walking Test

The Rockport Walking Institute has developed a walking test to assess maximal cardiorespiratory fitness (VO_2max) for men and women. It is helpful to do this test with a workout partner. Classes often do this test in two groups. A heart rate monitor (if available) and a watch are needed for this aerobic test.

1. Find a 1-mile course that is flat, uninterrupted, and correctly measured. A quarter-mile track is preferable for the outdoors.

2. Walk 1 mile as quickly and comfortably as possible and have your workout partner record your time at the finish mark to the closest second. For example, if a person finishes in 13 minutes and 35 seconds, the time is converted to the nearest hundredth minute by dividing the seconds (35) by 60 seconds. Thus, the time is 13.55 minutes.

© Jacob Covell

3. If using a heart rate monitor, get your heart rate the instant you cross the 1-mile mark. If taking a pulse, upon crossing the finish mark immediately take a heart rate by counting your pulse for 15 seconds. Multiply that number by four to get your heart rate for one minute.

4. You can also do this test inside, especially during unpleasant weather. Walk 1 mile as fast as you can by adjusting the speed of the treadmill. Make sure you do not jog or run and keep the treadmill grade at 0% for the test. Record the time from the computer display and take your heart rate with a heart rate monitor or by taking your pulse.

5. Calculate your VO_2max using the following equation.

6. VO_2max (ml/kg/min) = 132.853 − (0.0769 × weight) − (0.3877 × age) + (6.315 × gender) − (3.2649 × time) − (0.1565 × heart rate)

Where:

a. Time is expressed in minutes and 100ths of a minute
b. Weight is in pounds (lbs)
c. Gender Male = 1 and Female = 0
d. Heart rate is in beats/minute
e. Age is in years

Example VO$_2$max Calculations for a Female and Male:

For a 22-year-old Female who weighs 140 lbs who completed the Rockport Walk Test in 13 minutes and 35 seconds, or 13.55 minutes, with a heart rate of 150 beats per minute the calculation would be as follows:

$$132.853 - (0.0769 \times 140) - (0.3877 \times 22) + (6.315 \times 0) - (3.2649 \times 13.55) - (0.1565 \times 150)$$
$$\text{VO}_2\text{max (ml/kg/min)} = 45.73 \text{ ml/kg/min}$$

For a 22-year-old Male who weighs 140 lbs who completed the Rockport Walk Test in 13 minutes and 35 seconds, or 13.55 minutes, with a heart rate of 150 beats per minute the calculation would be as follows:

$$132.853 - (0.0769 \times 140) - (0.3877 \times 22) + (6.315 \times 1) - (3.2649 \times 13.55) - (0.1565 \times 150)$$
$$\text{VO}_2\text{max (ml/kg/min)} = 52.05 \text{ ml/kg/min}$$

Use the charts below to classify your cardiorespiratory fitness.

7. Record score and rating in the *Student Profile Guide*.

MALES: CARDIORESPIRATORY FITNESS CLASSIFICATION: VO$_2$MAX (ML/KG/MIN)						
Age	Superior	Excellent	Very Good	Good	Fair	Poor
20–30	>60	54–59	48–53	45–47	37–44	≤36
31–40	>56	50–55	45–49	39–44	34–38	≤33
41–50	>50	46–49	40–45	36–39	30–35	≤29
51–60	>46	42–45	37–41	33–36	28–32	≤27

FEMALES: CARDIORESPIRATORY FITNESS CLASSIFICATION: VO$_2$MAX (ML/KG/MIN)						
Age	Superior	Excellent	Very Good	Good	Fair	Poor
20–30	>50	46–49	42–45	36–41	32–35	≤31
31–40	>46	42–45	38–41	33–37	28–32	≤27
41–50	>41	38–40	34–37	28–33	25–27	≤24
51–60	>37	32–36	29–31	26–28	22–25	≤21
Tables derived from graphs by Shvartz, E. and Reibold, R.C. Aerobic fitness norms for males and females aged 6 to 75 years: A review. Aviation, Space, and Environmental Medicine, 61, 3–11						

Muscular Strength and Endurance

Abdominal Strength and Endurance Test

1. Lie on your back with your hands either supporting your head or across your chest.

2. Keep your legs bent at the knees, with the feet flat on the floor about 6 to 10 inches from your buttocks.

3. To perform the "crunch," curl your trunk so that your shoulder blades come off the floor. (Your lower back stays on the floor.) Keep the movements smooth.

4. To take the test, count the number of "crunches" you can do for one minute.

5. Record results and rating in the *Student Profile Guide*.

© Jacob Covell

RATING FOR ABDOMINAL STRENGTH AND ENDURANCE TEST	
Category	Results
Excellent	60 crunches or more
Very Good	50 to 59 crunches
Good	42 to 49 crunches
Fair	34 to 41 crunches
Poor	Less than 34 crunches

Upper Torso Muscular Endurance

The push-up test measures upper-body muscular endurance, specifically in the chest (pectoralis major muscle group), shoulder (anterior deltoids), and arms (triceps). Here are the steps to follow:

1. Begin by lying face down on mat or floor with hands placed shoulder width apart. Keep fingers pointed forward and elbows pointed backward.

2. Push upward to a full extension with the arms, keeping the body straight.

3. Lower so the chest to the thighs slightly make contact to the floor or mat.

4. The push-up test is not timed, so students are encouraged to complete each push-up at a comfortable rate, until fatigue or no more CORRECT push-ups can be performed.

5. Stopping or resting is not allowed during the push-up test. This ends the test.

6. Push-ups performed with the spine sagging downward or buttocks protruding upward are not counted.

© Jacob Covell

PUSH-UP PERCENTILE NORMS FOR MEN AND WOMEN		
Percentile	Norms for Men	Norms for Women
< 20	< 15	< 3
20–39	15–19	3–6
40–59	20–25	7–9
60–79	26–31	10–14
80–100	32–64	15–26

Adapted from: Arupendra Mozumdar, Gary Liguori & Ted A. Baumgartner (2010). Additional Revised Push-Up Test Norms for College Students, Measurement in Physical Education and Exercise Science, 14:1, 61-66, DOI: 10.1080/10913670903484835
Norms are based on college males and females (ages 18–19 yrs).

Flexibility

Sit-and-Reach Test

Flexibility is specific. This means that the degree of flexibility in one joint will not necessarily be the same in other joints of the body. Because a lack of flexibility in the lower back, back of the legs, and hips is a contributing cause for 80 percent of the low back pain in the U.S. adult population, this flexibility test was chosen.

1. Sit with your legs extended in front of you. Keep your feel perpendicular to the floor. Place a ruler along your legs on the floor.

2. Slowly stretch forward, reaching toward (or past) your toes and hold. (Do not bounce!) Keep your legs straight but not locked.

3. It is best to do this several times for practice, gently stretching further toward your point of limitation.

4. Record results and rating in the *Student Profile Guide*.

© Jacob Covell

RATINGS FOR THE SIT-AND-REACH TEST	
Category	Results
Excellent	7 inches or more past the toes
Very Good	4 to 7 inches past the toes
Good	1 to 4 inches past the toes
Fair	2 inches from in front of the toes to 1 inch past
Poor	More than 2 inches in front of the toes
A limitation of this sit-and-reach test is that it does not differentiate between a person with short arms and/or long legs and someone with long arms and/or short legs. However, this test is appropriate to monitor flexibility changes over time.	

Body Composition

Skinfold Caliper Measurement

Approximately one-third of the fat in the body is located just under the skin and is closely correlated to total body fat. Researchers have demonstrated that this skinfold fat is distributed differently in men and women and, for that reason, skinfold measurements are taken at different body locations. Skinfolds should not be taken immediately after exercise, because the shift of body fluids will increase the skinfold size.

There are several practical and inexpensive skinfold calipers available for body composition analysis. To take a skinfold measurement,

1. Grasp the anatomical site with the thumb and index finger.

2. Lift the skinfold away from the site to make sure no muscle is caught in the fold.

3. Place the caliper one-half inch below the thumb and index finger.

4. Allow the caliper to stabilize for a few seconds before reading. Take at least three measurements, and record the average.

5. Total the average of your skinfolds.

6. Determine your percentage of body fat by placing a straightedge from your age to the sum of the three skinfolds on the nomogram. The recommended percentage of body fat is 16 to 28 percent for a woman (18–34 years) and 5 to 15 percent for a man (18–34 years). There is an error factor of plus or minus 3 to 5 percent with skinfold body composition assessment.

7. Record the results and rating in the *Student Profile Guide*.

Did You Know?

Your body has about 47 days of storage fat.

Did You Know?

The loss of muscle mass with age and inactivity is called sarcopenia.

Did You Know?

The cell structure of the skeleton completely rejuvenates itself every 10 years.

Skinfolds are conventionally taken on the right side of the body. Here is how to find the anatomical skinfold sites:

- ○ **Chest**—the fold over the side border of the pectoralis major
- ○ **Abdomen**—vertical fold adjacent to the umbilicus
- ○ **Thigh**—vertical fold on the front part of the thigh midway between the hip and knee joint
- ○ **Triceps**—vertical fold on the back of the arm midway between the shoulder and elbow (arm held straight and relaxed)
- ○ **Suprailium**—diagonal fold above the crest of the ilium

Anatomical Skinfold Sites

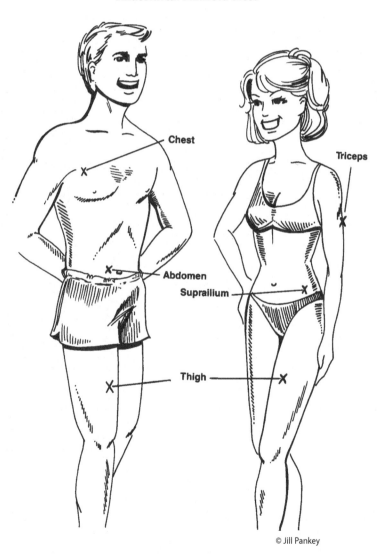

Chest

Triceps

Abdomen

Suprailium

Thigh

© Jill Pankey

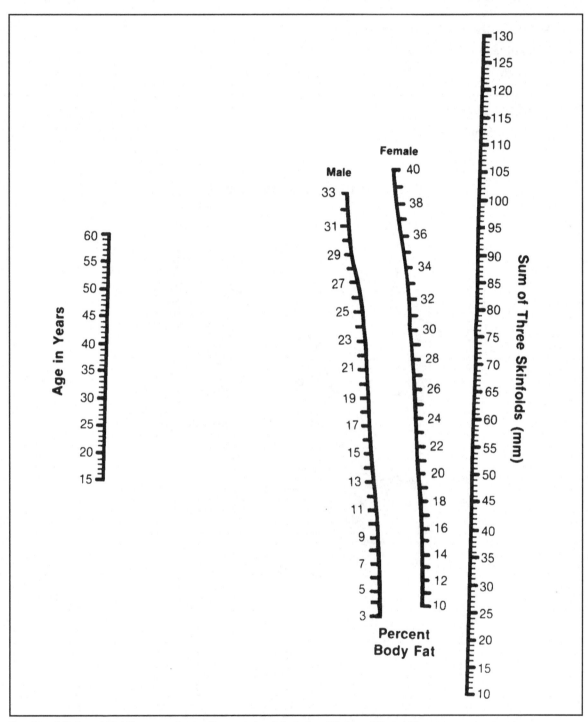

From Baun, W.B., Baun, M.R. A Nomogram. Reprinted by permission of the *Society of Health and Physical Educators*, www.shapeamerica.org

The "S.P.O.R.T." Principle

Fitness conditioning involves the "S.P.O.R.T." principle: Specificity, Progression, Overload, Reversibility, and Training Effect.

Specificity: Specificity takes the guesswork out of training. Your body will adapt to the specific type of training you choose. If you want to run marathons, you've got to train long distances. If you wish to build muscles, you must do intense weight training. Identify your goals and get started.

Progression: Challenge your body's abilities gradually and regularly. Let your body adapt to its new capability, and then you can progress some more. (Injuries happen from trying to do too much, too soon, too hard, and too fast.)

Overload: You "overload" by increasing the intensity, duration, or frequency of your established level of exercise. For instance, you may do aerobics longer, more times a week, or at a more intense level. When your exercise program becomes easier and somewhat routine, it is often a good time to overload. Overload your exercise program in increments of about 5 percent of your present ability.

Reversibility: You can't store the benefits of exercise. If you stop exercising there will be a marked decrease in skill, endurance, and strength from your previous level. So keep it up!

Training Effect: As you specifically train for a certain activity, you gradually and progressively improve your body's fitness capacity. The resulting increase in muscular and cardiorespiratory conditioning is the training effect.

Your final phase is to **MAINTAIN** this newly acquired level of health throughout your lifetime. You can do it!

© Jacob Covell

The Formula for Aerobic Fitness

To benefit from a sound cardiorespiratory program, follow the "F.I.T." formula. "F.I.T." stands for Frequency, Intensity, and Time.

Frequency: For optimal results, perform your aerobic activity three to five times a week (preferably every other day). If you choose to exercise more, make sure you rest at least one day each week to prevent any injuries from overuse!

Intensity: Your intensity should be 50 percent to 85 percent of your personalized training zone. For beginners in good health, 60 percent to 70 percent of your training zone is encouraged.

Time: The time or duration should gradually build up to between 20 and 60 minutes of continuous or intermittent activity (10 minute bouts accumulated throughout the day).

> **Did You Know?**
>
> A person's maximal heart rate gradually decreases with aging.

Heart Rate Monitoring

Monitoring your heart rate is a very simple, practical, and safe way to understand your exertion during aerobics. You will improve your cardiorespiratory system if you train at 60 percent to 85 percent of your personalized target zone. To estimate your target zone, you must first calculate your maximum heart rate and your resting heart rate. Your maximum heart rate (the fastest your heart will beat) can be estimated with the equation $208 - (0.7 \times \text{Age in Years})$. Resting heart rate is defined as the average heart rate (per minute) prior to initiating any physical activity. It is often measured in the morning, after waking up, and prior to

PERSONALIZED TARGET ZONE		
Your Estimated Maximum Heart Rate (MHR)	$208 - (0.7 \times \text{Age in Years})$	
Your resting heart rate	−72	
Subtract resting heart rate from estimated MHR	115	
Multiply by	60%	85%
Equals	69	98
Add resting heart rate	+72	+72
Equals exercise heart rate	141	170
	Target Zone	

PERSONALIZED TARGET ZONE WITH A 30-YEAR-OLD PERSON		
Your Estimated Maximum Heart Rate (MHR)	208 − (0.7 x Age in Years) = 187	
Your resting heart rate		
Subtract resting heart rate from estimated MHR		
Multiply by	60%	85%
Equals		
Add resting heart rate		
Equals exercise heart rate		
	Target Zone	

physical activity. Here's how a 30-year-old individual with a resting heart rate of 72 would estimate her/his personalized target zone.

Did You Know?

The mitochondrion is where all energy reactions take place in cells.

1. Find your pulse with your index and middle fingers pressed gently on your wrist (on the inner edge of the wrist below the base of the thumb) or neck (below the ear along the jaw) and count for 10 seconds.

2. Multiply by 6 to find the beats per minute. Pulse monitoring at the wrist is recommended because you can inadvertently press too hard on the neck and cause a slowing of the heart rate.

3. Monitor your heart rate before, after three to five minutes of aerobic exercise, and on completion of an aerobic section. Keep moving while you take your exercise pulse.

Some students find it easy to calculate their personalized target zone for a 10-second count. To do this, divide your exercise heart rate by 6. For instance, if your personalized target zone is 150 beats per minute to 180 beats per minute, your 10-second count would be determined as follows: 150/6 = 25; 180/6 = 30. So, if you do a 10-second pulse check while exercising, your heart rate should be between 25 and 30.

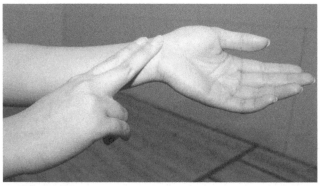

Finding the Pulse   © Jacob Covell

Perceived Exertion

You can also monitor exercise intensity through the use of perceived exertion. With perceived exertion, you interpret various body sensations such as heart rate, muscle and joint sensations, breathing intensity, and body temperature, and subjectively estimate your exercise intensity. A model that corresponds exercise heart rate with perceived exertion has been developed by Gunnar Borg, a Swedish physiologist. Notice that by adding a "0" to the numbers of the perceived exertion scale, it correlates to your exercise heart rate intensity. This is a great way to learn to listen to your body and compare your results to your counted heart rate. The American College of Sports Medicine recommends training in the 12 to 16 range of the perceived exertion scale to improve your aerobic capacity.

Talk Test

A very easy and accurate way to know if you are in your optimal aerobic training intensity is to perform the 'talk test'. If you can cite the 'Pledge of Allegiance' (or any 35 word phrase) with mild difficulty while doing your aerobic workout you are probably in the desired aerobic exercise intensity range.

Rate of Perceived Exertion Scale

6	
7	Very, very light
8	
9	Very light
10	
11	Fairly light
12	
13	Somewhat hard
14	
15	Hard
16	
17	Very hard
18	
19	Very, very hard
20	

From Borg, G. "Perceived Exertion: A Note on History and Methods."
Medicine and Science in Sports and Exercise 5:90–93, 1983.

All about Strength, Function, and Core

It has been well documented that the implementation of an appropriate resistance training program elicits many health benefits throughout a wide range of age, gender, fitness level and health status. These benefits include positive adaptations in muscular strength, muscular endurance, body composition and successful management of several chronic diseases, including diabetes mellitus, obesity, hypertension, bone and joint diseases (osteoporosis and osteoarthritis), and depression. The American College of Sports Medicine (ACSM) currently recommends that a healthy adult perform resistance training 2–3 days per week involving the major muscle groups of the body. Several training variables exist in designing high-quality resistance training programs such as various movement patterns, number of sets, number of repetitions, training load and rest periods. One principle approach for the organization of a training program is periodization. Periodization training may be characterized as alterations of volume (repetitions × sets), intensity (load), exercise selection and rest (between sets and workouts) in distinctive cycles to optimally improve musculoskeletal fitness.

Your overall strength is determined by numerous factors, including the intensity of training you regularly do, the predominant muscle fiber type of your muscles, hormonal levels, tendon insertion points, body proportions, and neurological efficiency. Here are some key terms and concepts to know about strength training.

A **concentric muscle action** (or contraction) describes a muscle going through a shortening motion as it overcomes the resistance.

During **eccentric muscle actions** (or contractions), the muscle lengthens as it resists the load. So, if you examine a person doing a biceps curl exercise, the upward phase of the movement is the concentric action, and the lowering phase of the movement is the eccentric action.

An **isometric action** (or contraction) is the amount of strength an individual can exhibit at a single point in the range of motion. With isometric actions, there is no limb movement or change in the joint angle. Just holding a weight in one position is an example of isometric strength.

Speed strength is a term that is interchangeable with the term power. Speed strength refers to the maximum force exhibited over a distance at a certain speed of movement. Examples of speed strength in sports include throwing a javelin and striking a punching bag.

Absolute strength is the maximal amount of weight that an individual can lift at one time. It is sometimes referred to as the one-repetition maximum, abbreviated 1RM.

Relative strength is a useful method for comparing the strength between different individuals. It is the ratio of the amount weight lifted to total body weight. For example, if a person can do a one repetition maximum biceps curl with 50 lbs. and weighs 130 lbs., what is the relative strength for this muscle group? To solve, set up a ratio and compute: 50 lbs./130 lbs. = .38. Relative strength is reported as a percentage, so multiplying by 100 will make this answer 38 percent for the relative strength of the biceps muscles.

Functional strength is a very popular term now used in fitness and sports. In fitness, functional strength applies to doing exercises that will enhance a person's ability to execute everyday activities. Some professionals also use the term **meaningful exercise** to describe functional strength. With functional strength, exercises are chosen that are task-specific to help a person perform better in daily life. Numerous exercises throughout this text offer significant functional strength benefits.

In sports, functional strength is used to enhance an athlete's sports performance. For recreational and competitive athletes, trainers and coaches try to duplicate the range of motion (or a portion of the range) with an exercise. For instance, a push-up is excellent for developing the strength of the shoulder joint, yet not the best functional exercise choice for training a golfer. When working with a golfer, the trainer might design an exercise that goes through more of a diagonal pathway, such as the motion of swinging a golf club.

Core strength or core stability training is a relatively new type of strength training in the health and fitness industry. Core training involves exercises that strengthen the deep spinal muscles. These are the deep abdominal and lower back muscles surrounding the spine, often referred to as the intrinsic muscles. The purpose of core training is to spare the spine from damage. Stability training creates a stable and mobile lower back. Development of core strength leads to a greater enjoyment of exercise participation and improvement in exercise performance. Several exercises in this text have been included to improve core strength.

© Jacob Covell

How Do Muscles Grow?

Muscles are of great interest to exercise enthusiasts. Your muscles attach to the skeleton and contract continuously during exercise. Muscles are powered by ATP, which comes from the aerobic and anaerobic energy systems. Your bones provide the structure for the muscles to do their work, enabling your body to move. Think of muscles as the engines driving your body's movements and the skeleton as a complex arrangement of levers, fulcrums, and force arms that carry out the movements. As you continue to challenge the muscles of your body, they rapidly learn and adapt to work harder and function better. Muscle growth, which is called muscle hypertrophy, occurs when your muscle fibers increase in their diameter size. In people, the mechanisms for the muscle size to increase is due to a thickening of the contractile proteins as well as an addition of more contractile proteins. In addition, there is an increase in the fluid (called sarcoplasm) region of the muscle. Note that in people there is no change in the number of muscle fibers, with hypertrophy, just the contractile proteins and fluid within the muscle fiber.

It is important to note that strength gains that occur the first couple of months of any resistance training program are primarily neural adaptations. In the early training phases of resistance training the muscle is acquiring greater input signals from the nerves, referred to as neural drive.

What Training Methods Promote Muscle Growth?

Some of the following body building training methods promote muscle growth.

Descending Weight Sets or Drop Sets

Here is an example of doing descending weight sets or drop sets. An exerciser may do 8 repetitions of dumbbell lateral raises with 30 lbs to momentary muscular fatigue (MMF), where she/he can't do another repetition, and then put the dumbbells down and complete 8 repetitions with 25 lbs to MMF and then drop to 8 repetitions of 20 lbs to MMF. A sequential drop of 10–25% in weight would be appropriate with this technique.

Eccentric Training

With eccentric training the exercisers lifts the weight in 1 second and lowers the weight in 3–4 seconds. One popular eccentric training technique is the 'supramaximal technique,' where the exercise enthusiast lifts a weight (with the aid of a workout partner or personal trainer) that is 105% to 120% of their normal weight and then lowers the weight slowly in 3–4 seconds.

© Jacob Covell

Forced Repetitions

With the spotting aid of a workout partner or personal trainer, complete 2–4 extra repetitions after reaching MMF on a set.

Super Sets

Super sets are any two sets that are performed in sequence (with no rest between exercises). Possible super set strategies (and examples of each) include agonist/antagonist (biceps curl and triceps extension), opposite action (chest fly and seated row), upper body/lower body (chest press and leg press), lower body only (lunge and heel raise) and upper body only (fly and chest press).

Did You Know?

The only joint in the human body with 360 degrees of rotation is the shoulder.

Did You Know?

Cessation of cigarette smoking is the single most preventable cause of death.

Did You Know?

The average foot walks more than a thousand miles a year.

Did You Know?

The single most important thing you can do to prevent the transmission of infectious organisms is washing your hands often.

The Ten Rules of Strength Training

Doing your exercises is not enough. It's doing them right that really counts. Follow these 10 rules for effective results.

1. **Control your movement.** Avoid fast, jerky movements that rely too heavily on momentum and may be harmful to your muscles and joints. A safe recommendation for resistance exercise is to perform the ascending motion for two seconds and the descending motion for four seconds.

> **Did You Know?**
>
> Eccentric exercise has been shown to improve a person's endurance capacity.

2. **Perform all exercises through the complete range of motion.** The benefits of strength, endurance, flexibility, skill, and performance are best achieved when exercises are performed through the full range of movement. Sometimes small range-of-motion movements are incorporated with the full range movements. (Exception: to avoid stressing the neck, do not take the head straight back.)

3. **Always exercise opposing muscle groups.** You need to balance the strength of opposing muscles. (See THE MUSCLE SYSTEM for a list of opposing muscle groups.)

4. **Concentrate on the muscles you are working.** Focusing on the specific muscle groups you are working will help you know when and how much to overload.

5. **Do the exercises properly.** The quality, form, and technique of the exercise is very important. Don't just try to see how many repetitions of an exercise you can do!

6. **Breathe normally.** Always exhale as you exert. Do not hold your breath!

7. **Don't exercise to the point of pain.** Pain is a warning sign—STOP before you hurt yourself. For optimal results, challenge yourself to the point of momentary muscular fatigue to sufficiently overload the muscles.

8. **Vary your program and exercises.** This prevents boredom, staleness, and overtraining.

9. **Exercise major body parts early in the workout.** Work your larger muscle groups, such as your legs and chest, before isolating your smaller muscle groups. That way the fatigue in the smaller muscle groups will not affect the performance of the heavier, more-difficult exercises.

10. **Be faithful to your warm-up and cooldown routines.** The warm-up prepares the body for the workout to follow and helps to decrease the risk of injury. It should include low-intensity movements very similar to the workout activity. The cooldown helps the body recover toward a normal resting level. Stretching exercises are recommended to help promote mind and body relaxation and to prevent muscle soreness.

The Importance of Recovery from Exercise

Exercise enthusiasts should be aware of the importance of recovery from exercise. Recovery from exercise training is an integral component of the overall training program; indeed, it is essential for optimal improvement and performance. As the exerciser's rate of recovery improves, he or she can use higher training volumes and intensities without the detrimental effects of overtraining. Recovery includes the following processes: (1) normalization of physiological functions (e.g., blood pressure, cardiac cycle), (2) return to homeostasis (i.e., a resting cell environment), (3) restoration of energy stores (blood glucose and muscle glycogen), and (4) replenishment of cellular energy enzymes (e.g., phosphofructokinase, a key enzyme in carbohydrate metabolism). Muscle recovery occurs during and primarily after exercise and is characterized by continued removal of metabolic end products (e.g., lactate and hydrogen ions). For exercisers to achieve optimal exercise performance, one has to be proactive in planning recovery as part of the training program. Although no consensus exists about a central recovery strategy, monitoring and observing your exercise performance is always helpful in adjusting and planning for this essential ingredient of training. The recovery process varies by the individual due to multiple factors—for example, training status (trained or untrained); level of fatigue; and the person's ability to deal with physical, emotional, and psychological stressors. In addition, realizing the importance of the quantity and quality of recovery sleep may empower you to enhance your training outcomes.

© Jacob Covell

SECTION 2
Training Tips and Injury Prevention

© Jacob Covell

Maximize Your Results, Minimize Your Risks

Not all exercises are good for you. Here are some unsafe or poorly executed exercises with their preferred alternatives. The exercise model with the LIGHT colored top is doing the incorrect version of the exercise.

1. **Twisting Hops** The combination of twisting the spine while hopping on the floor can be quite stressful on the back. The force of hopping alone equals two to three times your body weight.

   Alternative: Jump rope hops do not require any twisting and are more controllable.

© Jacob Covell

© Jacob Covell

2. **Fast-Twisting Waist Exercises** The fast side-to-side twisting of the torso imposes a shearing stress on the vertebrae of the spine.

   Alternative: Do them slowly as a warm-up stretch. Twisting crunches are more effective waist work.

© Jacob Covell

3. **Toe Touches** The straight-legged toe touch position stretches the ligaments behind the knees too much and stresses the lower spine. Bouncing touches are even worse!

   Alternative: The seated pike stretch (with slightly bent knees) and the seated half-straddle stretch are much better for you.

© Jacob Covell

4. **Windmill Stretch** This stretch also places too much stress on the ligaments supporting the spine. The twist adds stress to your back.

   Alternative: Try a seated side straddle stretch for greater control and safety.

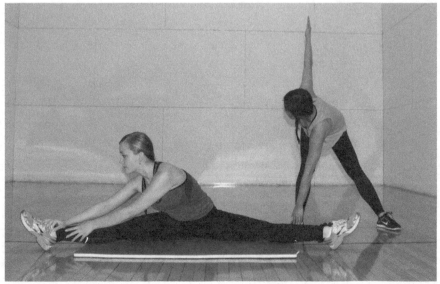

© Jacob Covell

5. **Deep Knee Bends** Deep knee bend variations can overstretch the ligaments supporting the knee and compress the cartilage.

   Alternative: When squatting, keep the knees from protruding past the toes, and lower your buttocks to just above your knees.

© Jacob Covell

6. **Lunges with Protruding Knees** The lunge is often incorrectly performed. A bent knee that juts past the ankle places stress on the knee.

   Alternative: Make sure the front knee stays over the ankle.

© Jacob Covell

7. **Hurdler's Stretch** This exercise can overstretch the muscles in the groin and the ligaments of the bent knee.

   Alternative: The seated center straddle stretch and half-straddle stretch are better options.

© Jacob Covell

8. **Head Throws in a Crunch** Often the head is "thrown forward" during a crunch.

   Alternative: Keep your head in a neutral or normal position. Focus on the ceiling when performing this exercise.

© Jacob Covell

9. **Swan Lifts** The combination of arching the lower spine as the muscles are contracting can injure the back.

   Alternative: Keep the lower body on the floor and only lift the upper body, as in the back extension. Or, simultaneously lift one arm in front while lifting the opposite leg in back. Repeat the movement lifting the opposite limbs.

© Jacob Covell

10. **The Plow** This movement places too much stress on the discs and bones of the neck. It may inhibit breathing and blood flow.

   Alternative: The seated pike stretch (with soft knees) is safer.

© Jacob Covell

11. Gymnastics Bridges The gymnastics bridge, designed to stretch the upper back and shoulders, is usually performed with an overarched back.

Alternative: Perform a pelvic lift with the spine in neutral position.

© Jacob Covell

12. Side Straddle Stretch If you allow the opposite hip to come off the floor while stretching to the side, you place the hip and spine in poor alignment.

Alternative: Keep the buttocks and legs firmly on the floor.

© Jacob Covell

13. Neck Extensions and 360-Degree Head Rolls Taking the head straight back, as in neck extensions or full head rolls, may place too much stress on the disks of the neck vertebrae.

Alternative: Neck rotation and lateral flexion are much safer. It is okay to bring the head forward and back, but avoid taking it too far past its neutral position when moving posteriorly.

© Jacob Covell

> **Did You Know?**
> The muscle cells in the heart are called myocardial cells.

> **Did You Know?**
> The most abundant tissue in the human body is skeletal muscle.

> **Did You Know?**
> The three types of muscle fibers are Type I, Type IIa and Type IIx

Twelve Most Common Exercise Mistakes

The following are some of the most common mistakes that occur in exercise programs.

1. **Overtraining** In their zeal to achieve fitness, people often try too hard. Possible signs of overtraining are injury, weight loss, mental dullness, disturbed digestion, loss of appetite, early exhaustion during a workout, fatigue during the day, or elevated heart rate upon awakening in the morning, or after a workout. Stress quality, not quantity!

2. **Poor Exercise Technique** Exercises performed incorrectly can lead to injury and poor performance. Poor technique is most frequent during the latter stages of a workout, when fatigue is starting to occur.

3. **Improper Equipment** The exercise clothes you wear, the shoes on your feet, the surface you are training on, and the equipment you are using can all **improve** or **impair** your performance.

4. **Insufficient Warm-up** Too often, the main activity is begun without proper warm-up (or after a quick, insufficient warm-up). This can lead to injury.

5. **Extra-Long Workouts** See signs of overtraining.

6. **Lifting Weights That Are Too Heavy** This leads to improper exercise technique, predisposes you to injury, and is not the progressive overload needed for optimal results in strength and endurance. Realize your limits.

7. **Forgetting Muscle Groups** For complete body symmetry make sure you work **all** your muscle groups.

8. **Unrealistic Goal Setting** Set realistic short- and long-term goals.

© Jacob Covell

9. **Forced Breathing** Proper breathing during exercise is easy to remember—**exhale** as you **exert.** Do not force your breathing.

10. **Exercises That Are Too Bouncy and Fast** Fast and bouncy movements stimulate your opposing muscle groups to contract and hinder the movement. Control is the key!

11. **Inadequate Aerobic Cooldown** Blood pressure may drop significantly from an abrupt cessation of vigorous aerobic exercise. This may also lead to fainting and irregular heart beats. Slow down gradually; don't just stop!

12. **Insufficient Stretching at the End of the Workout** Slow stretching following a workout helps reduce muscle soreness and improve flexibility.

Did You Know?

The adult human body has approximately 50 trillion cells.

Did You Know?

The largest muscle in the human body is the gluteus maximus.

© Jacob Covell

Did You Know?

The only food that can be metabolized anaerobically is carbohydrate.

Injuries

In Case of Injury

Let's face it, when you pursue an active lifestyle you will occasionally overdo it. And even if you are careful, inadequate equipment or exercising on an improper surface can lead to injuries. You can usually tell when you have an injury; pain and swelling appear in an area and gradually worsen. What do you do? R.I.C.E. (Rest, Ice, Compression, Elevation) is the answer. Most of these problems are muscle, ligament, and tendon injuries. The R.I.C.E. approach will limit the injury and accelerate the healing.

Rest:
Rest prevents you from reinjury and decreases the circulation to the area. "Time heals."

Ice:
Ice should be applied immediately to the injured area to keep the swelling down. An ice pack may be applied for 10 to 20 minutes periodically through the first 24 hours. Direct ice massage can be used for 7- to 10-minute sessions with the same effects. Heat can be applied after 48 hours, in conjunction with ice, to increase the circulation and enhance the body's process of removing the excess blood and fluid.

Compression:
Compression helps reduce the swelling and internal bleeding. Ace bandages are a good way to do this. Be careful not to obstruct circulation by overtightening!

Elevation:
Elevation helps reduce the internal bleeding and excessive fluid entry to the injury. If possible, elevate the injured area above the level of the heart at all opportune times until the swelling subsides.

See your physician if necessary. Persistent pain, major swelling, and significant discoloration all require elevation. The **cause** of the injury must also be **corrected** so reinjury does not occur. (Maybe you need new shoes, less weight, shorter workouts, etc.) Begin your rehabilitation process of stretching and strengthening and return to your former level of activity when your body is READY!

© Jill Pankey

Common Aerobic Injuries

Shin Splints

The most common aerobic injury is a pain between the knee and ankle, commonly referred to as "shin splints." Shin pain can be caused by a number of conditions, but impact shock is probably the major cause. Rest, ice, and exercise to increase muscle strength/flexibility are standard treatments. Footwear (specifically the arch support), floor surface resiliency, movement selection, and the structure of the workout should be reevaluated for safety and effectiveness. If this pain continues, see your physician.

Knee Injuries

A variety of knee injuries that affect the joint structure may also occur from repeated impact forces of aerobic exercise. Proper footwear, resilient workout surface, sufficient warm-up, and the progressive increase in exercise intensity will help to prevent these injuries.

> **Did You Know?**
>
> About 40 percent of running injuries are knee injuries.

Ankle Sprain

An ankle sprain is the most common of all injuries. It usually occurs when the weak ligaments on the outside of the joint are injured by an accidental rolling outward of the ankle. Rest, ice, compression, and elevation are standard treatments; physician referral may be necessary. Safe movement selection, proper warm-up, and concentration on the activity itself will help prevent this type of injury.

Muscle and Ligament Inflammation

Another common injury that occurs from the repeated impact of the foot striking the ground is an inflammation of the muscles and ligaments supporting the foot. Overtraining and improper warm-up often lead to this ailment. Rest, ice, compression, and elevation are recommended treatments. Proper footwear and safe training procedures are preventives.

> **Did You Know?**
>
> Learning the technique and the proper use of equipment should come first, before increasing the weight or intensity.

> **Did You Know?**
>
> The idea of "no pain, no gain" is a myth. It's okay to challenge yourself, but don't push too hard.

Guide to a Better Back

It's a pain! Why do you get this lower-back pain and what can you do to prevent back problems? Although there may be a number of different contributing factors to low back pain, it's essential to realize that when you stand upright, most of your body weight falls on the lower back. Weak abdominal and back muscles from underuse and/or poor posture may not give the spine the support it needs, leaving the back prone to pain or injury. Your goal to a healthy back is to keep the muscles of the spine, buttocks, and upper legs strong and flexible, be aware of preferred posture, and control your weight.

Healthy Back Tips

Standing and Walking

Maintain your normal back curve, but avoid the swayback posture. Stand tall, feeling lifted throughout the lower abdominal region. Try not to stand still too long. If you must, put one leg up on a support or at least bend alternate knees. Ladies, limit your high heel wearing time because these shoes accentuate the back curve and create stress on the spine. Use your abdominal muscles to support your body weight as you stand or move.

© Jacob Covell

Lifting

Bend your knees, not your back, when lifting. Bring objects toward your body and avoid over-the-head lifts. Avoid rotating your body when lifting or lowering an object. Instead, change your foot placement while maintaining the object directly in front of you.

> **Did You Know?**
>
> 80 percent of Americans encounter a lower-back problem sometime in their daily life.

© Jacob Covell

Sitting at Your Computer Station

Sit in an adjustable chair that keeps your back upright or slightly forward. The adaptable backrest should maintain your body's natural low back curve. Your knees should be slightly lower than your hips. Your feet should be placed solidly on the floor or a footrest. Your keyboard should be at elbow level, with the bend at your elbows near 90 degrees. Your hands and wrists should be straight and relaxed. For some people, wrist rests are preferable. Your eyes should be approximately at a midscreen height of your monitor with your head about an arm's length from the screen.

© Jacob Covell

Sleeping

Try sleeping on your side on a firm mattress with your knees slightly bent or on your back with a pillow under your knees. If you must sleep on your stomach, place a small pillow under your abdominals to correct for a sagging spine.

© Jacob Covell

Did You Know?	Did You Know?
The longest and strongest bone in the human body is the femur.	Nerve cells are the longest cells in the human body.

Back Pain Relief

Back injuries require the attention of a specialist. For relief of small aches, lie on your back on a padded surface and elevate your feet (with bent knees). Place a small pillow or folded towel under your neck and rest in this position for 10 to 15 minutes.

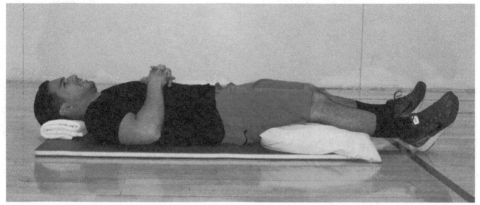

© Jacob Covell

Five Exercises for a Healthy Back

1. **Pelvic Tilt** Lie on your back with knees bent, arms on chest, and feet on floor. Press the lower back into the floor by tightening the abdominal muscles and slightly lifting the buttocks off the floor. Hold for 10 seconds and repeat 8 to 15 times.

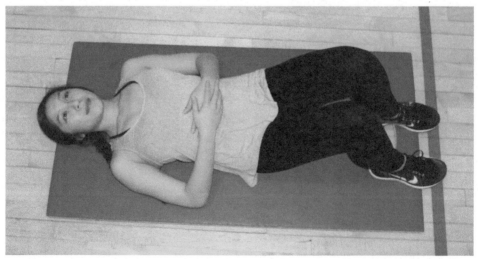

© Jacob Covell

2. **Hamstring Stretch** Lie on your back, with both knees bent and one foot on the floor. Grasp behind the lifted knee, bring it toward the chest, and hold for several seconds. Repeat 3 to 5 times on each leg.

© Jacob Covell

3. **Tuck-Hold** Tuck both knees to chest using your arms to create a tight tuck position. Then, press your lower back into the floor. Keep your back flat. Hold for 15 seconds and repeat 5 to 10 times.

© Jacob Covell

4. **Slow Crunch** Lie on your back with your knees bent at a 45-degree angle and your head supported at the base of the neck by your hands. Slowly lift your chest as you press your lower back into the floor; then slowly lower. Try lifting your buttocks slightly off the floor as you raise the chest. Repeat 8 to 25 times.

© Jacob Covell

5. **Prone Prop** While on your front, lift your chest off the floor and hold by propping your elbows on the ground. Open your legs slightly.

   Variation: Same as prone prop, only straighten your arms. For both, relax your hips and abdominals and hold for 8 to 15 seconds and then lower. Repeat 3 to 5 times.

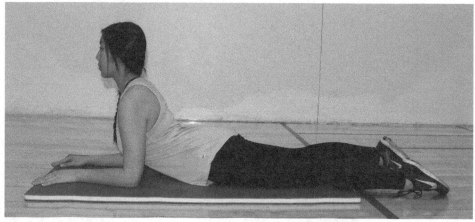

© Jacob Covell

Good Posture Promotes Good Health

What Is Good Posture and What Is Faulty Posture?

The word 'posture' comes from the Latin verb 'ponere' which means to put or place. It refers to the position of the human body in space. Good posture can be defined as a state of skeletal and muscular balance and alignment that protects the supporting structures of the body from progressive abnormality and injury. Whether erect, lying, squatting or stooping, good posture allows the muscles of the body to function most proficiently. With good standing posture the body's joints are in a state of stability with the least amount of physical energy being used to sustain this upright position.

Contrariwise, poor posture, often referred to as faulty posture, is an unsatisfactory link of various skeletal structures of the body. It may produce strain on the supporting body framework structures. With faulty posture there is less efficient balance of the body over its base of support. Therefore, any restriction, imbalance or misalignment of the skeletal structures will have an adverse affect on the movement effectiveness of the person.

Test Your Posture

Test your posture by standing with your hips, back and head against a wall while looking at yourself in a mirror. Place your heels a couple of inches away from the wall. Test for the following:

Head: Not rotated or tilted

Shoulders: Level with no depression or elevation

Lower back: There should be a small space between your lower back and the wall

Pelvis: The hips should be level

Lower extremities: Straight and not bowed

Feet: Facing parallel or with slight out-toeing

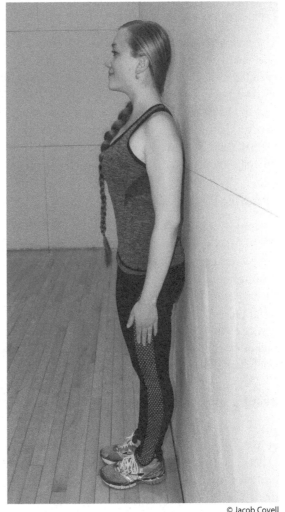

© Jacob Covell

> ### Did You Know?
>
> Good posture allows the muscles to work more efficiently. The body uses less energy which helps to prevent muscle fatigue.

Water: Nature's Most Important Nutrient

Water 101: The Basic Facts About Water in the Body

Water is colorless, tasteless and odorless. Because of its numerous and diverse functions in the body, it is often regarded as the most important nutrient. Water is the most abundant constituent of the body, accounting for 50% to 60% of its mass. It is intricately involved in numerous functions of the body including the transport of oxygen, nutrients and waste products into and out of the cells. The body uses water as a coolant, helping to regulate body temperature during exercise, fever and in hot environments.

What Is the Proper Fluid Replacement to Sustain Endurance Exercise?

Failure to hydrate appropriately during exercise is a chief contributing factor to poor performance during endurance events, particularly in hot and humid conditions. The next three sections, prehydrating before exercise, hydrating during exercise, and rehydrating after exercise, summarize key points from current research on fluid replacement.

Prehydrating Before Exercise

The prehydration goal is to make certain that any fluid and electrolyte insufficiency is corrected prior to starting a cardiovascular exercise bout. Hydrating before the exercise can begin progressively about 4 hours before the workout session. About 5–7 mL/kg body weight (1 kg = 2.2 lbs) should be sufficient. So, if a person weighs 150 lbs, that weight is 68 kg; therefore 7 mL/kg × 68 kg = 476 milliliters of fluid. Since 8 ounces is equivalent to 237 milliliters, 476 milliliters is about 16 ounces, or two glasses of water.

© Jacob Covell

Hydrating During Exercise

Hydration recommendations during exercise can be quite variable depending on a person's sweat rate, mode of exercise, exercise duration, weather conditions, opportunities to hydrate, training status, heat acclimatization and exercise intensity. Exercisers are encouraged to monitor their pre- and post-workout body weights during different workouts and try to match the weight loss (via sweat) with fluid replacement during the exercise. To sustain endurance exercise performance lasting over 1 hour, carbohydrate consumption (with a mixture of sugars such as glucose, fructose, maltodextrine, and sucrose) may be beneficial. The carbohydrate concentration should be up to 8%, and not beyond, because a higher concentration may impede gastric (stomach) emptying.

Rehydrating After Exercise

After exercise, the goal is to replenish any fluid or electrolyte shortfall. Most scientists suggest a resumption of normal meals and snacks (that contain adequate sodium) with sufficient water to restore the body. As a general rule of thumb, for each kilogram (2.2 lbs) of weight post-exercise below the pre-exercise weight the body will need about 1.5 liters of fluid. Converting kg to lb, for each pound of sweat you lose in exercise, drink about 25 ounces of fluid post-exercise for replenishment.

Nutrient Timing: A Cutting Edge Training Tip

Exercise enthusiasts regularly seek to improve their strength, stamina, and muscle power through consistent exercise and proper nutrition. In the areas of nutrition and exercise physiology, nutrient timing is 'buzzing' with scientific interest. With appropriate nutrient timing you will be able to more effectively repair muscle tissue damage, restore physiological function, replenish glycogen (stored form of glucose) stores, and promote muscle growth . . . that pretty much says it all.

Nutrient timing is the application of knowing when to eat and what to eat before and after exercise. It is designed to help athletes and exercise enthusiasts achieve their most advantageous exercise performance and recovery. There are two distinct phases in the nutrient timing system.

The Energy Phase: What to Do Before Exercise?

Muscle glycogen is the primary fuel (followed by fat) used by the body during exercise. Low muscle glycogen stores result in muscle fatigue and the body's inability to complete high intensity exercise. Both aerobic and anaerobic exercise decrease glycogen stores, so the need for carbohydrates is high for all types of exercise during this energy phase.

Prior to aerobic exercise, protein intake combined with carbohydrate ingestion has been shown to stimulate protein synthesis post-exercise. This same nutrient combination prior to resistance training can increase the body's capacity to perform more sets, repetitions and prolong a resistance training workout. A combined carbohydrate to protein supplement drink in a 4 to 1 ratio is recommended within 30 minutes of exercise. This will best fuel the energy needs of the body for the workout.

The Anabolic Phase: The 30- to 45-Minute Optimal Window After Exercise

The anabolic phase is a critical phase occurring up to 30 to 45 minutes post-exercise. It is during this time that muscle cells are particularly sensitive to nutrient stimulation. It is also the time that specialized hormones begin working to repair the muscle, decrease its inflammation and promote muscle growth. Refueling with carbohydrate after a workout is essential. An absolute recommendation is to consume at least 50 g of carbohydrate and 10–15 g of protein with fluid soon after the exercise session. This will increase protein synthesis for cell growth and repair. It will also replenish the depleted glycogen stores in muscle that were used for energy. There are several recovery drinks on the market a person can purchase. Interesting, research has also shown that a glass of low-fat chocolate milk also has an adequate nutrient composition breakdown to initiate cell growth and repair.

© Angela Aladro mella/Shutterstock.com

Understanding Muscle Soreness

All types of muscle contractions may potentially lead to delayed onset muscle soreness (DOMS). DOMS is classically characterized as the muscle soreness and swelling that becomes evident 8 to 10 hours after exercise and peaks between 24 and 48 hours. It tends to diminish in 72 hours. DOMS is a multifactoral physiological phenomenon, which scientists have proposed several explanatory theories. One premise is the connective tissue theory, which suggests there is a disruption of the non-contractile elements in the muscle cell. Another theory, known as the cellular theory, focuses on disruption of particular components in the sarcomere (the basic units of muscle cells). And most recently, a newer theory suggests that the release of too many calcium ions (from a membrane in the muscle known as the sarcoplasmic reticulum) results in a disruption within the muscle cell. With the numerous theories about what causes DOMS, it is safe to say that there is still much to be learned through research. All the theories clearly indicate that exercise-induced DOMS is a multifaceted event in muscle. Although many strategies to lessen muscle soreness (once it occurs) are promoted in the media, the best approach is to stay active, hydrate well, eat healthy and get plenty of sleep (for the body to heal itself).

What Is the Repeated Bout Effect in Eccentric Training?

One area of research that has much promise, in relation to DOMS and particularly eccentric exercise (where the muscle is loaded while lengthening), is the repeated bout effect (RBE). With the RBE, the exerciser initially completes a LOWER INTENSITY eccentric training bout. Then, about one week later the exerciser completes a HIGHER INTENSITY eccentric training bout. This RBE approach will result in reduced DOMS response to the HIGHER intensity eccentric training bout. What causes the RBE to work is not fully understood. However, there are theories suggesting it is a contribution of adaptations from neural input to the muscle, restructuring of connective tissue in muscle and cellular adaptations with the muscle cell.

© Jacob Covell

SECTION 3
Fitness Gear and Where to Train

© Jacob Covell

In Search of the Perfect Walking, Running, and Fitness Shoe

You want a shoe with flexibility, that supports your arches, cushions your heels, adds extra impact absorption at the balls of your feet, and fits well. Here's what to check out:

- **The outersole** should be flexible, yet durable.
- **The midsole** (between the outer and inner sole) should provide good stability and cushioning to absorb shock, yet allow for foot flexibility.
- **The innersole:** A high-shock-absorbent material is recommended. If the shoe you like doesn't have this, purchase an innersole separately.
- **The toe area:** This is the one place on the shoe where roominess counts. When you exercise, your foot swells. Allow for it. Can you wiggle your toes?
- **Forefoot cushion:** The greatest amount of force the foot must absorb is behind the ball of the foot. There must be good cushioning here.
- **Forefoot flexibility:** The shoe should bend (as the foot does) at the ball of the foot. Too stiff a forefoot will cause lower leg discomfort. This area needs to be flexible yet stable.
- **Arch support:** Make sure the arch provides comfortable support.
- **The heel counter:** This should be an inflexible material surrounding the heel area, holding it in place. The more it prevents excessive rolling and twisting, the better it is.
- **The shoe heel:** Look for an outer heel that makes a flush contact with the ground. If the inner heel height is too low, it will cause an excessive pull on the calf and Achilles tendon. The heel should provide good cushion without being too hard or too soft. Shoes are now designed in high-top ankle support. These help out a lot.
- **See the experts:** It's best to go to a specialty running or fitness store where a qualified salesperson can help you select a pair of shoes that offer your feet the support they need.
- **Measure your feet:** You may think you know your size, but it's best to get your feet measured each time you buy new shoes. Your feet change over time.
- **Comfort:** When you go shopping, take along the socks and any inserts that you've been using. That way you can make a realistic evaluation of how well the new shoe will fit your feet. Try on as many different models and pairs as possible. Do a test walk or run in the store, moving around for about 10 minutes. Don't purchase them if it feels uncomfortable. Also, because your feet swell during the day, it is best to purchase shoes in the afternoon or evening.

© ronstik/Shutterstock.com

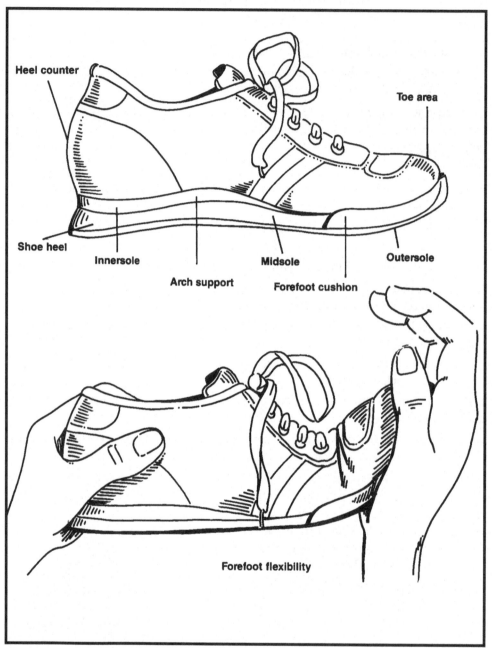

Heel counter

Toe area

Shoe heel

Innersole

Arch support

Midsole

Forefoot cushion

Outersole

Forefoot flexibility

© Jill Pankey

How to Choose a Sports and Fitness Facility

Try to visit the prospective sports and fitness facility during the time you would be using the facility. Shop around using the following as a helpful checklist.

1. Is the location convenient to your home, work, or school?

2. Is it a workout gym, a social club, a coed facility, or a fitness center for families? What are you looking for?

3. Does the facility look clean, organized, seasonally air-controlled, and suitably lighted? Specifically check out the locker room and showers for cleanliness!

4. What facilities should you look for?
   - Well-equipped exercise rooms containing updated equipment. Are there enough weight-resistance machines, stationary bikes, treadmills, rowing machines, free weights, and space to accommodate the members?
   - An aerobic exercise room with a proper floor. Does it have a floating wood design or is it carpet, wood, or linoleum over cement (which is much more unsafe)? Does it have enough space for the class sizes? Is it air-conditioned?
   - Accessible racquetball or squash courts. What is the court reservation procedure? (If you have to reserve over 48 hours in advance, you know that they are getting heavy use.) Do the court floors and walls look very marked up? Do you have to pay for court time?
   - Well-maintained pool. Is it heated year-round? Is the size suitable to your needs?
   - Available track facilities. Is there an indoor or outdoor track?
   - Relaxing spa facilities. Is there a whirlpool, sauna, steam room, massage room, and cold plunge?
   - Well-kept locker room. Do you get a locker and key every time you use the facility? Or do you bring your own lock or rent out the locker? Does the club provide towels, soap, shampoo, hair dryers, and other grooming amenities?

5. What kind of staff does it have? Are there trained personnel in physical education, exercise physiology, nutrition, or sports medicine? Does the staff have a professional, friendly, and helpful attitude?

6. What type of programs do they run? Are there enough classes in a variety of workouts? Are there additional fees? Can you take a class any time you wish?

7. Do the club hours fit your needs?

8. **Examine the fees carefully!**
   - Are they affordable? Is there a payment plan?
   - Is there an initiation fee? Is it refundable? Is this a one-time charge or a yearly charge? Are there any monthly dues in addition? How much?
   - Be leery of contracts and "too good to be true" promotionals. Read all the small print before you sign.

○ Be wary of "lifetime" memberships—is it your lifetime or the facility?

○ What are the cancellation policies? Must you sell your membership? Do you get a prorated refund?

○ Read with caution any "preopening" sales packages.

9. Does the club allow you to put your membership on hold for a short period (such as for a vacation) without having to pay the monthly dues?

10. How much does it cost to bring a guest to the facility? Does the facility give out guest passes?

11. How long has the sports and fitness facility been in operation?

12. How long has the present management been with the fitness center?

13. Ask if the fitness center belongs to any national trade organization with an established code of ethics for staff and clients.

14. Before joining, talk to some members as they enter or on leaving the facility to get their opinions of the fitness center.

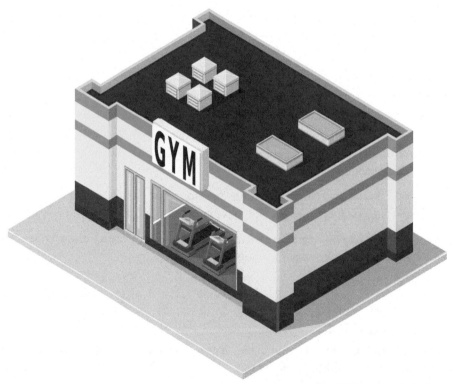

© Grimgram/Shutterstock.com

Creating a Home Gym

You don't have to be rich to create a convenient home gym. Even if you belong to a workout club or fitness center, your schedule or occasional desire for workout privacy may warrant the purchase of home exercise equipment. Here are some tips to get you started.

1. Make sure you have enough space. A wall mirror helps you view your exercise technique and serves as a great motivator. Music helps too!

2. Make sure the lighting and air ventilation are adequate.

3. Before purchasing any equipment, identify your fitness needs. Do you want a jump rope, treadmill, stationary cycle, rowing machine, or step for cardiorespiratory fitness? Do you want equipment for specific exercises for your abdominals, legs, and buttocks? Having identified your fitness needs will prevent you from purchasing equipment of no practical use to you.

4. Look for equipment that features effective safety measures and provides progressive exercise guidelines.

5. Shop around. It's amazing how the cost of the same equipment varies from store to store! Examine the warranty and service agreements closely.

6. Watch out for attractive, shiny, lightweight equipment that lacks durability and stability.

7. Try the equipment out. Not all equipment feels the same. With mail-order equipment, review the return policies and procedures carefully before purchasing. Are the shipping charges reasonable?

8. Build your exercise area to fit your program. Buy a little equipment at a time and add as you see fit.

9. Stay away from products that guarantee phenomenal results in a short time.

10. When purchasing equipment on sale, see if the product is being discontinued. If it is, there may be a newer, better style available at the same price.

11. For display purposes, fitness store equipment is usually free standing and movable. Check to see which products need to be firmly secured to a wall or floor, and how they need to be secured.

© Iriana Shiyan/Shutterstock.com

Finding the Right Instructor

All instructors have their own teaching style, and classes have their own special characteristics. Here's what to look for in an instructor and class to make sure it meets your needs.

1. Take a trial class or observe the instructor and class during the time you would normally attend.

2. Look for **quality** and not **quantity.** Just because a class does numerous repetitions or the instructor is "tough" doesn't mean it's a good class.

3. Does the instructor make an effort to teach, correct, explain, and give clear directions? Can you hear the verbal instructions? Does the instructor modify exercises for the students who have special needs?

4. If there is a mirror, does the instructor face it throughout most of the class? Mirrors are wonderful instructional aids, but direct eye contact is one of the most effective means of communication and interaction.

5. Look for a well-rounded workout: a thorough warm-up, a gradually increasing aerobic section, a winding down of the aerobics, a complete body-firming section, and a cool-down stretching segment.

© Jacob Covell

6. Does the workout seem to flow smoothly from one section to the next?

7. Is the class easy to follow? Could you see the instructor easily or was it too crowded?

8. Does the instructor inspire and motivate you? Did you enjoy the workout?

9. Was the workout challenging enough for you? Does the club or studio offer a variety of different levels and styles of classes?

10. Did you feel comfortable with the class atmosphere?

11. Could you hear the music? Was it too loud?

12. Does the class follow a prescribed exercise program? The American College of Sports Medicine recommends aerobic activity three to five times a week for between 20 and 60 minutes, at 55 percent to 90 percent of your maximum heart rate.

13. Is there any type of medical screening for participants prior to participation?

14. Is the cost of the class or program within your budget?

15. Is the class in a convenient location?

16. What training, credentials, and education does the instructor have? The credibility of an instructor who boasts of "being certified" cannot always be substantiated. Inquire about any specific training, experience, and education the instructor has had.

17. Many of the readers of this text may wish to pursue a fitness certification. The IDEA Health and Fitness Association (www.ideafit.com) has created an all-inclusive directory of fitness certifications and training groups. This robust directory of organizations not only shows basic information and the certification types that each group offers, but also highlights the organization's upcoming classes and events, reviews, CECs/CEUs, exercise videos, testimonials and blog.

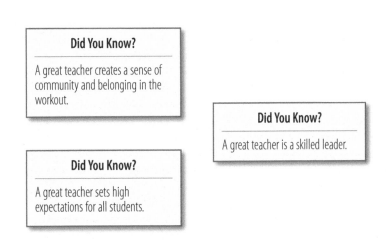

Did You Know?

A great teacher creates a sense of community and belonging in the workout.

Did You Know?

A great teacher is a skilled leader.

Did You Know?

A great teacher sets high expectations for all students.

SECTION 4
Let's Work Out

© Jacob Covell

Start Moving More to Combat Sedentary Behavior

Before I introduce your workouts, I'd like to encourage you to start getting up more in your daily life. Yes, that includes standing up from your chairs. If your home is your castle, its chairs have become the throne. It won't bring you bountiful riches, though—at least not of the good-health variety. Over the past few years, a large group of scientists from around the world have been studying what happens to our body when we sit too much. It is called the science of sedentary behavior. The word sedentary comes from the Latin word *sedere*, meaning "to sit." In the US, sedentary behavior takes up a great percentage of the waking day for many people. In fact, adults, students, and children in the US spend the majority of their non-exercising waking day engaging in some form of sedentary behavior, such as riding in a car, working at a desk, eating a meal at a table, playing video games, working on a computer, and watching television. You will probably not be surprised to learn that a sedentary lifestyle can have hazardous health effects. Researchers increasingly believe that, as the saying goes, sitting has become the new smoking.

Findings about the harmful effects of too much sitting have their early research roots in the 1950s, when researchers observed that men who worked physically active jobs had less heart disease during middle age than men in physically inactive jobs. The researchers also observed that when physically active men did develop heart disease, it was less severe and later in life. Leaping forward half a century, a large study from Canada found that there is a strong association between sitting and mortality risk from cardiovascular disease (and several other diseases too). This study looked at the mortality rates of 7,278 men and 9,735 women aged eighteen to ninety years over a twelve-year period. Surprisingly, the study discovered that even if a person completes her/his thirty minutes of moderate intensity exercise a day but remains seated during the rest of the day, she/he has an increased risk of heart disease. The bottom line: long periods of sitting during your waking day are unsafe to your health.

Why is it so unhealthy to sit for sustained periods of time on a daily basis? Scientist believe when you sit too much during your waking day, the "lousy" cholesterol (the LDL cholesterol) starts to accumulate more plaque in your arteries. Simultaneously, the good cholesterol (the HDL cholesterol) decreases, making it less available for cleaning up the plaque. Once a lot of plaque builds up in your arteries, you are vulnerable to cardiovascular disease.

All of the new research on the perils of a sedentary lifestyle underscores the critical importance of getting up and moving much more throughout your waking day. To help you accomplish this, I'm going to reveal a NEW slogan and goal I'd like you to shoot for every day: *For every 30, get your 3*. Here's how it works: For every 30 minutes you sit, I want you to get at least 3 minutes of movement. Yes, more is better, but to start let's shoot for the "for every 30 get your 3." I realize some classes (or jobs), due to their nature, do not allow you to take a movement break every 30 minutes. I encourage those of you in such a situation to find creative ways to achieve your movement goals over the course of your day. However, many of you will be able to get up out of your chairs and move every 30 minutes without any restrictions during a large part of your waking day. You get to decide how far and how fast you move—but just move. So start right now—and get up and move! Go for it, and then come back to reading *Anybody's Guide to Total Fitness*. I will do the same.

[A few minutes pass] . . . and we're back. See, didn't that feel great?

To help you get a move on, here are some options for breaking up sustained sitting periods at work:

1. Standing up and walking around your school location or home office every thirty minutes.

2. Standing up and moving every time you drink some water.

3. Walking to the farthest bathroom in your school facility when going to the restroom (if multiple bathrooms are available).

4. Walking around the room or building when talking on the telephone.

5. Getting a standing workstation where you can intermittently stand and work on your desktop computer simultaneously.

6. Going for a walk break with every coffee or tea break.

7. Substituting sending emails to student friends and colleagues by walking to meet them at the student union or library.

8. Making your next student meeting a walking/talking/discussing meeting.

Of course, excessive sitting doesn't happen only at school; it's just as much of a problem once you get home. Many people spend a lot of time—perhaps too much time—watching TV, viewing movies, and/or reading books in a chair. To help counteract the effects of this, please do some of the following at home:

1. Getting up and moving during every commercial.

2. Taking a brief walk break every thirty minutes.

3. Getting on a stationary piece of cardiovascular exercise equipment (a.k.a. treadmill or indoor cycle) and using it for several minutes after each half hour of TV viewing or reading.

4. Standing up and moving for the opening segment of each TV show.

5. Getting up to walk around the room or house every time you read four, six, or eight pages.

Takeaways from the Sedentary Behavior Research

Our technologically advanced society has given us the opportunity to do everything we need from our chairs. While this may have some work productivity benefits, being sedentary for so long can be very damaging to your health. In addition to enjoying the many great workouts in this book, I want you to strive to fulfill your new movement slogan on a daily basis: for every 30 get your 3. You can do it! Please be empowered and encouraged to teach it to your family and close friends as well. Remember, the ultimate power lies in the lifestyle choices you make every day. Get up, move, and enjoy!

For every 30 minutes of sitting try to get 3 minutes of movement.

The Physiology of Working Out

Energy Systems Provide the Fuel for Exercise

As you embark on some of your many exercises and workouts, it is essential to understand how your body is responding and adapting to these workouts. To exercise and do work for daily life activities, your body uses a chemical compound called ATP (adenosine triphosphate) like a car uses gasoline. ATP is produced by metabolizing (or breaking down) the carbohydrates and fats from the foods you eat. Proteins are used only sparingly for fuel during exercise. Depending on the intensity and duration of the activity, you produce ATP through aerobic and anaerobic metabolism.

Aerobic (which literally means with oxygen) metabolism is the most efficient and main energy production system of the body. This metabolic pathway cannot work unless there is sufficient oxygen available in the tissues during exercise. Prolonged vigorous activity over 5 minutes activates your aerobic metabolism. During prolonged exercises such as cycling, cross-country skiing, and distance running, muscle contraction is dependant on the ability of the aerobic metabolic pathways to continuously regenerate ATP. Mitochondrial respiration (aerobic metabolism in the mitochondrion of the cell) becomes the primary supplier of ATP. Think of the mitochondrion as the 'energy power plant' of your body's cells. As noted previously, fats in the form of triglycerides are available for ATP production, but their breakdown is much slower than glucose and glycogen (which both come from carbohydrates). In fact, decreased levels of blood glucose and low levels of muscle glycogen are associated with the onset of fatigue in sustained aerobic exercise events.

© Jacob Covell

Anaerobic (without oxygen) metabolism is used for situations requiring quick bursts of energy, such as lifting weights, running short races, jumping, and throwing. Although anaerobic metabolism is less efficient than the aerobic metabolism, it can quickly generate the ATP needed at the muscle site for needed bursts of energy. Anaerobic metabolism may be called on during aerobic conditioning if the intensity increases beyond the ability of the aerobic system to deliver ATP (such as finishing a long run with a sprint or a section of high kicks during an aerobic program). The two anaerobic metabolic systems are the phosphagen and glycolytic (break down of carbohydrates without the assistance of oxygen) energy system.

During vigorous anaerobic exercise bouts, such as sprinting and high intensity resistance exercise, continued muscle contraction is dependent on the formation of ATP for the demanding exercise. Under these exercise conditions, creatine phosphate, a molecule which resynthesizes ATP and glucose breakdown (called glycolysis) is primarily responsible for maintaining ATP levels. It has been found that during intense muscle contraction, creating phosphate becomes depleted rapidly, resulting in an incomplete supply of ATP.

To make up for this ATP deficiency, glycolysis increases. However, the increased output of glycolysis results in the accumulation of by-products, including lactate and protons (hydrogen ions also shown regularly as H+), which have been identified as potential contributors to fatigue. Historically, researchers have associated lactate (or lactic acid) production during increased rates of glycolysis with the development of cellular acidosis, or what we commonly call 'the burn'. However, more recent research has shown the proton (H+) accumulation is the cause of acidosis in muscle.

The Cardiorespiratory System Delivers the Oxygen

The biochemical reactions involved in mitochondrial respiration depend on continuous oxygen availability for proper functioning. Enhanced oxygen delivery and utilization during exercise will improve mitochondrial respiration and subsequently the capacity for endurance exercise. The oxygen is delivered by the red blood cells to the working muscle and transported into the mitochondrion where it is used in the aerobic production of ATP. There are two major components of the cardiorespiratory system. The heart and lungs, which deliver the oxygen to the working muscle, are called the central component. The ability of exercising muscles to extract and utilize oxygen, which has been transported by the red blood cells, is referred to as the peripheral component. With consistent aerobic training both the central and peripheral component of the cardiorespiratory system improve spectacularly.

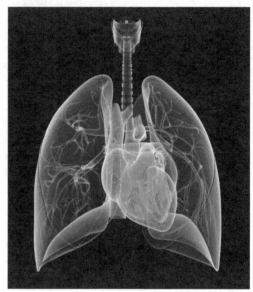

© Sebastian Kaulitzki/Shutterstock.com

The Muscles Are the 'Engines' That Do the Work

Your skeletal muscles attach to the skeleton and contract continuously during exercise. Your bones provide the structure for muscles to attach so that our bodies are able to move. Think of muscles as 'engines' causing the movement of your body and the skeleton as a complex arrangement of levers, fulcrums, and force arms that do carry out the movements. The muscles get numerous signals to contract from your nervous system. Muscles are incredibly intricate, with the ability to combine oxygen from the cardiorespiratory system with ATP from the metabolic system for you to do long-lasting exercise. Interestingly, your skeletal muscles work in pairs. One muscle will move a bone in one direction and its paired muscle will move the bone the other way. Your skeletal muscles contract voluntarily, meaning that you think about contracting them and your nervous system tells them to do so.

As you begin these exercises and workouts in *Anybody's Guide to Total Fitness* you will notice that you are breathing heavier and faster during your aerobic workouts. Your sweating is the body's way of dissipating the heat that is generated by your contracting muscles. That is why it is always important to drink water before, during, and after exercise. You are encouraged to try many of the different exercises and workouts in the book. Each will use different muscles of your body or the same muscles in different ways. This will enhance the benefits you receive from your exercise participation. Let's get started.

Exercise and Energy Balance

It is helpful to start this section off noting that both cardiovascular exercise and particularly resistance training have been shown to boost a person's metabolism. Traditional energy balance components of interest in weight management include discussions on resting energy expenditure (REE), the thermic effect of food (TEF) and activity energy expenditure (AEE). REE is the non-exercise energy needed throughout the day to maintain life. It represents approximately 2/3 of the energy needs of the human body. It varies broadly between people due primarily to body composition (fat versus muscle on the body), body size (the greater the body mass area, the greater the REE to stay alive) and some not fully understood other reasons. Remarkably, the brain, heart, kidney, and liver, which weigh relatively slight amounts of weight demand noteworthy amounts of energy for life sustaining needs, and contribute credibly to the body's total REE. The TEF is the energy expenditure designated to processing and digesting consumed foods. Dietary composition of protein produces the peak effect on TEF, which is followed by carbohydrate and then fat. AEE is the fuel utilized by the body via structured exercise and non-exercise movement (such as shopping, moving, and doing daily chores). AEE varies greatly between persons, as many people move a lot during their waking day and perform a considerable amount of daily exercise, while others live principally sedentary lifestyles.

© Mangsaab/Shutterstock.com

A positive energy balance refers to a person taking in more kilocalories than expending. Over time, a positive energy balance will result in overweight and/or obesity. Presently, scientists feel the body has a 'set point' to regulate body weight. The 'set point' theory suggests there is a highly organized feedback control system in the body (regulated by the hypothamamus in the brain) that tries to best regulate food intake and energy output.

Muscle tissue is metabolically active at rest, burning calories in this state. Contrariwise, fat tissue does not burn calories at rest. Thus having more muscle tissue will somewhat ensure that your resting balance energy expenditure will remain higher, particularly as you get older. As a person ages, the normal loss of muscle tissue is approximately 3 to 5% every ten years after the age of 25. Resistance training will help decrease this age-related decline in muscle mass, ensuring more caloric expenditure at rest, and lessening the chance of obesity.

Warm Up First

The purpose of the warm-up is to prepare the body for the more rigorous demands of the cardiorespiratory and/or muscular strength and conditioning segments of the workout.

WARM-UP DO'S AND DON'TS	
Do's	Don'ts
Move slowly and rhythmically.	Bounce, jerk, or force positions.
Focus on full body range of motion.	"Lock" your joints.
Perform all warm-up exercises on both sides.	

First Off: Active Start

Begin with three to five minutes of **easy** aerobics, brisk walking, or cycling to elevate the body temperature, stimulate circulation to the muscles, and loosen up the joints to prepare them for more strenuous exercise.

Then, try the following series of warm-up exercises:

Head
(For neck)

Action: Take head from one side, forward, and around to other side. Reverse. Also, turn head from side to side.

Tips: Avoid taking the head to a straight back position. Make sure these movements are performed slowly.

© Jacob Covell

> **Did You Know?**
>
> The average brain weighs 3 lbs.

© Jacob Covell

Shoulder Rolls
(For shoulders)

Action: Smooth circles with shoulders (arms down at side).

Tips: Circle in both directions.

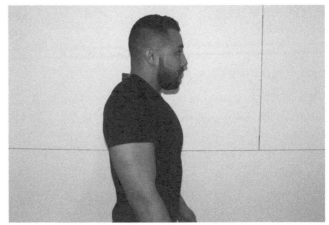

© Jacob Covell

Torso Side Stretch
(For side and hips)

Action: Reach one arm over your head and stretch your torso sideways. Stretch other side. Keep the knees slightly bent.

Tips: Be sure to face forward so you don't twist as you stretch. Support yourself with your extended arm on the thigh to avoid spinal stress.

© Jacob Covell

Torso Twist
(For spine)

Action: Twist gently and rhythmically from the waist.

Tips: Keep your knees slightly bent and control the movement.

© Jacob Covell

Arm Reaches
(For upper back)

Action: Reach with alternating arms over the head, lengthening the upper torso.

Tips: Keep your weight evenly balanced with your lower body. Look up slightly as you do your reaches.

© Jacob Covell

Upper Spine/Shoulder Stretch

Action: Place hands on thighs above knees. Keep your knees bent. Press one shoulder down and allow the trunk and head to rotate, stretching the upper back, shoulder, and neck. To other side.

Tips: Always keep your knees slightly bent and do not bend over too far forward.

© Jacob Covell

Lunge Stretch: High and Low
(For thighs and lower leg)

Action: Bend front knee and keep back leg straight.
High Lunge: Stretch the Achilles tendon and calf by gently bending and straightening the back leg.
Low Lunge: Stretch the hips down into the floor. Other side.

Tips: Keep the front knee over the ankle and the toes pointing forward.

© Jacob Covell

Aerobics: The Main Event

Following are some aerobic steps you can perform to lively music. Start gradually at a brisk walking pace, increase your intensity into your target zone, and then wind back down to a brisk walk. To improve your aerobic efficiency, build up to between 20 and 60 continuous minutes, three to five times a week. Be creative and "choreograph" your own routines! You can create variety by using various arm positions, lifting your legs to different heights, adding a clap, and traveling in a circle or in different directions.

AEROBIC REMINDERS
○ Wear good aerobic shoes.
○ Listen to your body.
○ Check your exercise heart rate to make sure you are in your personalized target zone. As well, periodically monitor your exercise intensity with the perceived exertion scale and talk test.
○ Gradually increase your exercise intensity.
○ Make floor contact with your whole foot.
○ Do not hop on one foot more than four times in a row.
○ Stay away from twisting hop variations (stress on the spine). Drink water during exercise; your thirst doesn't keep up with your body's need for water.
○ Important: gradually wind down your aerobics to a brisk walking pace. This is called the aerobic cool-down.

Did You Know?

10 billion white blood cells are made every day.

Did You Know?

95% of fat stored in the human body is in the form of a triglyceride.

STEP KNEE HOPS

**JOGGING IN
PLACE**

STEP KICKS   Photos © Jacob Covell

© Jacob Covell

SIDE LEG SLIDES

JUMP ROPE HOPS © Jacob Covell

JABS

© Jacob Covell

POWER RUNS

© Jacob Covell

JUMPING JACKS

© Jacob Covell

LUNGE CLAPS

© Jacob Covell

JUMP KICKS

© Jacob Covell

STRIDE RUNS

© Jacob Covell

Aerobic Kickboxing: A Knockout Punch

Aerobic kickboxing, kickbox fitness, box-step, and cardio-karate are a few class names that have become a staple core of the group-led exercise industry. Enthusiasts are enjoying the power from throwing kicks, punches, elbows, jabs, knee strikes, and combinations used in boxing and kickboxing. The athletic drills in these classes are mixed with recovery bouts of basic aerobic movements such as boxer-style rope skipping and easy jogging. Some programs utilize authentic boxing and martial arts equipment whereas others do a form of "shadow boxing." All classes are driven by high-energy music and have provided a new alternative to group-led exercise classes, which appeal to both women and men. Research by this author suggests that the energy cost of this type of exercise ranges from 6.5 to 8.4 kilocalories a minute for a 130-pound female.

With the popularity and excitement however, some new challenges have surfaced such as safety for the participants. A key concern is that instructors have the proper knowledge to teach correct punching techniques. The challenge involves integrating skill with a motivating workout environment. Several organizations have established their own standards of safety, but there are no nationally accepted guidelines among certifying groups. The best advice to participants is to make sure the class instructor has had some type of specialized training and/or certification. Instructors need to be aware of the appropriate development skills and precautions to use when teaching these martial arts workouts.

Aerobic Kickboxing Safety Guidelines

1. With all upper body jabs and strikes, keep your elbows from locking out.

2. Avoid performing complex upper body strike and lower body kick combinations.

3. Avoid high repetitions of any aerobic kickboxing move.

4. Do not do physical contact exercises without proper skill progressions.

5. Kicking and pivoting may lead to lower extremity injury. Always master the basic moves before progressing to advanced kickboxing movements.

6. Safe music speeds for aerobic kickboxing are from 120 to 135 bpm.

7. Be aware that the newness of kickboxing movements may lead to more delayed-onset muscle soreness when starting this type of program.

8. Give yourself plenty of floor space when doing your kickboxing movements.

9. Deliver punches from the body as opposed to from the shoulders.

© Jacob Covell

Aquatic Exercise Workouts

Water fitness classes (in 81° to 84°) are steadily growing in popularity with all fitness levels. These workouts have been shown to postively reduce percent body fat and improve muscular fitness. The three water depths used in water fitness classes are (1) shallow, which is navel to nipple; (2) transitional, which is nipple to neck; and (3) deep, where the feet are not touching the bottom. Lower body exercises in shallow water level incorporate more jumping and leaping exercise movements. In deep water exercise, where some type of buoyancy is used, the lower body challenge can be intensified with the use of aquatic exercise equipment to add more resistance to the movement. Always reduce the speed of the exercises in water as compared to similar movements on land. In fact, it is often preferable to self-adjust your exercise movement speed in water based on your own level of perceived exertion. Also, several types of aquatic equipment (such as fins, webbed gloves, and nonbuoyant bells) have been designed to provide a variety of different exercise options in aquatic exercise workouts. In aquatic exercise, attempt to keep your entire body in motion during the entire water workout. Try to always combine upper and lower body exercises and enjoy the variety of this wonderful workout.

© Rido/Shutterstock.com

Indoor Cycling Workouts

Indoor cycling classes are very popular aerobic workouts. Because of its non-weight bearing nature, indoor cycling workouts offer some orthopedic advantages for anyone having limitations with weight-bearing exercise. With indoor cycling, it is common to visualize you are on a 'virtual' outdoor race or scenic ride (with hills, curves, straight-aways, and valleys), where you pace your exercise intensity according to the demands of the situation. Motivational music and softer room lighting really enhance this type of aerobic workout. Because of the stationary nature of this workout, adequate air circulation is quite important. You can adjust your intensity with your wheel resistance, pedaling speed, and body position (seated or standing) while cycling. Make sure you are fitted correctly for your bike. Your downstroking knee should never lock out when extended and your upstroking knee should not exceed the level of your hip. Always wear cycling shorts with padded inserts to lessen any discomfort from the prolonged sitting. A hard-soled cycling shoe is recommended to decrease pressure on the feet while pedaling. Make sure your shoes provide plenty of movement space in the toe area to avoid numbness in the ball of the foot. Also, make sure you are fully aware of the operation and adjustments of the exercise bike before starting. Don't forget to bring your water bottle with you and a towel to wipe off your seat as you exercise. It is a heathful idea to vary your riding position during the workout to lessen the stress on your lower back. As well, don't place too much body weight on the handlebars during the standing position cycling. As these classes are sometimes quite strenuous, plan for a longer and more gradual cooldown when finishing this highly enjoyable workout.

> **Did You Know?**
>
> 31% of a woman's body weight is muscle.

> **Did You Know?**
>
> 38% of a man's body weight is muscle.

© Jacob Covell

Are You Ready for Some High Intensity Interval Training Workouts?

Introduction to High Intensity Interval Training

High intensity interval training (HIIT) workouts are enormously popular programs in the fitness industry. These training sessions typically include short bursts (from 6 seconds to 4 minutes) of challenging exercise (≥ 80% of maximal heart rate) alternated with relief breaks of varying length. The workouts include a limitless variety of exercises including body weight movements, power lifting, plyometrics, sprints, playground physical activities (e.g., sled pushes and pulls), multiple mode training (e.g., cycle ergometer, treadmill, elliptical training, etc.), heavy rope drills, and more. Characteristically, HIIT is depicted as an approach to training that provides several health, fitness, and performance benefits in a time-efficient manner.

How Much Can HIIT Improve Cardiovascular Fitness?

Comprehensive research reviews on high-intensity interval report that healthy young and older adult men and women can improve cardiorespiratory fitness from 4% to 46% in training periods lasting from 2 to 15 weeks in length. The improvement range varies depending on a person's initial fitness level. HIIT training appears to induce rather rapid changes in aerobic capacity. The scientific explanation for this increase in aerobic capacity from HIIT training is proposed to be primarily a consequential increase in stroke volume (volume of blood pumped by the heart per beat), which is induced by an increase in the heart muscles' contractile capability during near maximal exertion. All of the epidemiology and clinical studies show very similar results; that the vigorous exercise intensity from HIIT is also quite beneficial in positively altering one or more risk factors to coronary heart disease. Thus, for counteracting the effects of cardiovascular disease, the number one cause of death throughout the world, HIIT should be considered a most advantageous training intervention.

© Jacob Covell

What Is the Effect of HIIT on Insulin Resistance?

Studies indicate that insulin sensitivity can be improved 23% to 58% with HIIT training. The mechanism for this improvement appears to be well documented, with the ability of the exercising muscle contractions to stimulate the glucose shuttle transporters (known as GLUT4 translocaters) to take up glucose into the working muscle (from the blood), whether insulin is available or not.

What Is the Effect of HIIT on Cholesterol Levels?

HIIT has been shown to meaningfully improve HDL cholesterol (sometimes referred to as the good or healthy cholesterol) levels after a minimum of 8 weeks of training. Scientists suggest that HIIT with an accompanying moderate decrease in body fat (or body weight) is needed to see improvements in total cholesterol, LDL cholesterol, and blood triglycerides levels.

What Is the Effect of HIIT on Blood Pressure?

Researchers conclude that about 12 weeks of consistent HIIT training can lower elevated systolic and diastolic blood pressure (from 2% to 8%) in persons not on any hypertension medicine.

HIIT Program Development

I'd like to go over a few details to ensure understanding the HIIT workout designs ARE as effortless as possible. The title of each HIIT workout indicates its WORK/RECOVERY ratio and whether it's in seconds, minutes, or a combination of both. To get a better understanding of what I mean, let's analyze the title of an actual workout: "*Workout #5: 30s/30s HIIT.*" First, as you can probably figure out, this is the fifth HIIT workout in the book. Next, the "30s/30s" alerts you right away that the WORK interval of this exercise is 30 seconds and the RECOVERY interval is 30 seconds. If you see "3m/3m" in the workout title, it tells you the WORK interval is 3 minutes and the RECOVERY interval is 3 minutes. Basically, the title of each HIIT workout prepares you for the workout itself. Please note there are many interval training apps you can get on your mobile device to set times for your HIIT workouts. They are easy to program the times for the different HIIT workouts.

Below the title of each workout I have crafted a workout blueprint for you to follow. As you'll notice, most of the HIIT workouts actually let you choose up to three workout lengths, each falling between ten and twenty minutes in duration (not counting the warm-up and cooldown). So, counting the warm-up, cooldown, and workout, every HIIT workout in this book is about thirty minutes or less.

If you're wondering why they're short, here's why: The number one reason people state they do not work out is a lack of time. Simply put, most people say they just don't have enough time to fit exercise into their busy schedule. The great news is HIIT training has been shown in research to be a remarkably time-efficient type of training. That said, I welcome you to vary the length of each workout depending on how you feel. In each workout, I suggest appropriate intensities for the high intensity WORK intervals as well as the light intensity RECOVERY intervals using the perceived exertion and talk test gauges. On any day, and at any moment, feel empowered to modify the workout to best meet your desired level of exertion and duration. *You are in charge of every workout*!

For those of you doing swimming HIIT workouts, I suggest you do TWO laps at a comfortable but challenging intensity and time yourself. This will give you a time frame to work from when doing the HIIT WORK intervals. Do the same thing for your RECOVERY intervals: time yourself on two laps at a light to somewhat hard swimming intensity. You can't easily take a timer in the water with you, but you can gauge how many laps you do. Swimmers do this all the time.

Special Tip! Do not do more than three HIIT workouts a week to allow your body to fully recover and to prevent overtraining. Also, for variety, try doing HIIT on different modes of exercise. All of these HIIT workouts can be completed while walking, jogging, running, biking, elliptical striding, swimming, rowing, stair stepping, and/or using any type of cardio machine. Let's get started! Here are twelve fabulous HIIT workouts.

Workout #1: 60s/90s HIIT

Warm-up: Complete a 5–7-minute progressive warm-up at a perceived exertion intensity (RPE) level of 9–11 (light to mild-feeling intensity). Do the same exercise you will do for your HIIT workout.

	Interval	Duration	Intensity
	HIIT WORKOUT DESIGN		
BOUT 1	WORK Interval 1	60 seconds	RPE: Level 15: Feels challenging TALK Test: Moderate difficulty talking
	RECOVERY Interval 1	90 seconds	RPE: Level 10–13: Light movement to somewhat hard TALK Test: Mild to no difficulty talking
BOUT 2	WORK Interval 2	60 seconds	RPE: Level 15–16: Challenging to more challenging TALK Test: Moderate difficulty talking
	RECOVERY Interval 2	90 seconds	RPE: Level 10–11: Light movement TALK Test: Mild to no difficulty talking

Choose the length of this workout depending on how you feel!
Progression: Start off with the 10-minute workout.
    For a 10-minute workout complete 4 BOUTS
    For a 15-minute workout complete 6 BOUTS
    For a 20-minute workout complete 8 BOUTS
Cooldown: 3–5-minute progressive recovery at a mild intensity

Workout #2: 60s/60s HIIT

Warm-up: Complete a 5–7-minute progressive warm-up at a perceived exertion intensity (RPE) level of 9–11 (light to a mild-feeling intensity). Do the same exercise you will do for your HIIT workout.

	Interval	Duration	Intensity
	HIIT WORKOUT DESIGN		
BOUT 1	WORK Interval 1	60 seconds	RPE: Level 15: Feels challenging TALK Test: Moderate difficulty talking
	RECOVERY Interval 1	60 seconds	RPE: Level 10–13: Light movement to somewhat hard TALK Test: Mild to no difficulty talking
BOUT 2	WORK Interval 2	60 seconds	RPE: Level 15–16: Challenging to more challenging TALK Test: Moderate difficulty talking
	RECOVERY Interval 2	60 seconds	RPE: Level 10–13: Light movement to somewhat hard TALK Test: Mild to no difficulty talking

Choose the length of this workout depending on how you feel!
Progression: Start off with the 10-minute workout.
    For a 10-minute workout complete 5 BOUTS
    For a 15-minute workout complete 7 BOUTS
    For a 20-minute workout complete 10 BOUTS
Cooldown: 3–5-minute progressive recovery at a mild intensity

Workout #3: 60s/30s HIIT

Warm-up: Complete a 5–7-minute warm-up at a perceived exertion intensity (RPE) 9–11 (light to mild-feeling intensity). Do the same exercise you will do for your HIIT workout.

HIIT WORKOUT DESIGN			
	Interval	Duration	Intensity
BOUT 1	WORK Interval 1	60 seconds	RPE: Level 15: Feels challenging TALK Test: Moderate difficulty talking
	RECOVERY Interval 1	30 seconds	RPE: Level 10–13: Light movement to somewhat hard TALK Test: Mild to no difficulty talking
BOUT 2	WORK Interval 2	60 seconds	RPE: Level 15–16: Challenging to more challenging TALK Test: Moderate difficulty talking
	RECOVERY Interval 2	30 seconds	RPE: Level 10–13: Light movement to somewhat hard TALK Test: Mild to no difficulty talking

Choose the length of this workout depending on how you feel!
Progression: Start off with the 10-minute workout.
>   For a 10-minute workout complete 6 BOUTS
>   For a 15-minute workout complete 10 BOUTS
>   For a 20-minute workout complete 13 BOUTS

Cooldown: 3–5-minute progressive recovery at a mild intensity

Workout #4: 90s/30s HIIT

Warm-up: Complete a 5–7-minute progressive warm-up at a perceived exertion intensity (RPE) of 9–11 (light to mild-feeling intensity). Do the same exercise you will do for your HIIT workout.

HIIT WORKOUT DESIGN			
	Interval	Duration	Intensity
BOUT 1	WORK Interval 1	90 seconds	RPE: Level 15: Feels challenging TALK Test: Moderate difficulty talking
	RECOVERY Interval 1	30 seconds	RPE: Level 10–13: Light movement to somewhat hard TALK Test: Mild to no difficulty talking
BOUT 2	WORK Interval 2	90 seconds	RPE: Level 15–16: Challenging to more challenging TALK Test: Moderate difficulty talking
	RECOVERY Interval 2	30 seconds	RPE: Level 10–13: Light movement to somewhat hard TALK Test: Mild to no difficulty talking

Choose the length of this workout depending on how you feel!
Progression: Start off with the 10-minute workout.
>   For a 10-minute workout complete 5 BOUTS
>   For a 15-minute workout complete 7 BOUTS
>   For a 20-minute workout complete 10 BOUTS

Cooldown: 3–5-minute progressive recovery at a mild intensity

Workout #5: 30s/30s HIIT

Warm-up: Complete a 5–7-minute progressive warm-up at a perceived exertion intensity (RPE) of 9–11 (light to mild-feeling intensity). Do the same exercise you will do for your HIIT workout.

HIIT WORKOUT DESIGN			
	Interval	Duration	Intensity
BOUT 1	WORK Interval 1	30 seconds	RPE: Level 15: Feels challenging TALK Test: Moderate difficulty talking
	RECOVERY Interval 1	30 seconds	RPE: Level 10–13: Light movement to somewhat hard TALK Test: Mild to no difficulty talking
BOUT 2	WORK Interval 2	30 seconds	RPE: Level 15–16: Challenging to more challenging TALK Test: Moderate difficulty talking
	RECOVERY Interval 2	30 seconds	RPE: Level 10–13: Light movement to somewhat hard TALK Test: Mild to no difficulty talking

Choose the length of this workout depending on how you feel!
Progression: Start off with the 10-minute workout.
>   For a 10-minute workout complete 10 BOUTS
>   For a 15-minute workout complete 15 BOUTS
>   For a 20-minute workout complete 20 BOUTS

Cooldown: 3–5-minute progressive recovery at a mild intensity

Workout #6: 30s/45s HIIT

Warm-up: Complete a 5–7-minute progressive warm-up at a perceived exertion intensity (RPE) of 9–11 (light to mild-feeling intensity). Do the same exercise you will do for your HIIT workout.

HIIT WORKOUT DESIGN			
	Interval	Duration	Intensity
BOUT 1	WORK Interval 1	30 seconds	RPE: Level 15: Feels challenging TALK Test: Moderate difficulty talking
	RECOVERY Interval 1	45 seconds	RPE: Level 10–13: Light movement to somewhat hard TALK Test: Mild to no difficulty talking
BOUT 2	WORK Interval 2	30 seconds	RPE: Level 5–6: Challenging to more challenging TALK Test: Moderate difficulty talking
	RECOVERY Interval 2	45 seconds	RPE: Level 10–13: Light movement to somewhat hard TALK Test: Mild to no difficulty talking

Choose the length of this workout depending on how you feel!
Progression: Start off with the 10-minute workout.
>   For a 10-minute workout complete 8 BOUTS
>   For a 15-minute workout complete 12 BOUTS
>   For a 20-minute workout complete 16 BOUTS

Cooldown: 3–5-minute progressive recovery at a mild intensity

Workout #7: 30s/60s HIIT

Warm-up: Complete a 5–7-minute progressive warm-up at a perceived exertion intensity (RPE) of 9–11 (light to mild-feeling intensity). Do the same exercise you will do for your HIIT workout.

HIIT WORKOUT DESIGN			
	Interval	Duration	Intensity
BOUT 1	WORK Interval 1	30 seconds	RPE: Level 15: Feels challenging
			TALK Test: Moderate difficulty talking
	RECOVERY Interval 1	60 seconds	RPE: Level 10–13: Light movement to somewhat hard
			TALK Test: Mild to no difficulty talking
BOUT 2	WORK Interval 2	30 seconds	RPE: Level 15–16: Challenging to more challenging
			TALK Test: Moderate difficulty talking
	RECOVERY Interval 2	60 seconds	RPE: Level 10–13: Light movement to somewhat hard
			TALK Test: Mild to no difficulty talking

Choose the length of this workout depending on how you feel!
Progression: Start off with the 10-minute workout.
  For a 10-minute workout complete 7 BOUTS
  For a 15-minute workout complete 10 BOUTS
  For a 20-minute workout complete 13 BOUTS
Cooldown: 3–5-minute progressive recovery at a mild intensity

Workout #8: 3m/3m HIIT

Warm-up: Complete a 5–7-minute progressive warm-up at a perceived exertion intensity (RPE) level of 9–11 (light to mild-feeling intensity). Do the same exercise you will do for your HIIT workout.

HIIT WORKOUT DESIGN			
	Interval	Duration	Intensity
BOUT 1	WORK Interval 1	3 minutes	RPE: Level 15: Feels challenging
			TALK Test: Moderate difficulty talking
	RECOVERY Interval 1	3 minutes	RPE: Level 10–13: Light movement to somewhat hard
			TALK Test: Mild to no difficulty talking
BOUT 2	WORK Interval 2	3 minutes	RPE: Level 15–16: Challenging to more challenging
			TALK Test: Moderate difficulty talking
	RECOVERY Interval 2	3 minutes	RPE: Level 10–13: Light movement to somewhat hard
			TALK Test: Mild to no difficulty talking

Choose the length of this workout depending on how you feel!
Progression: Start off with the 12-minute workout.
  For a 12-minute workout complete 2 BOUTS
  For an 18-minute workout complete 3 BOUTS
Cooldown: 3–5-minute progressive recovery at a mild intensity

Workout #9: 3m/4m HIIT

Warm-up: Complete a 5–7-minute progressive warm-up at a perceived exertion intensity (RPE) level of 9–11 (light to mild-feeling intensity). Do the same exercise you will do for your HIIT workout.

HIIT WORKOUT DESIGN			
	Interval	Duration	Intensity
BOUT 1	WORK Interval 1	3 minutes	RPE: Level 15: Feels challenging
			TALK Test: Moderate difficulty talking
	RECOVERY Interval 1	4 minutes	RPE: Level 10–13: Light movement to somewhat hard
			TALK Test: Mild to no difficulty talking
BOUT 2	WORK Interval 2	3 minutes	RPE: Level 15–16: Challenging to more challenging
			TALK Test: Moderate difficulty talking
	RECOVERY Interval 2	4 minutes	RPE: Level 10–13: Light movement to somewhat hard
			TALK Test: Mild to no difficulty talking

Choose the length of this workout depending on how you feel!
Progression: Start off with the 14-minute workout.
>   For a 14-minute workout complete 2 BOUTS
>   For a 21-minute workout complete 3 BOUTS

Cooldown: 3–5-minute progressive recovery at a mild intensity

Workout #10: 3m/6m HIIT

Warm-up: Complete a 5–7-minute progressive warm-up at a perceived exertion intensity (RPE) level of 9–11 (light to mild-feeling intensity). Do the same exercise you will do for your HIIT workout.

HIIT WORKOUT DESIGN			
	Interval	Duration	Intensity
BOUT 1	WORK Interval 1	3 minutes	RPE: Level 15: Feels challenging
			TALK Test: Moderate difficulty talking
	RECOVERY Interval 1	6 minutes	RPE: Level 10–13: Light movement to somewhat hard
			TALK Test: Mild to no difficulty talking
BOUT 2	WORK Interval 2	3 minutes	RPE: Level 5–6: Challenging to more challenging
			TALK Test: Moderate difficulty talking
	RECOVERY Interval 2	6 minutes	RPE: Level 10–13: Light movement to somewhat hard
			TALK Test: Mild to no difficulty talking

Choose the length of this workout depending on how you feel!
Progression: Start off with the 9-minute workout.
>   For a 9-minute workout complete 1 BOUT
>   For an 18-minute workout complete 2 BOUTS

Cooldown: 3–5-minute progressive recovery at a mild intensity

Workout #11: 4m/3m HIIT

Warm-up: Complete a 5–7-minute progressive warm-up at a perceived exertion intensity (RPE) of 9–11 (light to mild-feeling intensity). Do the same exercise you will do for your HIIT workout.

HIIT WORKOUT DESIGN			
	Interval	Duration	Intensity
BOUT 1	WORK Interval 1	4 minutes	RPE: Level 15: Feels challenging TALK Test: Moderate difficulty talking
	RECOVERY Interval 1	3 minutes	RPE: Level 10–13: Light movement to somewhat hard TALK Test: Mild to no difficulty talking
BOUT 2	WORK Interval 2	4 minutes	RPE: Level 15–16: Challenging to more challenging TALK Test: Moderate difficulty talking
	RECOVERY Interval 2	3 minutes	RPE: Level 10–13: Light movement to somewhat hard TALK Test: Mild to no difficulty talking

Choose the length of this workout depending on how you feel!
Progression: Start off with the 14-minute workout.
    For a 14-minute workout complete 2 BOUTS
    For a 21-minute workout complete 3 BOUTS
Cooldown: 3–5-minute progressive recovery at a mild intensity

Workout #12: 4m/2m HIIT

Warm-up: Complete a 5–7-minute progressive warm-up at a perceived exertion intensity (RPE) level of 9–11 (light to mild-feeling intensity). Do the same exercise you will do for your HIIT workout.

HIIT WORKOUT DESIGN			
	Interval	Duration	Intensity
BOUT 1	WORK Interval 1	4 minutes	RPE: Level 15: Feels challenging TALK Test: Moderate difficulty talking
	RECOVERY Interval 1	2 minutes	RPE: Level 10–13: Light movement to somewhat hard TALK Test: Mild to no difficulty talking
BOUT 2	WORK Interval 2	4 minutes	RPE: Level 15–16: Challenging to more challenging TALK Test: Moderate difficulty talking
	RECOVERY Interval 2	2 minutes	RPE: Level 10–13: Light movement to somewhat hard TALK Test: Mild to no difficulty talking

Choose the length of this workout depending on how you feel!
Progression: Start off with the 12-minute workout.
    For a 12-minute workout complete 2 BOUTS
    For an 18-minute workout complete 3 BOUTSs
Cooldown: 3–5-minute progressive recovery at a mild intensity

Body Conditioning Workouts

The following pages include several different body conditioning training programs. They include:

1. A site-specific exercise section to choose specific exercises for body areas of interest.

2. A total body super sculpturing workout with hand-held weights.

3. A time-efficient, total body circuit training program, complete with instructions on how to progress the circuit.

4. Two new peripheral heart action training workouts.

5. The biomotor PHA functional power exercises and workout.

For best body shaping results, regularly vary your selection of these workouts to continuously challenge your muscles with different movement stimuli.

© Jacob Covell

Chest, Shoulder, and Arm Developers

Perform 10 to 30 repetitions of each exercise.

Biceps Curls
(Front of the arms)

Action: With a curl bar (called an EZ bar) or dumbbells. Use your biceps strength to move the bar or dumbbell from the starting position in a semicircular arc to your shoulders.

Tips: Keep the core engaged and do not let your torso move back and forth.

© Jacob Covell

Wide-Arm Push-ups or Push-ups
(Chest, shoulders, and arms)

Action: Place arms shoulder width apart or wider than shoulder width apart. Keep fingers facing forward.

Tips: Engage the core the entire time you complete your push-ups.

© Jacob Covell

Pike Push-ups
(Shoulders and triceps—back of the arms)

Action: A push-up with hips up and hands closer to feet. Legs together or open to a straddle.

Tips: Placing the hands closer together is more challenging.

© Jacob Covell

Dips
(Shoulders, chest, and triceps)

Action: With hands on bench or chair, bend and extend the arms.

Tips: Keep hands facing forward and legs extended forward.

© Jacob Covell

For a Stable Core: The Excellent Eight

Perform 15 to 40 repetitions of each exercise.

Regular Crunch
(Abdominals)

Action: Lift the back and shoulders off the floor. Push the small of the back against the floor. Rotate pelvis so buttocks are slightly off floor.

Tips: Feet are on the floor approximately six to ten inches from the buttocks. Hands may support the head at the base of the neck or lie across the chest. Focus on the ceiling.

Variation: Squeeze your knees together for inner thigh work as well.

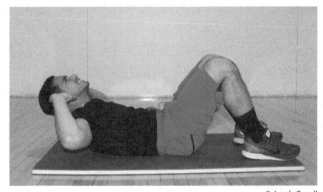

© Jacob Covell

Twisting Crunch
(Abdominals and obliques—sides)

Action: Alternate shoulders as you lift your upper back off the floor.

Tips: Vary your technique by either lifting first and then twisting or by twisting first and then lifting.

© Jacob Covell

Reverse Crunch
(Lower abdominals)

Action: Slowly lift buttocks off the ground a couple of inches.

Tips: Keep the knees bent.

Variation: Bring chest toward knee (as you lift the buttocks) for an even more challenging crunch. Press the heels into the buttocks to relax your hip flexors and work the abdominals more.

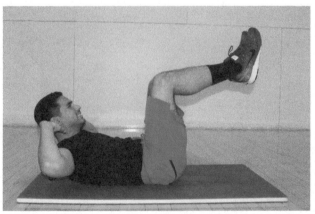

© Jacob Covell

Rope Pull Crunch
(Abdominals and obliques)

Action: Lift shoulder blades off the floor and alternate reaching the arms (as if pulling a rope).

Tips: Make sure the small of the back is pressed into floor.

© Jacob Covell

The All-Around Crunch
(Abdominals and obliques)

Action: Alternate with a twisting crunch to one side, a regular crunch straight up, and a twisting crunch to the other side.

Tips: Lift the legs so the thighs are perpendicular to the floor and bent at the knees. You may wish to place your feet on a chair.

Variation: Randomly mix the pattern of the side, up, other side to surprise your abdominal muscles—they have to work harder!

© Jacob Covell

Back Extension
(After working the abdominal muscles, it is correct to work the opposite muscle group: the lower back.)

Action: Slowly lift the head, shoulders, and chest off the floor from the prone position. The arms may help with the lift, remain at the sides, or be held close to the shoulders.

Tips: Keep the feet on the floor to protect the spine. Stretch up and out.

© Jacob Covell

Horizontal Side Bridge
(Deep abdominals and spinal muscles)

© Jacob Covell

Action: Do this exercise on a padded surface. Lie on your side with the knees bent at about a 90-degree angle. With the abdominals pulled in, push up with the elbow, lifting the torso off the ground. Hold for 6 to 12 seconds and then lower and repeat several times on both sides.

Tips: Keep the nonsupportive hand on the hip facing the ceiling.

Variation: For greater challenge, do the exercise with the knees off the floor and legs extended.

Rolling Side Bridge
(Deep abdominals and spinal muscles)

Action: Lie on your side with your legs extended. Pull in the abdominal muscles and push up to a side bridge. Roll slowly to a front prone position with both elbows on the ground and then roll to the other elbow.

Tips: Move very slowly and work up to repeating this entire sequence for up to 30 to 45 seconds or until the muscles fatigue.

Variation: For a more challenging side bridge, place the upper foot in front of the lower foot. This will cause more instability, making you work your intrinsic spinal muscles even more.

© Jacob Covell

Thighs, Hips, and Buttocks

These body parts are best worked together! Use elastic resistance or exercise equipment or wear leg weights for an adequate overload. Perform 15 to 30 repetitions of each exercise.

Back Thigh Lifts
(Back thigh, buttocks, and hip)

Action: Keeping an erect standing position with the resistance on one ankle, bring the leg toward the rear to a comfortable ending point.

Tips: For balance, place one arm on an immobile surface.

Variation: Do this exercise slightly toward the angle (between straight back and to the side). It works the same muscles and some people find it more comfortable.

© Jacob Covell

Hip Adduction
(Inner thigh)

Action: From a standing position, extend one leg to the side making sure you feel a moderate resistance on the leg. Pull the leg in front and across the midline of the body. Return slowly to starting position.

Tips: Try not to let the body twist during this exercise.

Variation: Hold leg across midline of movement for 3 seconds before returning to starting position.

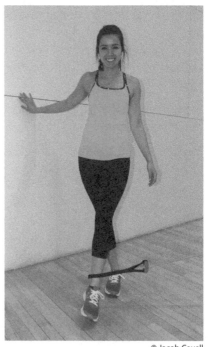

© Jacob Covell

Hip Abduction
(Outer thighs and hips)

Action: From a standing position with feet together and resistance strap around the outer leg, lift the leg straight to the side.

Tips: Do not let the body swing from side to side and keep your feet facing forward.

Variation: Hold the movement for 3 seconds out to the side before returning to starting position.

© Jacob Covell

Bird-Dog Exercise
(Buttocks and lower back)

Action: Starting on the hands and knees, slowly raise one arm and the opposite leg to a horizontal position and hold for 6 seconds. Lower the arm and leg and then repeat with the other arm and opposite leg. Repeat several times.

Tips: Pull in the abdominals while doing this exercise.

Variation: You can also do this exercise while lying in a prone position.

© Jacob Covell

Tightening Tips

○ Remember to repeat all exercises on both sides. Vary your exercise performance tempo.

○ There is a tendency in leg work to roll back at the hip and let the powerful quadriceps (front of the thigh muscles) do the work—watch your technique.

○ It is not necessary to lift the legs high for results.

○ Combine full range-of-motion exercises with "pulse" movements—take the leg to the top end of the range and perform small "pulse" movements.

Inner Thigh Extras

Inner Thigh Lifts—Knee Down

Action: Lie on side with head supported by bent arm or resting on straight arm. Bring top leg over extended bottom leg and relax top knee into the floor. Lift lower leg up and down.

Tips: Concentrate on lifting with bottom heel. Perform 15 to 30 repetitions. You may need to use ankle weights to effectively challenge your inner thighs.

© Jacob Covell

Wide Squats

Action: Stand with feet placed wider than shoulders. Keeping your back straight, bend your knees until your buttocks are slightly above knee height. Hold this position for 15 to 30 seconds.

Tips: Make sure your knees point directly over your toes.

Variation: While in this squat position go up and down very slowly and focus on using the muscles of the inner thigh.

© Jacob Covell

Super Sculpturing with Weights

If you really want to attain that sleek, firm, and shapely look, use weights. You can work all the major muscles of the body with hand weights. Perform 8 to 20 repetitions of each exercise, doing two to four sets of each exercise. Be sure to rest 30 to 60 seconds between sets.

Squat
(Buttocks and thighs)

Action: Stand with feet placed wider than shoulders. Hold weights into chest or next to shoulders. Keeping your back straight, bend legs and squat down with your buttocks no lower than your knee height and return to start.

Tips: Make sure your buttocks go back as you sit and your knees stay over your toes. Do this carefully if you have knee problems!

Variation: Change the width of your stance to work all the muscles completely.

© Jacob Covell

Long Lunge
(Thighs and buttocks)

Action: Stand with feet together and hand weights next to shoulder or down by your side. Step forward about two to three feet with one leg to a bent knee position. Keep the back leg extended, allowing it to bend slightly. Push back to a stand and repeat on other leg.

Tips: Keep your back straight and press into the bending leg.

Variation: Stand with feet together and hand weights by side. "Step back" into lunge position.

© Jacob Covell

Short Lunge
(Thighs and buttocks)

Action: Stand with one foot two to three feet in front of the other foot. Hold dumbbells on your shoulders. Bend both legs as the back knee comes within 3 inches of the ground and then straighten up. Do on both sides.

Tips: You may wish to turn front toes out slightly for better balance.

© Jacob Covell

Heel Raises
(Calves)

Action: Stand with legs wider than shoulder width, feet slightly turned out. Hold weights along sides. Lift heels high off the ground and then lower.

Tips: Perform this exercise on a thick book or block of wood to allow a larger range of motion.

© Jacob Covell

Chest Press
(Chest, shoulders, and arms)

Action: Lie on a bench or floor with hand weights held by shoulders. Extend arms straight up and back down to side.

Tips: Keep elbows out from body at the start for effective chest overload. Bend knees with feet on the bench (ground) or with knees pulled toward the chest to safeguard the lower back.

© Jacob Covell

Flys
(Chest and arms)

Action: Same position (on bench or floor) as chest press. Start with hand weights extended above chest and lower arms perpendicularly away from body and then back up.

Tips: Keep arms slightly bent throughout the exercise and palms facing each other.

Variation: Modify the position of the hand weights as they extend over the chest.

© Jacob Covell

Crunches with Weights
(Abdominals)

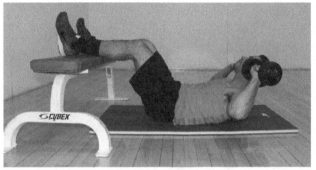

Action: With back on the floor, weight(s) held to the side of the head or on chest, lift upper back off the floor and lower. Place lower legs on bench or chair.

Tips: Press the heels onto the bench as you lift up.

Variation: Twist side to side on the crunch.

© Jacob Covell

Standing Rows
(Upper and middle back)

Action: Stand with legs shoulder width apart and upper body slightly forward. Slightly bend at the knee. Weights (barbell, EZ bar, or dumbbells) are extended in front of the body. Pull elbows as far back as they will go and return to start.

Tips: Do not been forward too much, as this may stress the spine.

Variation: Stand in lunge position with weight in one hand. Bend over at waist and place other hand on bent knee for support. Pull arm straight back and lower.

© Jacob Covell

Shoulder Press
(Shoulders and triceps)

Action: May be done standing or sitting.

Shoulder: Start with hand weights held next to shoulder. Press weights straight over head and return to start.

Tips: Make sure you keep your back stable during the exercise.

Variation: Alternate pressing one arm and then the other arm to concentrate on each side.

© Jacob Covell

Side Lateral Raises
(Shoulders and back)

Action: Hold hand weights next to your side. Keeping arms slightly bent, elevate weights laterally to shoulder height and lower.

Tips: Do not "lock" elbow joints or raise arms above shoulders.

Variation: For more upper back work, sit in a chair and bend forward at hips. Lift weights to shoulder height with bent arms and lower.

© Jacob Covell

Dumbbell Kickbacks

Action: Grasp dumbbell in one hand and place other hand (and same side knee) on bench. Keeping your back straight and core engaged, bend the working arm to a 90-degree angle. Slowly straighten the working arm and then return to starting position. Complete desired number of repetitions on one arm and then complete on other side.

Variation: Instead of placing one knee on bench, you can place both legs on floor and just place hand on bench for stability and balance.

© Jacob Covell

Bicep Curls
(Biceps—front of arms)

Action: Stand with legs shoulder-width apart and knees bent. Bring weights to shoulder and lower.

Tips: Keep the hands in a "palm-up" position.

Variation: Alternate lifting one arm and then the other. Or do the curls in a lunge position.

© Jacob Covell

Super Sculpture Tips

○ Find a hand weight that's comfortable, yet challenging.

○ For variety, vary the number of repetitions, the sequence of exercises, the number of sets, or the weight.

○ For best results perform this routine two or (preferably) three times a week.

○ As the weight gets easy to work with, gradually overload with a heavier weight, more repetitions, more sets, or less time between sets.

○ Try a circuit training format (time effective and good for muscular endurance training): perform a set of each exercise and then move to the next exercise without resting. Perform two to four circuits.

○ Refer to *A Circuit Workout* for more on circuit training.

Did You Know?

The longest nerve in the body is the sciatic nerve.

Did You Know?

99% of the calcium in your body is in your teeth.

Did You Know?

Joint cracking you hear sometimes in exercise or movement is a rapid release of gases into joint space.

START

FINISH

SQUATS

SHOULDER PRESS

WIDE-ARMED PUSH-UPS

BIRD-DOG EXERCISE

BACK EXTENSIONS

Circuit training is one of the most popular forms of training because you constantly move and change from one exercise to another. No rest is needed between exercises because you are working different muscle groups at each station. Circuit training can be performed with or without weights. By placing an aerobic station between each exercise (except for those done lying on the floor), you can burn additional calories and improve your level of fitness.

POWER LUNGES

SIDE LATERAL RAISES

STANDING ROWS

Perform 15 to 30 repetitions at each station for a 45-second work interval. Then move to the next station. Go through the circuit two to three times. Try working out to music. Make sure you warm up before you start and stretch out when you finish. You can progressively overload by the following means (but choose only one method at a time):

1. Increase the number of stations.

2. Repeat the circuit another time.

3. Increase the number of repetitions at each station.

4. Increase the load of weights.

5. Increase the pace of the workload.

BICEP CURLS

CRUNCHES

TRICEP EXTENSIONS

Introducing Peripheral Heart Action Training: A New Idea in Exercise

Peripheral heart action (PHA) training is a system of conditioning developed by Dr. Arthur Steinhaus in the 1940s. The concept of this training is to keep blood consistently circulating during the resistance training session. Typically, six exercises are performed sequentially (and with no rest between exercises) at a medium intensity to alternately stress the upper and lower body muscles. Interestingly, despite the early introduction of PHA to the fitness world, very little investigation has been conducted to examine its effect on cardiovascular and autonomic function (branch of nervous system that controls internal organs and regulates heart rate, respiration, and cardiac function). Recently, Piras and colleagues compared the cardiovascular and autonomic function effect of PHA to high intensity interval training in a young, untrained population.

© Jacob Covell

Let's Explore This New Study

Eighteen healthy volunteers (nine women and nine men, twenty-four years) were randomly assigned to a PHA group (ten participants) or a HIIT group (eight participants which served as an active exercise control group). All participants were disease-free non-smokers, not on any prescribed medications. The participants were recreationally active, but untrained, and their maximal aerobic capacity average was 32.89 ml/kg/min, which is a "poor" classification for their age and sex.

All volunteers did a pre- and post-test of several cardiovascular parameters within three to four days of a three-month training period consisting of three sessions per week of exercise, each day separated by one to two days of rest. All training sessions were supervised by one of the study researchers. Muscular strength was assessed with 1-RM testing of the pectoralis major and minor, quadriceps, latissiums dorsi, hamstrings, deltoids, hamstrings, and gastrocnemius.

HIIT Training Group

For the HIIT training, the subjects completed a five-minute warm-up on a cycle ergometer and began the HIIT training with a one-minute high intensity work bout at the level of their maximal aerobic capacity. This was followed by a two-minute (no load on the cycle) recovery cycle interval. The work and recovery intervals were repeated five times with a five-minute cooldown at the end of the workout.

PHA Training Group

Each PHA session began with a five-minute warm-up and concluded with a five-minute cooldown. The PHA consisted of six exercises strictly ordered in this circuit sequence: pectoralis major, leg extension, latissimus dorsi pull-down, leg curl, shoulder press, and heel raise on a seated calf machine. There was no rest between exercises. All participants completed fifteen repetitions for each exercise that was at 55–60 percent of their 1-repetition maximum (1-RM). After the completion of one circuit the subjects rested one minute and then completed another circuit in precisely the same fashion until a total of four circuits were completed. Participants also wore heart rate monitors during the PHA training. Heart rates were held consistently during the PHA training at 60–80 percent of their maximal heart rate (calculated from their maximal aerobic capacity pre-test).

Results of the PHA Training Group

Most interestingly, the PHA training group showed an 8 percent improvement in maximal aerobic capacity, which is higher than that reported in traditional circuit training studies. The PHA concept of alternating upper and lower body exercises, performed at a medium exercise intensity (with no rest between exercises), appears to stimulate several variables of cardiovascular function. All of these improvements translate into greater cardioprotection from cardiovascular disease. In addition, the muscular strength benefits of this type of training are quite impressive. What's old is new again, and this new, promising PHA research suggests this type of training is going to be around for quite some time. Finally, as expected, it should be noted that the HIIT group showed an impressive 18.7 percent increase in maximal aerobic capacity.

PHA means
Peripheral Heart Action Training

Peripheral Heart Action Workout #1

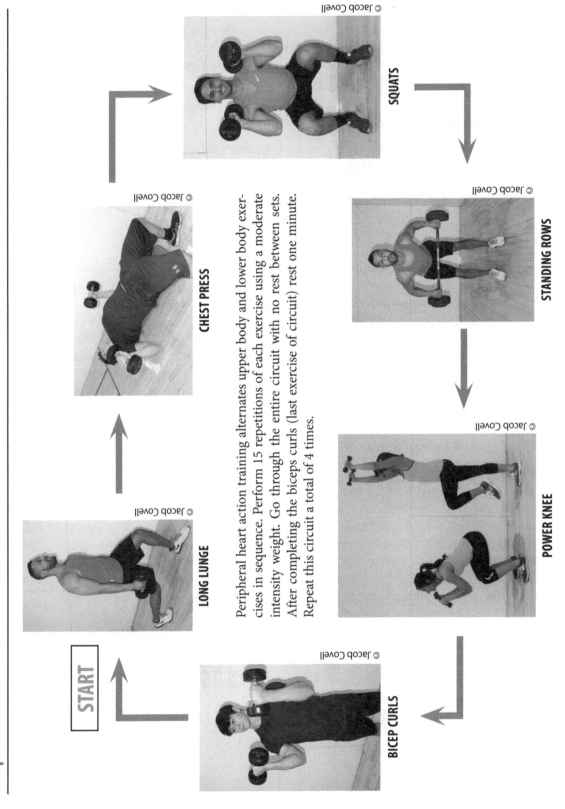

START

LONG LUNGE
© Jacob Covell

CHEST PRESS
© Jacob Covell

SQUATS
© Jacob Covell

STANDING ROWS
© Jacob Covell

POWER KNEE
© Jacob Covell

BICEP CURLS
© Jacob Covell

Peripheral heart action training alternates upper body and lower body exercises in sequence. Perform 15 repetitions of each exercise using a moderate intensity weight. Go through the entire circuit with no rest between sets. After completing the biceps curls (last exercise of circuit) rest one minute. Repeat this circuit a total of 4 times.

Peripheral Heart Action Workout #2

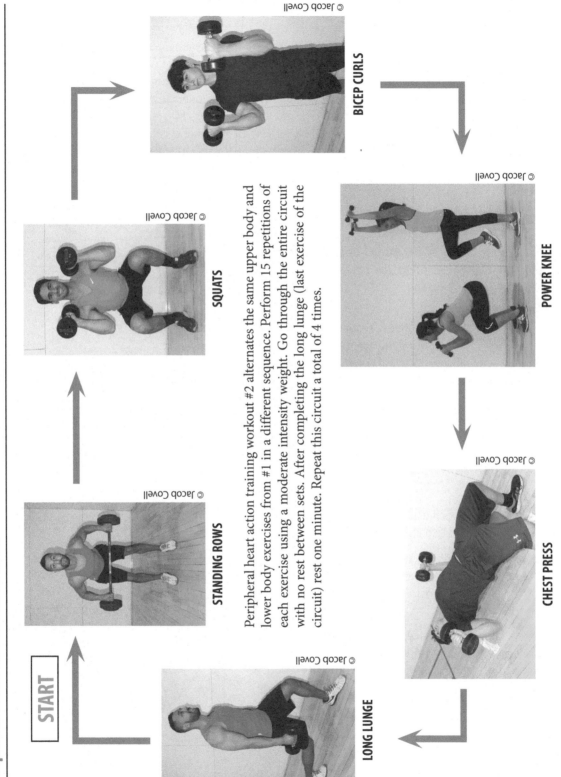

START

STANDING ROWS
© Jacob Covell

SQUATS
© Jacob Covell

BICEP CURLS
© Jacob Covell

POWER KNEE
© Jacob Covell

CHEST PRESS
© Jacob Covell

LONG LUNGE
© Jacob Covell

Peripheral heart action training workout #2 alternates the same upper body and lower body exercises from #1 in a different sequence. Perform 15 repetitions of each exercise using a moderate intensity weight. Go through the entire circuit with no rest between sets. After completing the long lunge (last exercise of the circuit) rest one minute. Repeat this circuit a total of 4 times.

Biomotor PHA Functional Power Exercises

The biomotor PHA functional power exercises are original movement combinations biomechanically designed to effectively challenge the body's functional balance and strength. These exercises are inspired by the concept of PHA, or pheripheral heart action training, which attempts to keep blood circulating continuously through the body by alternating upper and lower body sequencing exercises. This program offers creativity while also improving neuromuscular power and core stabilization. Begin with a comfortable starting dumbbell weight and gradually progress to heavier dumbbells. For variety, perform the biomotor PHA functional power exercises in random order, changing the movements after every eight repetitions.

Power Side
(Abductors, adductors, gluteals, quadriceps, hamstrings, deltoids, triceps)

Action: From a wide squat, extend legs lifting one leg off the ground as you straighten your arms. Return to squat and alternate sides.

Tips: Keep the lifting leg from rotating outward to effectively work the abductors. On all squats, be sure to keep the buttocks at or above standing knee height.

© Jacob Covell

Power Ski
(Abductors, adductors, gluteals, quadriceps, hamstrings, deltoids, pectorals)

Action: From a wide squat, extend legs to lift and flex one leg as you squeeze your elbows together. Return to wide squat and alternate sides.

Tips: Make sure you lift your knee to the side. Keep legs slightly wider than shoulder width in all wide squats.

© Jacob Covell

Power Knee
(Quadriceps, gluteals, hip flexors, deltoids, triceps)

Action: From a narrow squat position with legs close together, extend legs, lifting one leg with a bent knee as you extend the arms over the head. Lower to narrow squat and alternate sides.

Tips: Keep your back straight and the buttocks back as you sit in a narrow squat. Do not go as low in the narrow squat as you do in the wide squat.

© Jacob Covell

Did You Know?

The left side of your brain is a control center for logic and speech.

Power Deltoid
(Adductors, quadriceps, gluteals, hamstrings, deltoids)

Action: Extend your legs from a squat as you laterally raise your arms to shoulder height. Lower and repeat.

Tips: Raise and lower your arms (with control) making sure to keep them shoulder height or below in the top position.

© Jacob Covell

Power Row
(Spinal extensors, quadriceps, gluteals, hamstrings, trapezius)

Action: Extend your body and legs from a flexed squat position as you lift your elbows above your head.

Tips: Keep your hands close together, stopping them under your chin at the top position. To effectively work the spinal extensors, you need to find a comfortable yet challenging starting position where the trunk is flexed. Keep the head up and the back straight.

© Jacob Covell

Power Lunge
(Quadriceps, hamstrings, gluteals, biceps)

Action: From a standing position with arms by your side, step back into a lunge position and perform a bicep curl with your arms. Return to the starting position and repeat on other side.

Tips: Be sure to keep your bent knee over your ankle and your weight forward.

Variations: Turn your knuckles toward your shoulders and perform a reverse arm curl. You can also vary the degree of difficulty by keeping your knees slightly bent throughout the exercise.

© Jacob Covell

Did You Know?

Nerve impulses can travel 250 miles per hour.

Power Hamstring
(Hamstrings)

Action: Stand with one leg one and a half to two feet in front of the other leg with the toes facing forward. Hold weights down by sides. With your weight supported over your front leg, bend the back leg bringing the heel toward the buttocks and then lower the leg to the floor. Complete repetitions on one leg before switching sides. As the back leg bends, bring the arms up along the torso.

Tips: Do not allow the knee of the working leg to come forward. As you curl the leg, keep the upper body stable to support the lower back.

© Jacob Covell

Power Hip
(Gluteals, hamstrings, triceps)

Action: Stand with feet slightly wider than shoulder width. Bring the weights just under the shoulders. Lift the back leg toward the diagonal plane. Lower leg slowly to floor. As the leg goes back diagonally, the arms extend out to the side and return as the leg lowers to floor. Complete repetitions on one leg before switching sides.

Tips: Squeeze the buttocks as you lift and lower the leg. Try to do the action with a smooth rhythm throughout the range.

© Jacob Covell

Did You Know?

In most adults the spinal cord is about 17 inches long.

Biomotor Functional Power Workout

The following is a recommended sequence of exercises for a muscular endurance workout. You will effectively work your body's muscular system, progressing from larger (more energy demanding) muscle groups to smaller (more specific) muscles. To overload, vary the number of repetitions, the number of sets, the movement tempo, or the weight. Perform exercises half-time using music with 140 to 150 beats per minute.

- **Standing Power Moves:** Power side, power ski, power knee, power row, power deltoid, power lunge, power hamstring, power hip
- **Gastrocnemius/Anterior Tibialis:** Heel raises with feet facing out, forward, and in; toe lifts for anterior tibialis
- **Pectorals:** Standing flys with bent arms (arms high and low), chest/elbow squeezes
- **Rhomboids/Trapezius:** Standing row, single arm row, reverse fly (standing or with one knee on the floor)
- **Abdominals:** Crunch, twisting crunch, rope pull crunch, all-around crunch, reverse crunch (all abdominal exercises with or without hand weights)
- **Specific Gluteals, Abductors, Adductors:** Prone leg lifts, outer leg lifts, inner thigh lifts
- **Deltoids:** Shoulder press (in seated position)
- **Triceps/Deltoid/Chest:** Wide-arm push-ups, pike push-ups, triceps extension on knees (or seated)
- **Biceps:** Bicep curls and alternating arm bicep curls

Stability Ball Training for the 'Core'

Originating in Europe, stability ball training is quite popular throughout the United States. Although originally used in rehabilitation, stability ball training is now used in group-led exercise classes and by home fitness buffs. These round, beach-ball-looking devices provide an unstable base for exercises to be performed. The unstable nature of the ball allows more muscles to be challenged when performing exercises on or with the stability ball. Ball size varies; however, a good rule of thumb when selecting a ball is that when the individual is seated on the ball, her/his hips should be level with the knees. The firmness of the ball is another element to consider. A softer ball has a larger base or surface area, making it easier for the client to maintain balance. Firmer balls definitely provide more balance challenges. With specialized training, you can learn numerous exercises with stability balls. Because 80 percent of Americans suffer from a degree of low-back pain, the exercises shown with the stability ball have been chosen to strengthen the trunk and core musculature. The core muscles stabilize the spine and run the entire length of the torso. Do 8 to 16 repetitions of each exercise.

© Jacob Covell

Supine Trunk Curl
(Rectus abdominous, internal and external obliques)

Starting Position: Supine incline position with arms crossed over the chest or hands placed at the side of the head.

Action: Slowly curl your trunk, letting your shoulders and upper back lift off the ball. Return to starting position and repeat.

Tips: Support your head if your neck becomes fatigued. Think of bringing your ribs to your hips.

Variation: Change your feet position to vary the challenge of balance. The closer the feet are together, the more difficult it is to balance. Also, vary the position of your arms from across the chest, by the side of the head, or extended above the head.

© Jacob Covell

© Jacob Covell

Supine Oblique Rotation
(Rectus abdominous, internal and external obliques)

Starting position: Supine incline position with arms crossed over the chest or hands placed at the side of the head.

Action: Begin by bringing your ribs to the hips. As you curl your trunk, rotate one side of the upper body toward the other side. Return to starting position and repeat, rotating to the other side.

Tips: Always start each exercise with the trunk curl first. Press the lower back into the ball as you do the exercise.

Variation: Change your feet position to vary the challenge of balance. The closer the feet are together, the more difficult to balance. Also, vary the position of your arms from across the chest, by the side of the head, or extended to the side of your torso.

© Jacob Covell

© Jacob Covell

Prone Trunk Extension
(Erector spinae, gluteus maximus)

Starting Position: Start prone with your trunk on the ball. Place your hands to the side of your head, by your side, or wrapped around the ball. Allow your trunk to round over the ball. Spread your legs and keep both feet solid on the floor.

Action: Slowly extend the spine, lifting your chest slightly off the ball until the spine is straight. Return to starting position and repeat.

Tips: Keep your neck in a neutral position. Do not overextend your spine.

Variation: Regularly change your arms from by your side, next to your head, or extended over your head.

© Jacob Covell

© Jacob Covell

Side-Lying Lateral Flexion
(Internal and external obliques, erector spinae, quadratus lumborum)

Starting Position: Start in a side-lying position on the ball with the bent leg firmly planted on the floor. Place one hand on the ball and bend the arm on the ball, placing the hand on the side of the head. Allow the trunk to round over the ball.

Action: Laterally lift the trunk slowly. Once you reach the top of the motion, return slowly to the starting position and repeat.

Tips: Do not allow your hips to roll forward or backward. Keep your head in its neutral position, not allowing it to dip down, forward, or backward.

Variation: As you get stronger, put both hands to the side of the head with your elbows to the side.

© Jacob Covell

© Jacob Covell

Barefoot Running Program: Have You Tried It Yet?

For many people, running provides a feeling of wellbeing. Many enthusiasts experience feelings of euphoria and stress relief after a good run. Despite its popularity, the incidence of running injuries is relatively high. The majority of running injuries are at the knee, followed by the lower leg, the foot, and the upper leg.

A popular new approach to running is barefoot training. Some fitness professionals feel we spend too much time wearing shoes and thus it weakens the foot and leg structures. To strengthen these structures try walking barefoot around the house and perhaps start a barefoot training program. Here's how to go about it.

Developing a Barefoot Running Program

Step 1. Begin by doing different activities of daily life without shoes such as gardening, walking to the mailbox, and barefoot walking around the house.

Step 2. Next, do some exercise activities on an even grass surface or indoor surface. Perhaps do some walking, jogging, calisthenics, and games (e.g., volleyball or frisbee) on a grass field or indoor track.

© Stuart Jenner/Shutterstock.com

Step 3. Try doing 10 minutes of brisk barefoot walking before and/or after a regular workout.

Step 4. Gradually start doing 5-minute bouts of barefoot running before and after a regular workout.

Step 5. Increase slowly from 5 minutes to 10 minutes to 15 minutes of barefoot running before and/or after a regular workout.

Step 6. For variety, do your barefoot training indoors and outdoors (grass and/or sand).

Step 7. Progressively transition barefoot training to a harder surface (such as a sidewalk) with brisk walking. However, be very aware of rocks, glass, and harmful surface disturbances such as holes and rough spots.

Step 8. Cold environments can be a deterrent to barefoot training. Perhaps the use of a fitness facility, indoor location, mall, or school gymnasium (where the temperature is more reasonable) would be much more suitable during inclement weather conditions.

Step 9. Importantly, injured runners should not begin doing any barefoot training until the symptoms of their injury have subsided. Also, barefoot running is not recommended for people with diabetes because there may be a loss of protective sensations in the feet with this disease.

Step 10. Several shoe companies are now promoting new 'barefoot' shoes that protect the foot from harmful surfaces. Many people prefer this option for their barefoot training. Give it a try . . . you may enjoy it.

© Jacob Covell

POWER SIDE

START HERE

POWER RUNS

45–60 SECONDS

© Jacob Covell

POWER KNEE

SIDE LEG SLIDES 45–60 SECONDS

Boot Camp Workouts Are Happening!

Boot camp workouts are time efficient workouts that challenge your entire body by moving rapidly from one exercise to another with no rest. Initially they were completed outdoors. Now, because of their popularity they are also done regularly indoors and outdoors. They are similar to circuit training workouts which move the exercisers from station to station. The workouts can have a number of movement themes including muscular strength, agility, speed, muscular endurance, power, and aerobic capacity. They also can be designed for different groups including children, seniors,

© Jacob Covell

POWER HAMSTRING

JUMP KICKS

45–60 SECONDS

© Jacob Covell

POWER LUNGE

© Jacob Covell

POWER KNEE

© Jacob Covell

**SKI HOPS
45–60 SECONDS**

POWER DELTOID

weight loss, women-only, men-only, and sport specific (i.e., cycling, rowing, skiing, etc.). The underlying theme with a boot camp workout is to challenge yourself continuously during the workout, to resemble what occurs in a real military boot camp. For *Anybody's Guide to Total Fitness,* I have incorporated several of the biomotor functional power exercises that alternate with spirited aerobic moves into a challenging boot camp workout for you to try. Do each exercise for 45–60 seconds and then do the aerobic move for the same length of time before moving to the next exercise. Repeat the boot camp 2–3 times: For safety, please put the dumbbells on the ground when you do your aerobic exercises. Make sure you begin with a thorough warm-up and finish with a cool-down after the boot camp workout. Take yourself to the limit.

**JUMP ROPE HOPS
45–60 SECONDS**

**LUNGE CLAPS
45–60 SECONDS**

© Jacob Covell

POWER ROW

Stretch Right!

A well-designed flexibility program focuses on all the muscle groups and joints of the body—not just the most frequently used body parts. Stretch properly to achieve maximum flexibility.

Stretching Tips

- ○ Stretch warm muscles, not cold ones.
- ○ Avoid bouncing (ballistic) movement. Stretch gradually into and out of the stretch.
- ○ Stretch to the point of limitation, not to the point of pain.
- ○ Concentrate on relaxing the muscles being stretched; slow breathing helps.
- ○ Stretches to improve flexibility should be held 15 to 30 seconds.
- ○ Always stretch opposing muscle groups.
- ○ Keep the muscles warm when stretching by wearing warm-ups or sweats.
- ○ Stretch daily and certainly after every workout.
- ○ Increases in flexibility take time; you must be patient.

Neck

Action: Very slow circular movement of head toward each shoulder and chest.

Tips: It is not recommended to take your head back too far—you may possibly stress your neck.

© Jacob Covell

Shoulders (Two stretches)

1. **Action:** Holding a towel or rope over your head, stretch the arms back.

2. **Action:** Sit on the knees with the front of the feet flat on the floor. With towel behind back, bring the chest to the knees as you stretch the arms away from the body.

Tips: This is also a very good stretch for the spine and the front of the lower leg!

Variation: Change the width of your grip on the towel.

© Jacob Covell

© Jacob Covell

Hips, Side, and Back

Action: While sitting, bring one leg over other leg. Keep the bottom leg extended (but relaxed at the knee). Rotate the torso to both sides by pushing against floor with hands.

Tips: Stretch up through your spine.

© Jacob Covell

Lower Back

Action: While lying on the back, grab behind the knees and pull legs toward chest. May be done with legs tucked or slightly extended, but not locked.

Tips: This also stretches the hamstrings.

Variation: This stretch can be performed in the seated position.

© Jacob Covell

Abdominals and Chest

Action: From a prone position, lift the shoulders and chest off the ground and support the upper torso with elbows or extended arms.

Tips: Reach up and out with the upper body.

© Jacob Covell

Seated Butterfly Stretch
(For inner thigh)

Action: Bring both heels together and into body. Press knees toward the floor.

Tips: Grab your ankles, not your toes. Stretch torso forward as well.

© Jacob Covell

Half-Straddle Stretch
(For hamstrings and lower back)

Action: With one leg straight and the other leg bent, reach your chest forward toward the straight leg and hold. Do both legs.

Tips: Keep the back straight and relax.

© Jacob Covell

Straddle Stretch
(For hamstrings, inner thigh, and lower back)

Action: Stretch forward with your upper body between your open legs.

Tips: Keep your knees facing up, legs straight, and back straight. Placing your hands on the floor behind your thighs is a good modification for those a little less flexible in this position.

© Jacob Covell

Quadriceps and Hip Flexors

Action: While lying on your side, grab below the knee and stretch the leg back.

Tips: Focus on bringing the leg back and not out to the side.

Variation: Do the stretch standing against a wall, next to a chair, or in the prone position.

© Jacob Covell

Achilles Stretch and Calf-Stretch

Action: Stand in a lunge position with toes facing forward. To stretch the calf, bend front leg and keep back leg straight. To stretch Achilles tendon (and soleus), bend the back knee, keeping the heel on the floor.

Tips: Sometimes it is best to do these against the wall or an immovable object.

© Jacob Covell

Did You Know?

The soft inner part of long bones where blood cells are made is the marrow.

Did You Know?

The 12 pairs of nerves attached to the brain are the cranial nerves.

Mind-Body Fitness

What Is Mind-Body or Mindful Fitness?

The fitness industry's growth in the past 15 years has included many new dimensions in programming. Several of these innovative programs distinctively address an area of interest referred to as 'mind-body' or 'mindful' fitness. Mindful fitness is described as increased mental development and personal enlightenment through the participation in some form of movement that includes muscular strength, flexibility, balance, and coordination. With mind-body fitness modalities, the exerciser attempts to blend a mindful or cognitive process with some type of physical movement of low-to-moderate postures or exercise intensity. Mind-body fitness is performed with an inwardly directed focus. Attention of the practitioner is on breathing, posture, and body awareness throughout all physical movements. Whereas any traditional cardiovascular and resistance exercise program may include inner-focus elements, with mind-body exercise this inner-attentiveness is the predominant theme throughout the exercise. In mind-body exercise, participants emphasize more effort on self-monitoring, self-awareness, and perceived exertion as opposed to following the commands of the certified exercise leader. Thus, with mind-body exercising, the inner-focus elements are the process and the end product. Tai Chi and yoga are influential foundations of the evolving mind-body fitness programs. Because of the lower intensity demands of mind-body exercise programs, they have a wide-reaching adaptability for persons of multiple fitness levels and bodily movement challenges.

Results of recent research indicate there is considerable and meaningful evidence supporting several mind-body programs for interventions with cardiac rehabilitation, insomnia, headaches, incontinence, chronic low back pain, symptoms of cancer, and post-surgical outcomes. However, more research is needed to understand the mechanisms of these interventions so that specific factors may be identified for clinical use with clients suffering some of these health consequences.

Characteristics of Mind-Body Exercise Programs

Traditional exercise programs focus attention on some type of performance-oriented outcome such as muscular strength, muscular endurance, flexibility, body composition change, or cardiorespiratory endurance. The following are five common components of mindful exercise programs.

1. **Meditative/contemplative.** This represents a non-judgmental, present-moment introspective component. It focuses on the moment and is non-competitive.

2. **Proprioceptive awareness.** Proprioception is characterized as a sense of movement and position of the body, especially the limbs. Proprioceptors are sensory organs (such as muscle spindles and Golgi tendon organs) that are capable of receiving stimuli originating in the muscles or tendons. Much attention in mind-body fitness programs is developing this sense with the muscles as the body goes through directive movement.

3. **Breath-centering.** Interests in evaluating and understanding the biological mechanisms associated with breathing are ongoing. The breath is a centering activity in mindful exercise. It comes from the word 'pranayama', loosely translated, the science of breath. Many of the mind-body disciplines include various breathing techniques.

4. **Anatomic alignment** (e.g., spine, pelvis, etc.) or proper physical form. With the various mind-body disciplines, body position, technique, and alignment are centermost to the correct performance of the postures. In many ways, this is very analogous to the importance of body position and technique regularly incorporated in performing stretching and resistance exercises.

5. **Energycentric.** Energycentric is a descriptive mindful exercise term used to characterize the perception of movement and flow of one's energy force. This type of positive energy is inclusive in most mind-body programs.

Yoga for Mind, Body, and Spirit

Though its exact origin in India has yet to be identified, yoga has existed for at least 3,500 years. Translated, yoga means union and refers to one of the classic systems of Hindu philosophy that strives to bring together and develop the body, mind, and spirit. Hindu priests who lived frugal lifestyles, characterized by discipline and meditation, originally developed yoga. Through observing and mimicking the movement and patterns of animals, priests hoped to achieve the same balance with nature that animals seemed to possess. This aspect of yoga, known as Hatha yoga, is the form with which Westerners are most familiar and is defined by a series of exercises in physical posture and breathing patterns. Besides balance with nature, ancient Indian philosophers recognized health benefits of yoga, including proper organ functioning and whole well-being. These health benefits have also been acknowledged in the modern-day United States, with millions of individuals regularly participating in yoga.

There are several different forms of Hatha yoga that are popularly practiced. Iyengar yoga incorporates traditional Hatha techniques into fluid and dancelike sequences. It uses props such as chairs, pillows, blankets, and belts to accommodate persons with special needs. Ashtanga yoga is a fast-paced, athletic style that is the foundation for the various power-yoga classes. These classes resemble more vigorous workouts as opposed to relaxation sessions. Bikram, or hot yoga, is done in a sauna-style room that's over 100 degrees, so the muscles get very warm for extending and stretching. Jivamukti is both physically challenging and decidedly meditative. Kripalu yoga centers on personal growth and self-improvement. Although each type of yoga will have its unique benefits, documented benefits from participation in yoga include the following:

© Jacob Covell

- ○ Increase in flexibility
- ○ Increase in muscular endurance
- ○ Increase in balance
- ○ Improvement in posture
- ○ Increase in caloric expenditure
- ○ Increase in self-worth and self-control
- ○ Reduction of stress

The Pilates Method of Movement Training

The Pilates Method was developed by German immigrant J. H. Pilates in the early 20th century. Pilates is a methodical system of slow, controlled, specific movements that involve a deep internal focus. This method is essentially divided into two modalities, floor or mat work and the work on the resistance equipment that Pilates developed, such as the Universal Reformer. Equipment is generally learned in a one-on-one or small group setting whereas mat work can be taught in either a group or private setting. With either modality, but especially with the Reformer, the principle goal is to achieve efficient functional movement and improved movement capability. In many

© lightwavemedia/Shutterstock.com

ways, Pilates is a form of movement re-education where each participant learns to overcome faulty compensatory movement patterns. These inefficient movement patterns are broken down into components by using springs (using a Reformer) and changing the body's orientation to gravity. Pilates exercises are designed to enhance more efficient movement patterns by placing the student in a position that minimizes undesirable muscle activity, which can cause early fatigue and lead to injury. Pilates equipment was constructed to adapt to many human anatomical variations. For example, the springs, ropes, and foot bar of the Reformer can be

> **Did You Know?**
>
> Each brain cell can communicate with 25,000 other brain cells.

adjusted such that similar properties of movement sequencing can be applied to a variety of body types and limb/torso lengths. Pilates work involves substantial mental focus with harmonized breathing during the muscular contractions of the movements. The Pilates method may be utilized for rehabilitation, post-rehabilitation, general fitness and athletic performance. Pilates exercise is advantageous for those who desire low-impact exercise to improve posture, flexibility, and functionality. Research shows that various Pilates programs can be beneficial in improving flexibility, core strength, muscular fitness, and increased caloric expenditure.

© holbox/Shutterstock.com

SECTION 5
Successful Weight Management

© Gustavo Frazao/Shutterstock.com

As you probably know, obesity is a major health issue in many countries throughout the world—including our own. According to World Health Organization (WHO) data from 2018, the rate of obesity in the world has nearly tripled since 1975. More than 1.9 billion adults, eighteen years and older, were overweight in 2016, a staggering statistic. Of this group, over 650 million were obese. As alarming as this is, contained within this list of key facts and statistics is the following statement from the WHO: "Obesity is preventable." I want you to always remember that inspiring, valuable message.

Losing weight, and maintaining the weight loss, is definitely a worldwide challenge facing millions of women and men. But it is important to emphasize that even small changes in body weight can result in consequential health benefits. Studies show that a 5–10 percent loss of initial body weight, which is very doable, is associated with meaningful improvements in cholesterol levels, blood pressure (when elevated), and in the management and prevention of type 2 diabetes. For that very reason, a target goal of many weight-loss programs is for participants to lose at least 10 percent of one's initial weight, and then maintain that loss for a minimum of one year. I assure you, this is a realistic and achievable goal.

Before we get started, it's probably best to get a major weight loss disclaimer out of the way: It is clear from countless research articles and weight loss books that there is no one best approach to successful weight loss. Indeed, in the long run, you and every other person who strives to meet weight management goals will eventually find what works best for you. However, the research does show there are some evidence-based strategies that work very well for many people, and there are some important dietary and exercise approaches that are most beneficial health-wise. These are the strategies we are going to go over in *Anybody's Guide to Total Fitness*. Think of these approaches as some of the tools of the weight management success toolbox.

Launching "Inch by Inch, It's a Cinch"

In this section I will go into further detail about my "inch by inch, it's a cinch" philosophy. I've used this method for years while working with people trying to meet their weight management, fitness, and health goals. This philosophy is actually based on the small-changes approach, a scientific approach to behavior change. The small-changes approach encourages people to make modest but progressive behavior changes to lose weight and prevent the gradual regain of weight that has been lost. Importantly, this strategy is meant to make you think about your diet and physical well-being as part of your lifestyle. The concept isn't suggesting that little changes will have an immediately greater impact than some aggressive approaches to weight loss. Quite the contrary! But, for many people, the small-changes approach is a part of an achievable lifestyle, which is much more sustainable over the long run compared to disruptive, aggressive strategies that upend your life. This is really the key to weight loss success and weight regain prevention. Lasting changes in health, weight management, and fitness rarely come from "quick fix" approaches. Don't allow yourself to become enticed—or, rather, hoodwinked—by the slick advertising and marketing of some rapid weight loss product or program. With any program you consider, see if there is evidence supporting the program beyond the testimonials you hear or read in the advertising.

"Inch by Inch, It's a Cinch"

That said, it is just fine if you want to do a personal "overhaul" to some aspects of your lifestyle. Most of us are self-improving regularly, whether we realize it or not, and sometimes changes we make definitely feel like a personal lifestyle overhaul. Fundamentally, however, I've found the "inch by inch, it's a cinch" philosophy to be an optimal way to achieve your long-lasting behavior change goals. As you progress, I encourage you to welcome new healthy habits into your lifestyle.

Is There Any Science to Using a Small-Changes Approach?

In 2009, a seventeen-member task force from the American Society for Nutrition, the Institute of Food Technologists, and the International Food Information Council was established to evaluate the efficacy of the small-changes obesity intervention for a large part of the overweight/obese population. According to results published by this task force in the American Journal of Clinical Nutrition, this approach to combating obesity is beneficial for the following reasons:

1. Small, realistic changes are easier to achieve and maintain than large ones. The committee drew from years of research and observation when it found that major behavioral and lifestyle changes are quite difficult to attain. Small changes such as 2,000 more steps of walking a day (which requires about 100 extra calories of energy expenditure) and simple food substitutions (such as replacing a 12-ounce regular soda with a diet soda, saving 150 kilocalories) are doable and maintainable.

2. Small changes can have an important impact on body weight regulation. Most people in the US steadily gain weight over time, because we increase the discrepancy between energy intake (food consumption) and energy output (exercise and physical activity). This discrepancy is sometimes referred to as an "energy gap," and it is estimated to be up to 100 calories (or more) each day, leading to overweight and obesity over time if it's not derailed somewhere along the way.

3. Small, successful lifestyle changes lead to an increase in positive self-efficacy. Self-efficacy is your impression about your ability to perform in a certain manner. Positive self-efficacy when it comes to weight management suggests that as you make small lifestyle changes and achieve certain weight loss goals, you become empowered, skilled, confident, and motivated to stay on course with your goals. In fact, this increased self-confidence in yourself may inspire you to tackle even greater weight loss goals than you originally thought were possible. It's a praiseworthy cycle: positive outcomes lead to self-confidence and self-efficacy, encouraging you to make even higher gains. What could be more empowering! Little by little, step-by-step, inch by inch, you become more and more confident in yourself and what you can achieve—at any age or stage in your life!

Is the small-changes approach right for you? Reflect for a moment. Trying to get fit or lose weight often feels overwhelming, like being lost in a giant obstacle course. This is particularly true if you have been sedentary for a long time. A big part of the problem is that many weight management programs tend to create an "all or nothing" approach, which often leads to failure and dropping out. I advise you to stay away from those programs. The small-changes approach surely deserves your genuine attention. Stay patient and goal-focused as you progress with your personal lifestyle modifications and changes. Eventually you will hopefully agree with me: "inch by inch, it's a cinch."

Lessons from "The Biggest Loser"

You are probably familiar with a popular television competition show "The Biggest Loser," but if you're not, here's a quick summary: During the course of a season, participants (who are overweight or obese) battled it out to see who can lose the most amount of weight via diet and fitness. By the end of the competition, the contestants lost dozens of pounds; in the fifteenth season, one contestant shed 150 pounds in just seven months. As you can imagine, losing so much weight over such a quick period of time requires some pretty drastic dieting and exercising measures. You might say the show's philosophy was the opposite of "inch-by-inch, it's a cinch."

Whatever you think of the show—and it generated no small amount of controversy—it has been valuable to researchers because the contestants were, essentially, participants of a real-life experiment. Studying them could, in fact, answer this important question: Do people who undertake "extreme" weight loss stay healthy and fit after the show is over (that is, long-term)?

Well, let's look at the research to find out. In 2016, a study was published in the journal *Obesity* summarizing the long-term weight-loss results of several contestants on the 2009 "Biggest Loser" season. The study followed fourteen contestants (six men and eight women) from the season for six years, finding that the majority had regained a substantial amount of weight. The study findings explain what happened, so we will explore them in greater detail in the next section.

Resting Metabolic Rate Changes with Weight Loss

First, though, let's take a quick pivot to talk briefly about your body's energy balance. Your total daily energy expenditure consists of three main categories: the resting metabolic rate (or RMR which is also referred to as resting energy expenditure [REE]), the energy needed to stay alive; the thermic effect of food (or TEF), the energy required for the digestion, absorption, transport, and storage of all the foods you eat; and the activity energy expenditure (or AEE), the energy the body utilizes during exercise and spontaneous physical movement (such as shopping, moving, doing daily chores, and fidgeting). Your RMR is the largest portion of the body's energy expenditure, comprising an enormous 60–70 percent of your total daily energy expenditure (TEE). You have a very complex body, with over 50 trillion cells, and it requires a lot of energy to stay alive.

Here's how this is related to "The Biggest Loser." The 2016 study discovered that rapid, severe weight loss causes a massive slowdown in the body's RMR. In science, this process is referred to as a "metabolic adaptation." As the researchers of the study explain, metabolic adaptation occurs when the body tries to counteract such drastic weight loss. In other words, the body slows down its RMR in hopes of gaining back the lost weight. For the obesity study, researchers measured contestants' RMR at the beginning of the 2009 "Biggest Loser" season, at the end of the thirty-week competition, and six years after that. (See Table 1 on the following page for details from the assessment.)

TABLE 1	Body Composition & Energy Expenditure Comparisons		
VARIABLE	**PRE-CONTEST**	**30 WEEKS**	**6 YEARS AFTER**
Body Weight (lb)	328	200	290
Body Fat (%)	49.3	28.1	44.7
Muscle Mass (lb)	166	142	155
Fat Mass (lb)	162	58	135
RMR (calories/day)	2,607	1,996	1,903
TEE (calories/day)	3,804	3,002	3,429
Values are averages of the six men and eight women "Biggest Loser" contest volunteers before the start of the contest (Pre-Contest), immediately after the contest (thirty weeks), and six years after the contest. Source: Fothergill et al., 2016			

On average, the fourteen contestants each lost 128 lbs in the thirty-week exercise and nutrition competition. At the six-year follow-up, researchers found the contestants gained back an average of 90 lbs. The contestants lost 24 lbs of muscle during the vigorous thirty-week exercise program, but gained back 13 lbs of muscle six years after the contest. Likewise, the contestants lost an average of 104 lbs of fat in the thirty-week contest, but gained back 77 lbs of fat at the six-year assessment. Perhaps the most startling result, and one that helps explain the contestants' weight regain, has to do with their RMR measurements.

At the completion of the thirty-week contest, the average measured RMR of each contestant was 611 calories lower than at the start of it. Surprisingly, at the six-year follow-up, each contestant's RMR was on average 93 calories LOWER than after the thirty-week exercise/nutrition intervention. Thus, from the pre-contest time to the six-year follow-up, each contestant's RMR was suppressed by an average of 704 calories. In other words, their bodies were trying hard to gain back the lost weight by severely slowing down their RMR. This is gripping—and surprising to learn.

Did the Contestants' Rapid Weight Loss Cause Their Weight Regain?

In a word: yes. Many weight management professionals maintain that "The Biggest Loser" participants' extreme, rapid weight loss experienced directly contributed to their subsequent weight regain. With the dramatic slowing of their RMR, their bodies were expending fewer calories on a daily basis, and they gained back a substantial amount of weight. Weight management and fitness professionals, myself included, believe it is unhealthy to lose massive amounts of weight so quickly, especially through the extreme fitness regiments contestants endure in the show, such as seven hours of exercise a day. This is one of the reasons I am such a strong champion for the "inch by inch, it's a cinch" philosophy in fitness and weight management. It allows for the body to gradually adjust to the small changes in body weight that occur over a period of time. Numerous studies have shown small, progressive changes are quite doable and sustainable over the long run.

Is It True That Dieting-Only Programs Can Actually Promote Weight Gain?

As the name implies, diet-only weight-loss programs do not include any type of exercise. To figure out how this approach fares, let's look to the science. In a 2012 study published in the *International Journal of Obesity*, researchers collected and reported on weight changes among 4,129 individual twins at 16-, 17-, 18-, and 25-year increments after the start of the study. In the report, the researchers confirmed that a dieting-only weight-loss program may lead to the opposite of the desired weight loss outcome. The authors hypothesize that restrictive dieting may lead some people to become preoccupied with food and trigger overeating. In addition, the researchers found that the suppression of the RMR and loss of muscle mass may spur post-dieting weight-rebound—the same conclusion of the study of "The Biggest Loser" contestants. As we discussed above, a post-dieting weight rebound appears to be a response from the body, which is reacting "defensively" to the weight loss. These reactions may be part psychological and part physiological, but the fact is that rebounding leads to regaining lost weight. In some cases, people will actually wind up weighing more than when they originally started their diet. All of which is to say: yes, it appears that dieting-only weight-loss programs can indeed lead to weight gain. The great news is there are several ways to combat this weight regain phenomenon, and we will cover them very thoroughly in the next paragraph.

Secrets from Real-Life Biggest Losers

Given how much consumer advertising is dominated by diet books and weight-loss products and programs touting sketchy, quick-fix solutions, one could be forgiven for despairing when it comes to viable long-term weight-loss programs that actually work. Despair not, however: the truth is, there are real-life biggest losers who have successfully maintained long-term weight loss. To learn what these real-life biggest losers have been doing right, we will turn our attention to the National Weight Control Registry (NWCR). This is an archive of thousands of women and men who have lost thirty pounds or more, and kept this off for at least a year or longer.

In the next paragraphs we will analyze the NWCR data to figure out what really worked for those who have attained successful long-term weight loss and prevented weight regain. My hope is that their experiences and lessons can serve as insightful guideposts for you on your own journey.

Introducing the National Weight Control Registry

The NWCR was established by doctors Jim Hill and Rena Wing in 1994. The registry was developed for the express purpose of categorizing and examining the behavior of individuals who have succeeded at long-term weight loss. All of the 10,000-plus members currently in the registry are at least eighteen years or older, have lost at least thirty pounds, and have maintained this weight loss for at least one year. Eighty percent of the people in the registry are women, and 20 percent are men. The "average" woman in the registry is forty-five years of age and currently weighs 145 pounds, while the "average" man in the registry is forty-nine and currently weighs 190 pounds. NWCR volunteers (there is no compensation for participating) are recruited using national and local television, radio, magazine, and newspaper advertisements. Each new member first calls a toll-free number or completes a web application to determine their eligibility for the

NWCR, and then (if eligible to join) they are sent a consent form and detailed questionnaire packet that includes questions about the following: their lifetime maximum weight (and dates at this weight), current weight, education, ethnicity, age, gender, exercise habits, and methods of weight loss used. All registry members are tracked annually to determine any weight changes that have occurred as well as associated weight-related behavior modifications, if any.

Most NWCR members have lost an average of 66 pounds and kept this weight off for 5.5 years. (Praise where praise is due—that is exceedingly impressive!) The range of pounds lost ranges from 30 to 300. Some of the registry members lost their weight rapidly, while others lost it rather slowly, over a period of up to fourteen years. Remarkably, 45 percent of registry participants lost the weight on their own, while the other 55 percent lost weight with the help of some type of program such as a commercial diet program, or with the guidance of a physician or nutritionist. Ninety-eight percent of the registry members report they modified their food intake in some way to lose weight, and 94 percent increased their physical activity, with the most frequently reported form of activity being walking. Most of the registry members watch fewer than ten hours of television per week. This tells us they are definitely combatting the challenges of sedentary behavior.

What Strategies Have Worked for These Long-Term Weight-Loss Winners?

If we dig into the data, we can uncover the four main strategies NWCR members rely on for successful weight loss maintenance:

1. Doing high levels of physical activity
2. Consuming a lower-calorie diet
3. Weighing themselves frequently (i.e., monitoring their weight)
4. Eating breakfast, typically low-fat and low in sugar

Additionally, there are certain personality traits that successful weight loss "losers" have in common, most notably a heightened sense of vigilance about maintaining their weight loss. For instance, survey reports of this population reveal that successful weight loss maintainers continue to act like recently successful weight-loss losers for many years after their weight loss. In other words, they are "laser focused" when it comes to maintaining their lighter weight, and keep up this laser focus day after day. Seventy-five percent of NWCR members weigh themselves at least once a week, and 44 percent of registry members weigh themselves daily, further demonstrating the importance of their regular body monitoring.

How Much Physical Activity Are Registry Members Doing?

Both men and women on the registry get a lot of physical activity each week, a fact that is probably unsurprising. Both sexes average up to one hour each day of physical activity at a "somewhat hard" intensity. That is like taking two brisk thirty-minute walks a day; one in the morning and one in the afternoon. If we use the talk test as a guide, when you are working at a "somewhat hard" intensity you can exercise and carry on a conversation with a little bit of difficulty.

Seventy-six percent of members report that walking is their main form of physical activity. Other physical activities reported by men and women in the registry include resistance training, cycling, and other aerobic activities. Previous research on this population shows that as registry members decrease their physical activity, they have a tendency to regain some weight. So, regular exercise surely plays a key role in the prevention of weight regain for this population.

What Happens to NWCR Registry Members Who Regain Weight?

Researchers examined registry members who regained >5 pounds after one year of weight loss success to determine what predictors might indicate a member's likelihood of weight regain. They found that those who regain weight tend to periodically lose control of their eating. As well, those with higher levels of depression showed greater odds for regaining weight. It also appears that an increase in the percentage of calories from fat in a member's diet is associated with some weight regain.

However, perhaps the most important (if not most inspiring) finding is that members who were successful at maintaining their weight loss for two or more years had significantly greater chances of keeping weight off throughout the subsequent years. If women and men can succeed at maintaining their weight loss for two years, they can reduce their risk of subsequent weight regain by nearly 50 percent. Although this phenomenon is not fully understood, one explanation is that people who maintain their weight for at least two years have developed successful long-term coping skills that further equip them to manage their weight loss.

What Sparks Most People in the NWCR to Initially Start Their Weight Loss Plan?

It appears that the majority (83 percent) of the men and women in the NWCR have some type of prompt or trigger that sets off their weight loss initiative. The three most common prompts for weight loss and continued maintenance include medical conditions (23 percent), reaching an all-time high in body weight (21.3 percent), and observing oneself in a mirror or a picture (12.7 percent). Medical reasons were generally described as conditions that would lead to a heart attack if nothing were done. The next two motivators that follow the top three include wanting to live a longer life and/or having more time to spend with loved ones. In my view, it's interesting that simply getting a slimmer body isn't what motivates the majority of registry members.

Quite a few NWCR members acknowledge that they had previously made several failed attempts to lose weight before finding what really works for them. Many can attest that they are quite familiar with "yo-yo" dieting (losing and regaining weight in a cyclical manner). This is important for everyone starting a fitness, health, and/or weight loss program to know: There are a lot of up and downs, just like a roller coaster, before you really find what works best for you when it comes to exercise and weight management. The majority of the NWCR registry members kept their motivation up during these trying times and finally succeeded. You will too!

What Do NWCR Members' Diets Have in Common?

We can learn a lot from the commonalities between NWCR members, especially when it comes to diet. To start, members appear to share an appreciation for consistency and a determination to stick with a dietary regimen. Fifty-nine percent of members say their eating habits were the same on weekends (and holidays) and weekdays, while 39 percent of participants noted they followed stricter diets during the week as compared to the weekend. Notably, NWCR members who are more consistent with their diets during the week and weekend are 1.5 times more likely to maintain weight loss during the next year. This outcome seems to be validated by research. In a 2005 study published in the *American Journal of Clinical Nutrition,* researchers assert that allowing for "too much flexibility" in dietary behaviors may expose a person to high-risk situations, creating more opportunity to lose control and eat too much. So, during weekends, when you may enjoy special outings with your family, friends, and colleagues, please be aware of placing yourself in a tempting situation where you may overindulge. Enjoy, but perhaps remind yourself to use moderation.

Practical Advice from Real-Life Biggest Losers

To help you lose weight and achieve long-term weight control, here's a summary of the most important lessons we can draw from National Weight Control Registry's 10,000 real-life biggest losers.

1. No two people lost weight in exactly the same way in the registry. Accordingly, you must find what works best for you. In many ways, this gives you permission to explore different kinds of weight-loss options; just know that there is a weight management plan, strategy, or program out there that will work for you, even if it takes some time to find it.

2. All of the members on the registry have a sincere motivation for achieving their goals, whether it is a medical scare, an all-time high weight, or just wanting to spend more time with family and friends. Clearly, there are different factors that motivate people to be successful in weight management.

3. Whether they came to it on their own, or from joining a weight loss group or program, all members of the registry modified their diet in a way to take in fewer calories. How do you plan to modify your diet? What steps do you plan to take? If you're not sure, remember that this book includes a special chapter with one hundred ways to reduce calories in your daily life. Please take advantage of many of these fabulous ideas—they are my gift to you.

4. The majority of members of the registry complete up to one hour of "somewhat hard" intensity exercise on most days of the week. That is the equivalent of a thirty-minute brisk walk in the morning and one in the afternoon.

5. Regardless of how much time they spend exercising, most members do the same physical activity: walking briskly. Crucially, they keep up this exercise regime even after their weight loss, a strategy that definitely helps prevent weight regain.

6. A great majority of the members on the registry eat a healthy breakfast, typically cereal and fruit. Talk about giving yourself a healthy start!

7. Registry members weigh themselves frequently. Some check their weight daily, with most of them checking their weight at least once per week. What is best for you? Once a week? Daily? Decide and then start monitoring your weight.

8. Weight loss success is likelier to occur among members who don't let their dietary habits stray on the weekend. They are careful not to get out-of-control with their weekend food choices at parties, social events, and family outings. Plan ahead so you don't get caught off guard at these socials.

9. Most of the members on the registry have developed effective coping mechanisms to deal with any depression they may experience in their daily life. Depression is a widespread illness that affects millions of adults in the US every year, but the good news is that it can be treated. If you believe you are depressed, getting help is the best thing you can do for yourself. Please note that depression is often associated with weight gain.

10. It's not uncommon for NWCR members to experience the cycle of "yo-yo" dieting (the seesawing of weight loss and weight regain) on their road to successful weight management. Many NWCR members know what it is like to fail multiple times with dietary approaches. Weight management changes can be challenging for all of us. Have a positive attitude and be encouraged to reach out to your health practitioner, a certified personal trainer, or a registered dietician for guidance. Like the many thousands of people on the NWCR, you too can be healthy and happy.

11. Many members of the registry have effective self-monitoring techniques. Besides weighing themselves often, many keep dietary and exercise journals. This may be very helpful for tracking your own journey.

12. Members get back on track if they see they are "sliding" off their program. In other words, they do not let a small lapse turn into a big relapse. Likewise, I always encourage the people I work with to keep a "laser focus" on their goals. If they get offtrack, they should use the same laser focus to get back on their journey.

13. Members manage their emotions as they relate to diet and exercise. When faced with emotional challenges, they avoid using food as an escape.

14. The majority of the NWCR members watch less than ten hours per week of TV, a major victory in the battle to combat sedentary behavior. I encourage you to do the same.

15. NWCR members have developed an incredible vigilance when it comes to sticking with their exercise and dietary program. How inspiring. You can do this too!

16. Members who successfully maintain their weight loss for over two years significantly increase their odds for continued long-term success.

The most important message to take from these 10,000 real-life biggest losers is that losing weight and getting fit is really doable—for anyone. Learn from their success strategies and let their successes embolden you. Now is YOUR time to succeed. You can do it! Remember, inch by inch, it's a cinch!

The Balanced Eating Plan

The new 2015–2020 Dietary Guidelines for Americans (DGA) encourage a healthy eating pattern across a person's lifespan. The DGA outline basic steps for small shifts in your diet to improve your eating habits and the quality of your food consumption choices. The new guidelines emphasize that food and beverage choices matter. Overall, the DGA propose that each person choose a healthy eating pattern at an appropriate calorie level to achieve and maintain a healthy body weight, support nutrient adequacy, and reduce the risk of chronic disease.

All persons are encouraged to limit calories from added sugars, lower saturated fats intake and reduce sodium consumption. In regards to added sugars, the DGA calls for limiting added sugars to less then 10% of calories per day. Therefore, a person on a 2,000-calorie daily diet would have no more than 200 calories from added sugar (about the amount in a single regular 16-ounce soft drink). So, a major message from the new DGA is DRINK LESS sweetened beverages each day. Naturally occurring sugars such as those in fruits and milk don't count towards this limit, because they have valuable fiber and nutrients. Interestingly, for the first time the DGA discusses coffee, noting that coffee consumption can be part of a healthy eating pattern.

Importantly, the DGA warns against trans fats, such as those found in partially hydrogenated vegetable oils. Trans fats are no longer recognized as safe.

In reference to cholesterol, the DGA suggests the following: "As recommended by the Institute of Medicine, individuals should eat as little dietary cholesterol as possible when consuming a health eating pattern."

Key Recommendations of the New Dietary Guidelines for Americans

A healthy eating pattern includes:

1. A variety of vegetables from all of the subgroups—dark green, red and orange, legumes (beans and peas), starchy, and other. However, make sure you don't load up on starchy vegetables, such as white potatoes.

2. Fruits, especially whole fruits

3. Grains, at least half of which are whole grains. If your diet contains a lot of white bread, crackers, buns and rolls, baked goods, pasta and white rice, you most likely consume too many refined grains. Over-indulgence of refined grains is associated with diabetes, obesity and heart disease.

4. Fat-free or low-fat dairy, including milk, yogurt, cheese, and/or fortified soy beverages

5. A variety of protein foods, including seafood, lean meats and poultry, eggs, legumes (beans and peas), and nuts, seeds, and soy products. Make sure you limit red meats and processed meats, which are a source of sodium and saturated fats.

6. Oils, including those from plants such as corn, canola, olive, peanut, safflower, soybean, sunflower, as well as those naturally present in nuts, seeds, olives, seafood and avocados.

Let's review a few key points. A healthy eating pattern follows these guidelines:

1. Limits saturated fats and trans fats, added sugars, and sodium

2. Will consume less than 10 percent of calories per day from added sugars

3. Will consume less than 10 percent of calories per day from saturated fats

4. Will consume less than 2,300 milligrams (mg) per day of sodium

5. If alcohol is consumed, it should be consumed in moderation—up to one drink per day for women and up to two drinks per day for men—and only by adults of legal drinking age

Internet Resources on Healthy Eating Patterns

Below are some helpful internet resources if you wish to read more on specific topics:

The DGA (eighth edition) is posted in its entirety at this WEB site:
health.gov/dietaryguidelines/2015/guidelines

Healthy US-Style Eating Pattern:
health.gov/dietaryguidelines/2015/guidelines/appendix-3

Healthy Mediterranean-Style Eating Pattern:
health.gov/dietaryguidelines/2015/guidelines/appendix-4

Healthy Vegetarian Eating Pattern:
health.gov/dietaryguidelines/2015/guidelines/appendix-5

Dietary Approaches to Stop Hypertension (DASH) Eating Plan
http://www.nhlbi.nih.gov/health/health-topics/topics/dash

Water

Water is your most vital nutrient. More than 70 percent of muscle is water, whereas only 10 percent of body fat is water. Water is an important constituent of all body cells. It surrounds the cells, permeates bone tissue, and is the foundation element of the circulatory system. Among its important functions are transportation of nutrients, removal of the by-products of cell metabolism, temperature regulation, joint lubrication, and cell structure shape. In addition, water is a medium for life-sustaining chemical reactions in the body. Drink an average of 8 to 10 eight-ounce glasses of water a day.

Vitamins

A well-balanced diet does not have to be supplemented to meet the daily vitamin requirements. However, a deficiency of one or more vitamins will result in some kind of symptom or deficiency reaction, whereas too much of a vitamin may cause a toxic reaction. Vitamins are grouped into two groups based on their solubility. There are the water-soluble vitamins (B vitamins and C) and the fat-soluble vitamins (A, D, E, K). Toxicity is more likely to occur with fat-soluble than with water-soluble vitamins. The best way to get vitamins in your body is from the foods you eat. Avoid low-nutrient foods like soft drinks and foods high in calories and fat. Nutrient-dense foods like whole grains and fresh fruits and vegetables will provide adequate daily caloric intake, as well as vitamins and other micronutrients. Beliefs that extra amounts of certain vitamins will give extra energy, reduce stress, prevent a variety of ailments, or improve endurance have not been proven by controlled research.

Minerals

The minerals, or micronutrients, are inorganic substances that your body needs in small amounts each day. They facilitate numerous functions in your bodily processes such as enzymatic activities, electrolyte balance, and fluid transport. They also have structural roles in the body.

Following are some general eating guidelines to help you design your all-around best-balanced eating plan.

Diet Guidelines

Meat and Protein Foods

© marilyn barbone/Shutterstock.com

- Eat less red meat; reduce the serving size and frequency.
- Eat fewer processed and cured meats (like ham, bacon, sausage, frankfurters, and luncheon meats high in saturated fats, sodium, and artificial preservatives).
- Select lean cuts such as eye round, sirloin tips, shoulder, chuck, flank, tenderloin, and remove all visible fat before preparing.
- Eat poultry (white meat without the skin), which has less saturated fat and fewer calories than beef or pork.
- Eat fish, which is low in fat. However, tuna, salmon, and sardines canned in oil contain more fat and less protein, so purchase them canned in water.
- Nuts and seeds are rich sources of vegetable protein but also contain a high concentration of calories and fat (mainly the "good" polyunsaturated kind). Sunflower seeds, sesame seeds, walnuts, almonds, and peanuts are the best sources.
- Although eggs are an excellent source of high-quality protein, the yolks contain a concentrated source of fat and cholesterol. Limit intake to three or four eggs a week, or eat only the whites of the egg.

Dairy Products

○ Eat reduced- or nonfat dairy products such as skimmed milk, low-fat cottage cheese, plain yogurt, and low-fat cheeses. Reduce the amount of cream, ice cream (ice milk has about half the fat of ice cream), whole milk, whipped cream, and cream cheese. These products contain excess fat and calories.

© alexpro9500/Shutterstock.com

Fats and Oils

○ Use more polyunsaturated vegetable oils such as safflower, corn, and sunflower.

○ Avoid hydrogenated or trans fats (processed fats that are more saturated such as buttery crackers, french fries, fish sticks, and pastries).

○ Oils like olive oil, canola oil, avocado oil and sunflower oil are made up of different percentages of primarily mono- and poly-unsaturated fats, and are considered healthier choices.

○ Avoid palm oil and coconut oil, which are also high in saturated fat.

© JPC-PROD/Shutterstock.com

Fruits and Vegetables

○ Eat raw fruits and vegetables daily. Many vitamins and minerals are destroyed in the cooking process.

○ Eat dried peas and beans, which in their natural state are excellent lowfat sources of protein.

© monticello/Shutterstock.com

Breads and Cereals

○ Eat whole grain breads and cereals, rather than refined ones. During the refining process, essential "B" vitamins and minerals are removed along with the bran (the outer layer of wheat kernel). Vitamin E is also lost when the wheat germ is expelled. Enriched breads and cereals replace many (but not all) of the lost nutrients.

© tommaso lizzul/Shutterstock.com

Healthy Eating Tips

○ Avoid eating large meals. A large meal elevates blood sugars and fatty acids. This extra food will usually be stored as fat in your body. Eat small meals at more frequent intervals throughout the day.

○ Foods that are cooked, stored in the refrigerator (or freezer), and then reheated later lose many of their vitamins.

○ Eat slowly and chew your food completely. Fast eating encourages overeating.

○ Avoid overusing the salt shaker.

○ Limit consumption of cookies, cakes, and candies; they contain excessive amounts of sugar and fat.

○ Read the label panels of foods to evaluate the nutrient content and look for hidden ingredients.

○ Include more fiber in your diet. The typical American diet is too high in calories, sugars, fats, and sodium.

○ Drink no more than two cups of coffee a day to avoid symptoms of anxiety such as nervousness, irritability, increased blood pressure, muscle tension, and difficulty sleeping.

○ Avoid skipping meals (especially breakfast). Many times when meals are skipped, people more than make up for it at another meal.

○ Spread your toast and bread with fruit-only jams instead of sugary jellies and butter.

○ Satisfy your sweet tooth with low-fat treats such as frozen juice bars, nonfat yogurt, fresh fruit, and angel food cake.

○ Toss your salad with gourmet vinegar and herbs instead of regular dressing.

○ Eat air-popped popcorn at movies or for a snack.

○ When buying peanut butter, choose the natural-style and pour the oil off the top.

○ Use nonfat milk instead of cream or nondairy creamers in coffee.

○ Give yourself permission to eat moderate amounts of the foods you enjoy on a regular basis.

○ Get plenty of fiber. It is associated with lowered risk for cancer, diabetes, and coronary artery disease. Increase the amount of oats, beans, lentils, fruits, and vegetable skins.

○ Add peanut butter and peanuts to your diet. Although there are fats in peanut butter, they are mostly monounsaturated while also being high in folic acid, thiamin, vitamin E, niacin, magnesium, zinc, and protein.

The Chocolate Fallacies

Everyone is entitled to enjoy eating chocolate in moderate amounts. However, some manufacturers would like to convince you that eating chocolate is more for health than pleasure. Here are some chocolate fallacies.

Fallacy #1: Eating chocolate doesn't make you fat.

In reality, no one single food does cause obesity. However, chocolate is a food with a lot of calories, so it is important to watch how much you eat for agreeable weight control.

Fallacy #2: Chocolate protects the heart.

It is true that one of the saturated fats in chocolate, called stearic acid, doesn't raise cholesterol. But chocolate has other saturated fats, such as palmitic acid, that do raise cholesterol. Also, it is meaningful to mention that stearic acid may help to promote blood clots, which can trigger heart attacks and strokes.

Fallacy #3: Chocolate helps to prevent cancer.

Chocolate does contain a high level of antioxidants, which are protective molecules for some cellular functions. Presently, many studies show the link between fruits and vegetables and a lowered cancer risk, but the studies on chocolate and cancer risk reduction are not here yet.

© bitt24/Shutterstock.com

Bottom Line

For many of us, chocolate is a sweet sensation that is an utter enchantment for our culinary desires. In moderation, it certainly provides great fulfillment, with few harmful effects. The research indicates that dark chocolate is a wonderful source of antioxidants, those molecules that neutralize those deleterious free radicals. Dark chocolate is also loaded with flavonoids, molecules with many health-related benefits. For those of you wanting to enjoy the great tast of chocolate, choose quality dark chocolate (dark chocolate with 70% or higher cocoa content) as it seems to have the best promise for health benefits, too.

The Stress, Cortisol, and Obesity Story

Today there are several products that tout the effectiveness of cortisol-combating supplements that propose to help people lose weight and feel less stressed by inhibiting the effects of cortisol. Cortisol has definitely become the 'prime-time' hormone of fascination, mystery, and confusion within the consumer industry, due to these misleading advertisements. It is a steroid (compound based from a steroid nucleus) hormone that is produced in the cortex of the adrenal glands located on top of each kidney. Exercise, fasting, food intake, and chronic life stressors cause the body to release cortisol. Cortisol regulates foodstuffs by helping to select the type and amount of substrate (carbo-

© Filipe Frazao/Shutterstock.com

hydrate, fat, or protein) that is needed by the body to meet the demands placed upon the body's systems. Cortisol also mobilizes energy by tapping into the body's fat stores and moving it from one location to another, or delivering it to hungry tissues such as working muscle.

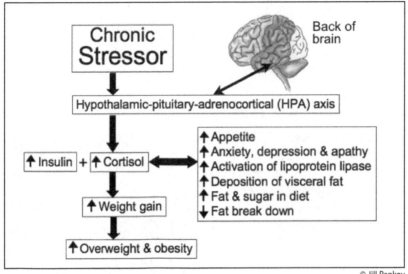

© Jill Pankey

With chronic stress the hypothalamus (which is the central control station for stress) directs the pituitary gland (below the hypothalamus) in the brain to send a signaling message hormone (known as adrenocorticotrophic hormone or ACTH) to the adrenal cortex (outer portion of adrenal glands on the kidneys), which results in the release of cortisol (see Stress, Cortisol, and Obesity Pathway figure). This reaction is referred to as the hypothalamic-pituitary-adrenocortical (HPA) axis, and it is most active during the early morning hours in humans. If the chronic stress (whether real or perceived) is of sufficient magnitude and duration the HPA does not wind down, as it should, resulting in a prolonged period of time that cortisol is elevated. Thus, chronic stress leads to daily increases of cortisol secretion. Cortisol is known to stimulate appetite during the intermittent recovery periods while a person is experiencing chronic stress in their daily life. Cortisol, with the help of slightly elevated insulin levels, has also been shown to activate lipoprotein lipase, the enzyme (lipoprotein lipase) that facilitates the deposition of fat. In the presence of slightly higher insulin levels, elevated cortisol promotes the storage of fat. Thus chronic stress consistently contributes to greater fat accumulation in the trunk area, which is called visceral fat. So, cortisol really isn't the problem! Stress is the problem. See the section on Stress Maintenance on how you can beat stress.

Did You Know?

The cell structure of your skeleton rejuvenates itself completely every 10 years.

Ten Tips for Weight-Loss Success

Americans spend over $35 million dollars a year trying to lose weight. It's no secret that diet books, diet pills, packaged foods, liquid diets, weight-loss groups, and hospital-sponsored programs abound, and yet at this junction in time no single program, plan, or treatment offers long-term effectiveness to large numbers of individuals. A winning weight-loss program will not be as concerned with loss of weight as it is with loss of body fat. Follow these tips for weight-loss success.

1. **Don't go on a crash diet or fast.** Very low calorie diets, often referred to as crash diets, lead to quick loss of muscle and fat. Only a small number of dieters will reach their goal weight, and fewer than 5 percent will maintain their new weight. Fasting exposes the body to a condition that actually increases

the activity of fat-depositing enzymes. Your body is reacting to what it perceives as starvation conditions and tries to protect itself from not being supplied the necessary foodstuffs.

2. **Go for fat loss—calories count!** The best diet to promote fat loss is a well-balanced, low-fat, heart-healthy, complex carbohydrate eating plan composed of a variety of foods to ensure good nutrition. It is important to educate yourself on which foods are high in fat and which are low. A rule of thumb for caloric expenditure is to consume roughly 16 calories per pound for moderately active people and no less than 1,200 calories a day. A complex carbohydrate, low-fat diet is also recommended for lowering the risk of high blood cholesterol, coronary artery disease, and high blood pressure.

3. **Exercise works.** The exercise program is essential to the success of any weight management plan and should be composed of aerobic exercise and resistance training. New research shows that persons who "Accumulate" 250–300 minutes of aerobic exercise during the week have the greatest weight loss success. This research shows that you can accumulate this total amount (250–300 minutes per week) in as little as 10-minute bouts of moderately intense exercise spaced throughout the days of the week. Of course, everyone is encouraged to gradually work up to this total amount of aerobic exercise per week. In addition, resistance exercise has been shown to impressively maintain your muscle mass during weight loss interventions. Thus, you will be preserving the most adaptable and metabolically active tissue in your body—muscle!

4. **Food choices.** Choose food that is low in calories but high in nutrients. Eat more complex carbohydrates such as whole-grain breads, cereals, rice, vegetables, bran products, and oatmeal. Substitute sugar-rich desserts with fruits. Drink plenty of water. It is a major component of your body and provides the environment within which the other nutrients may function. Eat low-calorie, nutrient-dense foods for snacks to help control your hunger between meals. Watch your consumption of alcohol. Alcohol has plenty of calories, but no nutrient value. Limit your salt intake to that which occurs naturally in food.

5. **Weight-loss goals.** Establish safe weight-loss goals. A loss of up to two pounds per week is a healthy recommendation for weight loss. Avoid seeking that slender fashion model figure. This may be too unrealistic and could lead to psychological distress and diet failure.

6. **Eating habits.** Many people eat till they are too full, mainly because the food tastes so good. Take responsibility and use good judgment at your meals. Also, it is not healthy just to eat when you are hungry. Instead of two or three large meals a day, eat five or six smaller ones, which better distributes your caloric needs throughout the day. Eat at a slower pace to avoid overeating and stomach discomfort.

7. **Food doesn't solve problems.** Unfortunately, conditions such as stress, emotional distress, or loneliness may lead some individuals to use food as a way of dealing with the problem. Attempt to disassociate food with these issues and seek professional counseling if necessary to establish appropriate intervention strategies. Food is an enjoyable fuel for life, not a mood-heightening support system.

8. **Behavior modification.** A major goal of any successful weight management program is to modify behaviors that may contribute to the problem. Begin by identifying those factors that may reinforce behaviors that are counterproductive to your body fat goals. Two helpful behavior modification measures involve the application of knowledge and values. Knowledge of accurate nutrition and exercise information is invaluable to complete your successful plan. Establishing new values enables you to develop behaviors that improve your quality of life and attain your body fat goals. Maintaining a positive attitude will certainly help.

9. **How to choose a good diet.** Choosing a safe and effective diet may be difficult with the hundreds of "miracle" diets on the market. Avoid programs that advertise unique fat-burning enzymes or fat-reducing formulas, as no known substances or formulas exist. Stay away from the quick and easy promises—there is no fast and easy way to lose excess fat. Steer away from those one-food diets, as they are deficient in essential nutrients. The program should be low in calories but complete in essential nutrients. It should incorporate a variety of food choices that you enjoy. Make sure the diet fits into your way of life. It should be designed to reduce no more than two pounds of fat per week. Finally, the diet you select should have lasting potential. Ask yourself if you can maintain it for a lifetime.

10. **Lifetime changes.** The dietary, exercise, and behavior changes you make should be sustainable for a lifetime. Develop a faithfulness and appreciation for exercise and health, not an obsession with thinness.

Sugar Controversy: Good Sugars versus Bad Sugars?

There is so much controversy on good sugars and bad sugars I decided to devote this final content in this successful weight management section to the ongoing sugar debate . . . to hopefully clarify many myths and misconceptions. Because of the scientific nature of this controversy, this section is presented a little more like a research review in order to appropriately and correctly address the salient issues about this sugar controversy.

Carbohydrates, which come primarily from plants, are a direct link to the Earth's food chain. Before the industrial revolution, carbohydrates were the major source of nutrients and energy for people throughout the world. In fitness, physiologists regularly extol the importance of carbohydrates as a vital fuel that drives exercise and sport performance. However, the evidence that added sugars in a person's dietary lifestyle presents several health risks is mounting. The purpose of this special section is to bring clarity to the important role of carbohydrates for exercise and present the health risks of American's sweet tooth sugar overload.

What Are Carbohydrates?

Carbohydrates are biomolecules that contain oxygen, carbon, and hydrogen atoms. They are made up of small building blocks referred to as monosaccharides (mono = one; saccharide = sugar). When we eat plants and digest them into monosaccharides, our body converts them to glucose, which the muscle cells use to produce energy. It should be noted that animals can also make carbohydrates, usually for use in their own body. The one meaningful exception is the natural sugar in milk, lactose, which is also a source of dietary carbohydrates. Glucose is the main carbohydrate in our blood, which we store in the form of glycogen in muscles and the liver.

Why Is Glucose the Preferred Fuel for Challenging Exercise Bouts?

It is important to note that energy that drives life and exercise is released when the chemical bonds in food substrates are broken. The energy in the food's molecular bonds is released in our cells to produce adenosine triphosphate (ATP), which is an immediately available source of energy for practically all bodily functions, particularly muscular contractions during exercises. At rest our body's energy demands are met fairly equally by the breaking of the bonds in fats and carbohydrates. During more intense exercise, glucose and glycogen are the preferred fuel because of their availability (glucose in blood and glycogen in muscle) and our muscle cells' highly developed enzyme system, which can chemically break them down rapidly to synthesize ATP.

Sugar Overload: Too Much Added Sweetness Has Its Perils

Cupcakes, cookies, muffins, doughnuts, chocolate, ice cream, soft drinks, fruit drinks, energy drinks, and more. The list of sweet temptations we have developed as a society is quite exhaustive, and now sounding off health alarms. In an invited commentary, Dr. Laura Schmidt (2014) clarifies that this sugar overconsumption to so many products during manufacturing is problematic. It is not due to eating too much fresh fruit, which has naturally occurring sugars, fiber, water, vitamins, and antioxidants. Schmidt explains that our health concerns originally were that too much sugar intake would lead to obesity and dental cavities, which has been prodigiously confirmed. The new concerns are these added sugars, predominantly sucrose and high-fructose corn syrup, which may be independent risk factors for cardiovascular disease, type 2 diabetes, abnormal lipids, and hypertension, highlighted in the next few sections.

The Sugar Burden on Cardiovascular Disease

Yang and colleagues analyzed national data (1988 to 2010) on the influence of added sugar consumption on cardiovascular disease (CVD). Their analysis shows that the CVD risk becomes elevated once added sugar intake surpasses 15 percent of daily calories. The researchers highlight, from their analysis, that regular consumption of sugar-sweetened beverages ($\geq$7 servings/week) is linked with increased risk of CVD mortality. Woefully, the risk increases with an increase in sugar intake. The researchers summarize that persons who consume approximately 17–21 percent of calories from added sugar have a 38 percent higher risk of CVD mortality.

Is There a Link with Sugar Intake and Type 2 Diabetes?

In their systematic review and meta-analysis from seventeen studies, Imamura et al. (2015) conclude that habitual consumption of sugar-sweetened beverages is independently linked with a greater incidence of type 2 diabetes. The researchers suggest that the consumption of sugar-sweetened beverages may be linked to 4–13 percent of type 2 diabetes incidence in the United States. Imamura and colleagues also state that artificially sweetened beverages and fruit juice are not healthy options for the prevention of type 2 diabetes. This data fully supports the recommendations for the healthy consumption of a wide variety of fruits, which have naturally occurring sugars that have not been linked to the incidence of type 2 diabetes.

Does Sugar Overconsumption Influence Blood Pressure and Blood Lipids?

Te Morenga et al. (2014) completed a meta-analysis of randomized controlled trials involving 1,699 participants that compared higher intakes of sugar to lower dietary sugar intakes in adults or children (who had no acute illnesses). Study results show that higher intakes of sugar are associated with harmful increased concentrations of triglycerides, total cholesterol, LDL cholesterol, and blood pressure. The researchers continue that the most likely explanation for the effect of higher sugars on blood pressure and lipids is in the fructose component. The researchers explain that overconsumption of dietary fructose, particularly from sugar-sweetened beverages, has been shown to increase liver fat synthesis, which results in increased concentrations of circulating triglycerides and cholesterol. In addition, the elevated liver fructose metabolism may lead to an increase of uric acid (uric acid is a waste product from the digestion of foods containing purines; e.g., dried beans, sardines, and certain meats), impairing the function of endothelial cells, resulting in a vasoconstriction of blood vessels and eventual high blood pressure.

Sugar Intake versus Sugar Recommendations

White (2018) summarizes estimates that the average American currently consumes about 19.5 teaspoons daily, which is approximately ~66 pounds of added sugar over the course of a year. In contrast, White notes that in 1790 that data suggest that the average yearly intake of sugar was 8 pounds annually. As a reminder, the average dose of sugar in one 16-ounce soda is about 16 teaspoons. White recaps that the American Heart Association recommends that adult females consume ≤6 teaspoons (~25 grams) and that adult males consume ≤9 teaspoons (~38 grams) of added sugar daily. Presently, Americans consume approximately three to six times more sugar that what is currently recommended.

Are There Unique Health Risks to High-Fructose Corn Syrup?

High-fructose corn syrup (HFCS), which was first introduced in the 1970s, is produced by a process that converts glucose to fructose. HFCS makes up a very large proportion of added sweeteners in beverages and many packaged foods (i.e., cereals, baked goods, desserts, flavored dairy products, and canned foods). Dornas et al. (2015) note that fructose is advantageous in processing because it is 1.5 times sweeter than sugar and inexpensive to produce. The researchers conclude, from their review, that HFCS definitely contributes to the development of several adverse health effects (i.e., insulin resistance, high blood fats, intra-abdominal fat accumulation, high blood pressure, and elevated uric acid). However, more research is needed to determine how excess HFCS causes these diseases, and the doses of HFCS that produce these negative health outcomes. With reliable data, evidence-based guidelines for HFCS intake may be proposed and recommended.

Sugar Restart Suggestions

The evidence clearly shows that added sugars are not just empty calories, they are very harmful calories. Health implications clearly indicate we should eat more whole foods as opposed to processed foods. Curbing the intake of sugar-sweetened beverages and sugar-laden yogurt would be a most healthful lifestyle change. In addition, choosing breakfast cereals with little or no sugar is a positive strategy. Interesting, added sweeteners to foods, which began as a way to combat high fat intake (and obesity) is now becoming an even bigger health problem. The bottom line message for fitness pros to clients is that healthy, unprocessed (or minimally processed) carbohydrates fuel our workouts and deliver beneficial vitamins, minerals, fiber, and phytonutrients. It's time to be mindful about all of the added sugars in foods, including foods not commonly thought of as sweet such as sauces, salad dressings, crackers, and breads. Perhaps the first step for many people in their sugar restart is not to avoid all sugar-sweetened products, just start limiting them in the daily diet.

ACSM Position Stand: Physical Activity, Weight Loss, and Weight Regain

Presently 69% of U.S. citizens are either overweight and/or obese. Weight loss in overweight/obese persons of as little as 3% to 5% of body weight (although 10% reduction is encouraged) has shown improvements in high-density lipoproteins (the good cholesterol), glucose utilization (for the prevention of diabetes), and reduction in blood fats and other risk factors of cardiovascular disease.

In the new ACSM position stand, the authors define weight maintenance as a <3% change in body weight, where as a 5% or greater change in body weight is considered a clinically significant change. The term "clinical" infers involving a medical observation, treatment, practice, or diagnosis.

How Much Physical Activity Is Needed for Clinically Significant Weight Loss?

It is recognized that most studies showing clinically significant weight loss (≥5% of body weight) demonstrate this with energy restriction (i.e., eating fewer calories) combined with physical activity to create a larger negative energy balance (i.e., more calories expended than consumed). Physical activity in the form of aerobic exercise between 225 and 420 minutes/week results in the greatest weight loss. For best practices, the ACSM position stand recommends accumulating 250 to 300 minutes of aerobic exercise each week. You can accumulate this aerobic exercise in ≥10-minute exercise bouts throughout each day. Also ACSM notes that regular resistance training (2–3 times a week) is a must for the maintenance and/or increase of muscle mass, as well as for an increase in daily energy metabolism (called resting metabolic rate).

© Jill Pankey

What about Weight Regain after Weight Loss?

It appears that many individuals are capable of losing weight with the long-standing challenge being how to maintain this reduced body weight. Consistent physical activity is the best predictor of sustained weight management after weight loss. And, when it comes to preventing weight gain, 'more is better'. The report specifies that individuals who have lost >10% of their body weight in 24 months, and did not gain it back, are participating in 275 minutes of aerobic exercise a week.

Adapted From: Donnelly, J.E., Blair, S.N., Jakicic, J.M., Manore, M.M., Rankin, J.W., & Smith, B.K. (2009). Appropriate physical activity intervention strategies for weight loss and prevention of weight regain for adults, 41(2), 459–469.

SECTION 6
Contemporary Health Issues

© Rawpixel.com/Shutterstock.com

Striving to be the healthiest person you can be is a very important goal in life. Your pursuit of optimal health emphasizes positive lifestyle practices and prevention strategies. Good health is determined by many of the choices you make in life about exercise, nutrition, weight management, alcohol use, smoking, substance use or abuse, and relationships. Developing your mind and managing your emotions are also closely interrelated with attaining optimal well-being. It is important that you take self-responsibility by engaging in activities that can positively affect your health. You deserve the opportunities that accompany good health. The purpose of this section is to briefly address some meaningful issues to help you make appropriate decisions regarding your personal health and well-being.

Wellness

Closely associated with optimal health is the concept of wellness. Wellness is an ongoing process of becoming aware of and making choices toward a healthy, fulfilling quality of life. Here are some of the different dimensions of wellness.

1. Social wellness emphasizes your interdependence with others.

2. Physical wellness encourages consumption of healthy foods, participation in activities that lead to optimal health (including exercise and self-care) and avoidance of unhealthy lifestyles (such as smoking and drug abuse).

3. Emotional wellness is the degree to which you feel positive and accepting about your own feelings. It includes your ability to realize your potential, your limitations and how you effectively cope with stress.

4. Intellectual wellness supports your pursuit of creative, stimulating activities and mental well-being.

5. Spiritual wellness involves seeking meaning and purpose in your life.

6. Occupational wellness emphasizes your preparation for a career that will provide enrichment and satisfaction.

7. Environmental wellness includes your respect for nature and the many species living in the world.

© Kendall Hunt Publishing Company

Self-Concept

Self-concept is how you feel about yourself. It is meaningful to note that someone with a low self-concept is more likely to adopt an unhealthy behavior such as smoking, alcohol, or substance abuse. A person's self-worth should come from the strength of his/her internal resources. Oftentimes an individual lets outside factors such as work, sports, school, or relationships determine his/her self-worth. This is very risky because these factors may be destructive to your self-concept. You need to acknowledge, to yourself, that you have positive attributes as well as faults, and that these qualities should not affect the decisions you make regarding your health. Clarify those physical, emotional, mental, and spiritual needs that must be met for you to be happy. Try to establish a link between your health behaviors and the fulfillment of these needs. This will help provide the direction and motivation for you to realize and sustain positive health outcomes.

> **Did You Know?**
>
> Self-concept is like a skill. You can develop it and master it.

Substance Abuse

Alcohol

The costs of alcohol problems in America have been estimated to exceed $70 billion per year, with the majority of these costs attributed to reduced productivity. It is second to tobacco as the leading cause of premature death.

Some general reasons people drink alcohol:

○ It often serves as a medium for friendship when people meet "for a drink."
○ It is frequently used to celebrate an event.
○ It is a means of dealing with stress, anxiety, emotions, or depression.
○ It is commonly used in social situations to lessen fears and make people feel at ease.
○ It is a lure successfully used by clever advertisers.
○ It is a behavior often introduced by role models.

Alcohol Continuum

Researchers have identified an alcohol continuum from which people may be able to evaluate or assess themselves or others.

> **Did You Know?**
>
> Alcohol is indicated in nearly half of all deaths caused by motor vehicle crashes and fatal intentional injuries such as homicides and suicides.

○ An *occasional drinker* drinks in small amounts, usually on special occasions.
○ A *light drinker* drinks regularly in quantities that are not intoxicating.
○ A *social drinker* drinks moderately, but in quantities that are not intoxicating.
○ The *problem drinker* drinks to the point of intoxication, following no specific pattern or even realizing what is happening.

- The *binge drinker* drinks heavily. Usually the drinking is linked to issues arising at work, home, or within his/her social life.
- The *chronic alcoholic* has problems associated with long-term, uncontrolled, and frequent drinking.

| Does Not Drink | Occasional Drinker | Light Drinker | Social Drinker | Problem Drinker | Binge Drinker | Chronic Alcoholic |

Women and Drinking

A variety of unique problems may arise when women drink. Females tend to have more body fat than men, and alcohol concentrations tend to be higher in people with more body fat. With less muscle mass than men and less water in their tissues (fat tissue has very little water), alcohol is absorbed into the bloodstream faster, even when all other absorption variables are constant. Therefore, a man and woman with the same body weight, who have consumed the same amount of alcohol in the same time period, will find the woman to be more intoxicated (primarily due to her body fat content). The negative effects to the fetus of a mother who drinks are well documented. Fetal alcohol syndrome is the second-highest cause of mental retardation in the United States. This is entirely preventable!

Drink Responsibly

The amount of alcohol in a person's bloodstream at a given time is referred to as one's blood alcohol concentration (BAC). The liver metabolizes 0.5 ounce of alcohol per hour. This is equivalent to the following drinks: 12 ounces of beer, 12 ounces of a wine cooler, 5 ounces of wine, or 1.5 ounces of liquor. It takes approximately one hour for any of these drinks to be metabolized by the liver and the BAC to return to normal. If more alcohol is consumed than is metabolized, the BAC will rise, and signs of impairment in motor skills, speech, equilibrium, and decision making will increase accordingly.

© Shaiith/Shutterstock.com

It is your responsibility to keep your BAC low and your behavior under control. Be aware of the reasons you may be drinking and make responsible decisions of how much you drink, what you drink, your limitations, your attitudes toward others who drink, and the consequences associated with alcohol use.

Tobacco

One out of every six deaths may be attributed to smoking. The use of tobacco is closely linked to diseases of the cardiovascular system, a number of cancers, respiratory infections, and ulcers.

Did You Know?

According to the Surgeon General, smoking is the single-most important preventable cause of death in the United States.

The active ingredients in smoking tobacco are nicotine, tar, and carbon monoxide. Nicotine, which is extremely addictive, stimulates the production of epinephrine. This causes the blood pressure and heart rate to increase and blood vessels to constrict. Tar, similar to that on city streets, is a sticky fluid that settles in the lungs and inhibits their functioning. Carbon monoxide is a deadly gas that retards the effective transportation of oxygen through the bloodstream.

The rate of female smokers is on the upswing whereas it is decreasing for the rest of the population. This increase in women smokers has been attributed to a desire of some females to have a slender image. This same desire makes it very difficult to quit smoking, as there usually is a small gain in weight that accompanies smoking cessation. The important point to stress is that smoking is a far greater risk to a person than gaining a few extra pounds.

Tobacco is consumed in five different forms:

1. cigarettes
2. low-tar and nicotine cigarettes
3. clove cigarettes
4. cigars and pipes
5. smokeless tobacco

© jps/Shutterstock.com

Although the low-tar and nicotine cigarettes are proposed to be safer, many of these smokers actually increase their cigarette consumption to satisfy their need for tar and nicotine. Smokeless tobacco (snuff or chewing tobacco) use is increasing, especially among young males. It is not a safe alternative for people who wish to quit smoking. Cancer of the cheek and gums is 50 times higher among smokeless tobacco users.

To quit smoking is a difficult process that requires breaking both a psychological and physical addiction to nicotine. It is very difficult for smokers to quit on their own. There are several programs available that utilize a number of approaches (behavioral, psychological, sociological, and pharmacological) that have proven to be successful in helping people stop smoking. With the cessation of smoking, a number of positive improvements in health rapidly occur. These include:

○ improvement in sense of smell and taste,
○ more efficient food digestion,
○ better circulatory and cardiorespiratory function,
○ better heart efficiency,
○ improvement in breathing capacity.

Other Drugs

Drug use can be found throughout every area of the country, in all social levels, at all income levels, and within many group affiliations. It is associated with a number of health problems including overdoses, drug-related violence, injuries, HIV infection (from shared needles), and birth defects. Oftentimes the use of drugs begins with harmless curiosity and results in substance abuse and dependence. Signals of drug dependence include the following:

1. emotional withdrawal,

2. decline in academic performance,

3. loss of interest in usual activities,

4. change in social groups,

5. concern with obtaining money, and

6. cranky behavior.

© Lurin/Shutterstock.com

There are several categories of substance abuse drugs, which include the following.

○ **Psychedelics.** The psychedelics or hallucinogenic drugs produce sensory and perceptual distortions of reality that may be pleasant or terrifying. Many of these drug episodes will last up to 12 hours and cannot be ended early.

○ **Opiates.** Heroin, long a part of the drug world, has similar but more powerful pain-relieving properties than morphine. Its main ingredient is opium, which is very addictive.

○ **Central nervous depressants.** Barbiturates are central nervous system depressants that may depress muscle control, speech, anxiety, and mood.

○ **Central nervous stimulants.** Cocaine and amphetamines are central nervous system stimulants. Amphetamines are occasionally used to curb appetite and to cope with difficult situations, such as cramming for tests. Babies of women who are cocaine users during pregnancy are more likely to have birth defects. Stimulant drugs often result in behavioral disturbances, irritability, hostility, and unprovoked violence. It should be noted that caffeine and nicotine are also central nervous system stimulants.

○ **Marijuana.** Marijuana is probably the most used illegal drug in the country. Attempts have been made to legalize it, with activists proclaiming marijuana less dangerous than tobacco or alcohol. However, the smoke in marijuana is harmful to the respiratory system. Although the long-term use of marijuana is unknown, chronic use of marijuana has been associated with infant mortality and neurological problems.

○ **Deliriants.** Designer drugs fall into this class. These are illegal drugs intended to replace some of the various street drugs.

A variety of programs are accessible to help people break their drug habits. Many treatment programs use substitution drug therapy. Counseling and support groups are also available. The most desirable solution to drug abuse is prevention. There are numerous ways to enjoy the gratification of a healthy life without having to depend on the dangerous stimulation of drugs.

Stress Maintenance

Stress is an inevitable part of living. When you feel too much stress you react with the "fight or flight response." This is the body's automatic response system that prepares you to "fight" or "flee" from an actual or perceived threat. A Harvard physiologist discovered the "fight or flight response." He describes it as a protective mechanism that is hard-wired in our brains. However, excessive stress and burnout can have emotional consequences.

One of the main causes of stress is a sudden, drastic, unwanted change: personal loss in the family, a job crisis, injury or illness, financial problems, and emotional problems all fall into this category. The tension from stress often leads to the worried, uptight sensation we call anxiety—you feel angered or frustrated. If these feelings continue to obstruct your ability to enjoy life, physical ailments such as ulcers and high blood pressure may result.

Being "stressed-out" may even lead to depression. Do you recognize the symptoms of depression?

- ○ restlessness
- ○ feelings of inadequacy and insecurity
- ○ inability to concentrate
- ○ sleeplessness
- ○ lack of interest in food, life, and social interaction

> **Did You Know?**
>
> The right side of the brain is the control center for creative thinking.

You can beat it! You can take charge!

Follow these guidelines:

1. Talk over your problems with a close friend or seek professional advice. You need to express your feelings!

2. See a physician if you have any physical ailments.

3. Do vigorous exercise regularly to vent anxiety and to combat depression.

4. Don't overload yourself. Set practical goals you can reach successfully and timetables you can meet.

5. Learn to relax. You need some peace and quiet each day just for **you!**

6. Organize your work and personal affairs. This will give you more efficient use of your time and will rid your life of clutter.

7. Take short breaks or a vacation. Time out will give you a better perspective.

8. Look ahead. Sometimes you can anticipate a job slump, a budding problem, or financial difficulties and be prepared.

9. Stay away from drugs and alcohol—they are just temporary relievers of tension, not cures for problems.

10. Improve your eating habits and your diet. Don't skip meals because you are too busy.

Stress Release Breathing Intervention

Here's a simple breathing drill you can do anytime to help lessen the effects of stress. Sit very comfortably and focus on relaxing your muscles in your body, especially those that are tensing up. Keep your breathing very slow and controlled. As you inhale say to yourself, "I am," and as you exhale say to yourself, "relaxed." Continue for 3 to 5 minutes.

Technology to Technostress

Although the benefits of technology are enormous, a new, unexpected type of stress is technostress. Technostress is the anxious feeling one gets by feeling reliant on technological devices (computers, fax machines, voice mail, remote control devices, cell phones, etc.). Thanks to technology, more people than ever before are adopting sedentary lifestyles, while spending hours at a time on a computer.

© Jacob Covell

What Are Some Symptoms of Technostress?

A common symptom is diminished concentration. People feel as though their memory is failing them, forget what they started to do, misspeak words, can't find the right words, or lose their train of thought. Impatience and irritability are also other symptoms. When you are technostressed it is difficult to find time to relax.

So, What Are Some Technostress Busters?

One simple suggestion is to go outside for a walk. Just being in the outdoors, in nature, appears to be most beneficial. Start an outdoor hobby such as gardening, hiking, or biking. All types of exercise are beneficial including aerobic exercise, resistance training, and flexibility training.

Avoiding Burnout

Everyone has the potential to suffer from burnout. The end result is a diminished capacity to function efficiently. Oftentimes the high demands needed for success, criticisms from others, and unrealistic expectations are underlying themes for burnout to occur.

© Jacob Covell

How to Avoid Burnout

1. Be careful of working extra long hours; in the long run this can lead to fatigue and loss of motivation.

2. Overextending yourself: try not to solve all of the world's problems. Get involved, but be realistic about your capabilities.

3. Too much stress, frustration, and anxiety in your daily life may lead to burnout.

Signs of Burnout

1. Attitude shift toward negativity; you may start putting less effort in current projects or an indifference toward your work.

2. Exhaustion; look for signs of frequent illnesses, fatigue, or even sadness.

3. Feelings of inadequacy; you may feel moody and less competent in areas in which you are really more talented, educated, and skilled.

Some Ways to Reduce Burnout

1. Be a good listener to your body. If you are regularly ill, exhausted, and fatigued, your body is warning you that something is wrong.

2. Realize you cannot do everything and be realistic on what you can accomplish.

3. Examine your work hours and perhaps incorporate some time-management strategies.

4. Don't overbook yourself.

5. Learn something new. Sometimes the boredom of work can take its toll. Go to some guest lectures or a seminar on a topic of interest. Pick up a new book to read.

6. Do something different. Perhaps you might find much satisfaction in having a pet or starting some type of hobby. Be willing to try something you've always considered, but never felt you had the time to do.

7. Do something different in your job. If possible try to do something different in your job that breaks you from the mode you might be experiencing. Students might want to buy some new video learning aids now available in most college bookstores.

Finally, try to draw a line in your life from who you are and what you do. Allow time for some of your friendships to grow and reestablish your lifestyle values for home and happiness.

> **Did You Know?**
>
> In humans, the four different types of blood are A, B, AB, and O.

The Eight Energy Bolsters

Do you ever get that feeling you want more energy? Do you know what to do? Here are some simple but effective tips you can do to bolster your energy.

1. Start by eating healthy and enough. Oftentimes the restrictive diets people attempt lead to early fatigue and low energy. Also, these same diets are often deficient in important vitamins and minerals your body needs to stay healthy.

2. Drink more water. A good rule of thumb is to drink about 1/2 to 1 cup of water every hour you are awake.

3. Get your carbohydrates. Without a doubt, carbohydrates are the most influential nutrients that regulate your energy. Eat plenty of whole-grain breads and cereals, rice, potatoes, pasta, and beans.

4. Take your vitamins and minerals. You may wish to consider a multivitamin if you know your daily diet seems insufficient. Key vitamins to focus on are vitamin C, calcium, magnesium, and potassium.

5. Keep an eye on iron. It is no secret that iron deficiency is a prevalent cause of fatigue in women. Don't forget that tofu and kidney beans are good sources as well as lean red meat.

6. Don't skip breakfast. Breakfast will help maintain your blood sugar levels that have dropped from your previous evening of sleep.

7. Sleep on. It is important to get the adequate sleep your body needs. Losing only one or two hours can sometimes sap you in the day and lead to weight gain.

8. Exercise. Aerobic exercise and resistance training improve several metabolic processes that can all lead to increased energy.

© Jacob Covell

Creative Problem-Solving

Whether it's solving a school issue, a personal challenge, or a family dilemma, resolving a problem can be quite stressful. When faced with this type of task, use these 10 ways to help resolve your predicament.

1. **Clearly define the problem.**

2. **Explore all possible solutions.**

3. **Be positive** and optimistic that you are going to successfully resolve this issue.

4. **Discuss and analyze** this problem and possible solutions with others who you respect. Choose colleagues who show a sincere interest in your well-being.

5. **Don't be overly critical** of any resolution ideas.

6. Allow yourself to **be imaginative** during this process.

7. Sometimes a new or different solution makes you feel apprehensive. **Feel confident** that it is OK, because you are using a fresh problem-solving approach.

8. **Summarize your options.**

9. **Choose a resolution** direction and put it into action.

10. **Observe and evaluate.** If the problem is not resolving, you may need to try another one of your options.

© Jill Pankey

Creative problem-solving is quite challenging. Reward yourself (with a book, show, or something special to you) for having gone through this process, as this method demands powerful analytical thinking and problem-solving skills.

Time Management Tips

Let's face it, time management for everyone can sometimes get pretty outlandish. With personal responsibilities, family responsibilities, work responsibilities, school responsibilities, and much more to do, it is no wonder many people find themselves overloaded. Use these eight tips to help you anticipate, organize, and take charge of your time.

1. **Start a master schedule.** Write down all your goals, commitments, and things to do. Make sure this master schedule is updated daily. This is also a good time to evaluate whether you have taken on too many projects and need to "put something on hold" for a later date.

2. **Organize and prioritize** your goals and commitments. Now that you have a master schedule, prioritize everything to keep you on track. Allow this organizational process to be very fluid, as goals and objectives often shift in importance.

3. **Focus on the big picture.** It is easy to lose a lot of energy micromanaging things that are of less importance. Focus your attention on what needs to be accomplished, in the order you have established.

4. **Be wary of regular distractions.** Telephones, pagers, cell phones, and e-mail can become distractions to accomplishing tasks. Sometimes it is best to allocate priority work times when you will not accept incoming communications and other possible distractions.

5. **Project breakdown.** Many people find it more productive and efficient to break down a large task into miniprojects.

6. **Establish a realistic time line for projects.** This may be the most difficult step. However, by creating a realistic time line you are helping yourself to avoid procrastination.

7. **Be an "objective detective" time manager.** An objective detective time manager can regularly anticipate the unexpected, such as more time needed for an assignment, and readjust his/her master schedule accordingly.

8. **Block into your life some daily "flex time."** Try to have some time each day that is allocated flex time to take care of projects that need more time or for you to get ahead on other coursework.

© Jacob Covell

Be a Great Communicator

Life is a constant state of communication with friends, colleagues, employers, teachers, and others. Here are eight suggestions to improve your professional and personal relations by being a more effective communicator.

1. Look at the other person. Always **make eye contact** with the person you are communicating with in a live conversation. This reflects self-confidence on your part.

2. **Listen actively** to the other party. Focus on the conversation without thinking of other things.

3. **Stay on track.** Some discussions start to digress when one or both parties begin to bring up unrelated issues or pointless past events.

4. **Avoid being judgmental.** Always try to be objective and comprehend the other person's point of view.

5. **Be sensitive and respectful.** In all conversations and discussions, appropriate respect and sensitivity to the feelings of others is appreciated.

6. **Clarify and then repeat.** Try not to assume anything in a conversation. Clarify important points and repeat statements to verify that what you heard was correct.

7. **Observe body language.** Oftentimes others may project their feelings with their body language. Observe the hands, face, and posture, and note how this person is expressing himself or herself nonverbally.

8. **Be supportive and constructive.** In all conversations make a point to be constructive and supportive in your feedback.

© Jacob Covell

Save a Life: Be a Stroke Detector

Most people do not know how to detect a person having a stroke, and yet every minute an American has one! Presently, with proper response time, medical researchers have developed helpful drugs that can resolve the clot causing the stroke. Here are the signs of someone having a stroke.

1. Sudden severe headache with no known cause

2. Unexplained dizziness or sudden falls

3. Some loss of vision, particularly in one eye or experiencing double vision

4. Sudden difficulty speaking or understanding speech

5. Sudden weakness or numbness of the face, arm, or on one side of the body

What Can You Do to Prevent a Stroke?

Each of us can take steps to prevent a stroke for loved ones and ourselves. An important first step is to lower blood pressure if it is too high. Do at least 30 minutes of moderate intensity exercise daily. If overweight, lose weight and eat plenty of fruits and vegetables daily. Smoking really increases the risk of stroke due to the noxious chemicals in smoke that make the blood vessels stiffer. If you smoke, STOPPING may save your life. You can prevent a stroke from occurring with your positive approach to a healthy lifestyle!

© Africa Studio/Shutterstock.com

Exercise Improves Brain Function!

Most recently, research on the favorable effects of exercise and brain function is emerging. Studies with physically active women and men indicate they have much less cognitive decline when they exercise regularly. Some scientists believe that physical activity may impart a neuroprotective effect in the brain, boosting brain health and cognitive (thinking, reasoning, remembering, imagining or learning) functioning.

The majority of the exercise and brain function research has been done using cardiovascular exercise as the intervention, and it is considered the most important form of exercise for improved brain function. Aerobic exercise induces the formation of new blood vessels in the brain during childhood and adulthood and improves brain circulation for better oxygen and nutrient delivery. In addition, programs combining aerobic exercise, resistance training, and flexibility are quite effective for cognitive function improvement, although the underlying mechanisms why are speculative at this time. Doesn't this brain and exercise research make you want to work out?

Ten 'Fascinating' Facts about the Brain

Here are some interesting bits of information about the brain.

1. The brain is 75% water.

2. The average number of thoughts that you experience each day is about 70,000.

3. Every time you blink, the brain 'kicks in' to keep things illuminated so the world doesn't go dark during the blink (which we do about 20,000 times a day).

4. While awake, your brain generates between 10 and 23 watts of power—or enough energy to power a light bulb.

5. You can't tickle yourself because the brain can distinguish between unexpected touch and your own touch.

6. Excessive stress can alter brain cells, structure, and function.

7. The brain uses about 20% of the total oxygen of the body at rest.

8. You continue to make new neurons throughout life as long as you use your brain in mental activities.

9. There are about 100,000 blood vessels in the brain.

10. The average brain, which weighs about 3 lbs, has approximately 100 billion neurons.

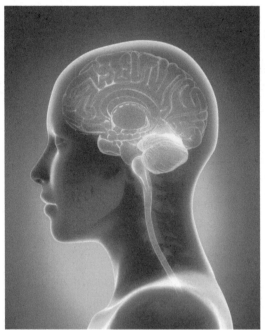
© CLIPAREA I Custom media/Shutterstock.com

Sleep: A Gift to Your Body and Mind

Scientists suggest that sleep provides the following 3 major functions: 1) it serves as the energy restoration (recharging) period from the daytime activities, 2) it affords bodily protection at night when sensory capacities are down-regulated, and 3) sleep affords the brain needed time to consolidate important experiences and memories for learning. Most men and women need 7–8 hours of sleep a night. Chronic sleep debt is commonly defined as sleeping between 4 to 7 hours a night.

Sleeping Hygiene Tips

The following are sleep hygiene tips to help you get the most favorable sleep.

1. Limit naps to a maximum of 30 minutes and try to do earlier in the day.

2. Avoid bringing food to bed.

3. Avoid bringing paperwork and work projects to bed.

4. Create a sleep-friendly bedroom by doing the following: use comfortable linens and pillows, put up darker shades, replace a worn-out mattress, and keep the bedroom cool during sleep.

5. Attempt to deal with stressful issues during the day and put them away at night (seek professional consultation if necessary to better deal with the stress).

6. Drink fewer fluids after dinner so the need to get up to go to the restroom is minimized.

7. Set a regular time to go to bed and a consistent time to awaken, and keep to this schedule.

8. Create a 'noise-free' sleeping environment.

9. Do not smoke or use any other products with nicotine before bed, as the nicotine keeps many people awake. Encourage clients who smoke to quit.

10. Cut down on caffeine consumption in the late afternoon and evening.

© Picsfive/Shutterstock.com

Five Vital Facts about Sleep Restriction

1. One-third of U.S. adults report chronic sleep restriction.

2. Chronic sleep restriction is particularly connected to motor vehicle accidents.

3. Sleeping more on the weekends to make-up for a loss of sleep during the workweek is not good sleep hygiene as it disturbs normal sleep-wake cycles.

4. Ever-present sleep restriction is associated with learning and memory loss.

5. Continual sleep restriction is linked to diabetes, depression, hypertension, and cardiovascular disease.

Did You Know?

Having high blood sugar will also elevate your risk for heart disease.

Did You Know?

88% of people in the US are right-handed.

SECTION 7
Fitness Facts and Fiction

© squarelogo/Shutterstock.com

Frequently Asked Questions

As a college professor, I get a lot of questions from my students related to weight management, exercise science, nutrition education, exercise physiology, and health. I realized over time that many of the same questions were coming up again and again, so years ago I started keeping a record of these questions. Without any further ado, here are many common questions about health, nutrition, weight management, and exercise, and their evidence-based answers.

Questions on Health

1. **How do I boost my HDL cholesterol?** Your HDL cholesterol is the "good" or "healthy" cholesterol. It's the scavenger that travels through the blood and removes excess plaque that is starting to clog up your arteries. One major way to boost your HDL is to quit smoking, if you smoke. Quitting smoking has been shown to improve your HDL cholesterol and lower your LDL ("bad") cholesterol. This is most impressive, as both of these changes reduce your risk of cardiovascular disease. Definitely continue with your cardiorespiratory exercise. Aerobic exercise programs have been shown to improve HDL cholesterol. Another great strategy to boost the effectiveness of HDL cholesterol is to replace saturated fats with healthier monounsaturated and polyunsaturated fats in your diet. And, if you drink, moderation is key. (If you don't drink alcohol, though, don't start.) Lastly, I want to note that scientists believe that even if your HDL numbers do not go up, lifestyle modifications—such as the ones suggested in this book—can still improve your HDL cholesterol's functioning in the body. Your lifestyle behaviors can progressively improve components of the HDL cholesterol structure, making it a more potent plaque forager.

2. **Will drinking coffee actually dehydrate me?** Recently, the Institute of Medicine published some guidelines on hydration and noted that caffeine-containing beverages did not significantly dehydrate people. The belief that for every cup of coffee you consume you need to drink a cup of water is a myth. The guidelines state that caffeine, colas, and tea may contribute to the body's fluid needs.

3. **Is it OK to drink beer after working out?** Alcohol is a diuretic, which means it stimulates urine production. Following a workout you want to replenish your body with lost fluids, not take more away from it. Consequently, drinking an alcoholic beverage before or after exercise is NOT recommended.

4. **Can I drink too much caffeine?** Most people have internal regulators that tell them when to stop consuming caffeine. However, experts from the Mayo Clinic suggest up to 400 milligrams (mg) of caffeine a day—roughly the amount in four cups of brewed coffee—appears to be safe for most healthy adults. Be aware of the symptoms of "caffeinism": breathlessness, headache, lightheadedness, and irregular heartbeat. Too much caffeine may also trigger a panic attack. For college students, caffeine-containing energy drinks have overtaken coffee as the primary source of caffeine. If you decide to consume one of these drinks, please check the label to make sure your caffeine intake is within recommended levels.

5. **What does it mean when a food has the American Heart Association logo on it?** The red heart with white checkmark means the food has no more than 3 grams of fat, 20 milligrams of cholesterol, and 480 milligrams of sodium. The food must also have at least 10 percent of the daily value for one or more of these nutrients: protein, vitamin A, vitamin C, calcium, iron, or dietary fiber.

6. **Is it true that tea is a healthy beverage?** Yes, black and green teas appear to lessen cholesterol's damaging effect on your arteries and protect against cancers of the skin and gastrointestinal tract. If you drink tea, make sure you steep it for at least three minutes to ensure the beneficial antioxidants in the leaves enter your beverage.

7. **What are trans-fatty acids and why are they bad for you?** Trans-fatty acids are unsaturated fats that have had hydrogen added to them, making them more saturated. This chemical process helps to extend the shelf life of many foods, such as crackers, cakes, cookies, chips, and unsaturated oils (such as corn and soybean). Regrettably, trans-fatty acids raise your total cholesterol and LDL (bad) cholesterol. They can also lower your HDL (healthy) cholesterol. In addition, trans fats are associated with increased risk of type 2 diabetes. When looking at food labels, the words hydrogenated and partially hydrogenated indicate there are trans fats in the food. Try to avoid these foods.

8. **Is there a difference between being overfat and overweight?** Yes, overweight is a term that is only concerned with pounds. Overfat is concerned with the muscle/fat relationship. For instance, many professional football players are overweight by the familiar height/weight charts but have a low percentage of body fat, which means they are certainly not overfat.

9. **Should I take a multivitamin?** Yes, this is an option to consider. Many people take a multivitamin because they are aware their diet is imperfect, which is a good reason to do so. If you take a multivitamin, make sure it has B-12. Your body doesn't make B-12, so you need to get it from animal-based foods (dairy products, eggs, fish, meat, and poultry) or from supplements. As you make the turn into your fifties, you absorb B-12 less effectively. A B-12 deficiency can lead to nerve damage. The average recommended amounts, measured in micrograms (mcg), is 2.4 mcg per day, 2.6 mcg per day if pregnant, and 2.8 mcg per day if breastfeeding. The other key vitamin to look for in a multivitamin is vitamin D. Many Americans get too little vitamin D from sunlight or food. The recommended levels are 600 IU until age seventy and 800 IU if you are older than seventy. If you are already taking some vitamins, I recommend you talk with your health practitioner before starting a multivitamin, as too many vitamins can become toxic to your body. However, I describe taking a multivitamin as being similar to an insurance policy. It is a daily guarantee to ensure your body gets the vitamins and minerals it needs. A multivitamin can make up for the shortfalls that happen when you don't get nutrition you need through food.

10. **Am I at increased cancer risk if I eat red meat?** Yes, according to research presented by the National Institutes of Health and National Cancer Institute. Eating a high consumption of red meat increases the likelihood of developing colorectal cancer. Minimize your intake of processed red meats such as sausage, hot dogs, bacon, and lunchmeats, as they have the strongest links to cancer development. Also, red meat consumption in early adult life for a woman is more associated with breast cancer risk than red meat consumption in midlife or later for a woman. As well, here's a note of safety for those of you who enjoy barbecuing your meats: Cooking meat at high temperatures causes chemicals called heterocyclic amines (HCAs) to form. These HCAs are carcinogens that can cause changes in your DNA, which may lead to cancer. There are several ways to minimize HCAs when you grill. For starters, you can eliminate 90 percent of the HCAs if you microwave your meat or chicken first for about 1.5–2 minutes. Then, just pour off the juices. Turning over the meat and poultry every minute cuts the HCAs by 75–95 percent because the surface temperature stays lower. Remember, however, the drier and more well done the meat, the more HCAs you get.

11. **Are sweet potato fries healthier that regular French fries?** It seems like sweet potato fries are showing up on menus in many restaurants, which raises this common question. Sorry, but sweet potato fries are still fries. The name "sweet potato fries" sounds like a healthy alternative, but it really isn't—both are loaded with calories and sodium. A better side dish option is a green salad or non-starchy vegetables like asparagus or broccoli.

12. **Is it possible to be fat but fit?** The paradox of being fat but fit has stimulated quite a bit of interest in medicine and fitness, and it's an important phenomenon to discuss, particularly as populations around the world are becoming more overweight. Dr. Jean-Pierre Després, the world acclaimed obesity and cardiovascular disease researcher from Laval University in Quebec, Canada, has addressed the fat but fit issue in his research. He asserts that reducing waist circumference by increasing cardiorespiratory fitness with exercise and incorporating movement to combat sedentary behavior will result in positive health benefits, even in the absence of weight loss. Dr. Després points out that most people who are fat but fit are in the overweight/moderate obesity range; they are not vastly obese. Fat but fit individuals tend to have less belly fat, the unhealthy danger zone for fat accumulation on your body. (Interestingly, HIIT exercise programs have been shown to selectively target unhealthy belly fat.) Finally, changing from a sedentary behavior to a physically active lifestyle is the major key when discussing this fat but fit question. In summary: yes, you can be fat but fit!

13. **Are nuts really that healthy?** Absolutely. A recent study published in *The New England Journal of Medicine* followed 119,000 women and men for twenty-four years, and it found that adults who regularly consume nuts were less likely to die of heart disease, cancer, and lung disease. Nuts are rich in unsaturated fats, protein, vitamin E, and fiber, and low in carbohydrates. Other studies have shown that nuts can improve blood pressure and cholesterol and reduce the risk of type 2 diabetes. This new study suggests that for optimal results you should eat a handful of nuts a day, which is about 3 tablespoons (or one ounce). Nuts pack a few calories (160–204 calories per ounce), but the research does not indicate you are going to get fat from eating them. Still, it is good to be aware of this if you are on a weight management plan, as the nuts do add to your caloric intake. Also, the thousands of men and women in this study ate all types of nuts, as well as peanuts, which is actually a legume. However, the researchers suggest that walnuts, almonds, and hazelnuts are particularly recommended for cardiovascular health. Here are some "nutty" ideas to consider for your daily life: Instead of snacking on sweets or chips, replace them with a handful of your favorite nuts. Also, top green salads with nuts instead of cheese or meats. Another great option is sprinkle some nuts on your favorite yogurt. Make sure you store nuts properly, as they can go bad. Keep them in an airtight container in your refrigerator or a sealed plastic bag in your freezer.

14. **What is the body mass index (BMI) measurement I've read about in weight management articles?** BMI is calculated as your weight in kilograms divided by the square of your height (in meters). Another simple BMI calculation is body weight in pounds multiplied by 703 and then divided by height in inches. Fortunately, there are many easy-to-use BMI calculators on the web. The World Health Organization has established guidelines for normal (18.5–24.9 kg/m2), overweight (25–29.9 kg/m2), and obese (>30 kg/m2) BMI in adults. One of the drawbacks of BMI, though, is that a muscular person will score higher, producing an inaccurate assessment that they are overweight or obese. Also, studies indicate that older people tend to lose muscle mass, possibly leading to an underestimate of the BMI. As we have discussed in this book, the ever-increasing worldwide obesity epidemic poses increased risk for coronary heart disease, hypertension, abnormal cholesterol, type 2 diabetes, sleep apnea, and cer-

tain cancers. This helps explain the popularity of BMI, which is a simple measurement tool for identifying people at risk. More recently, however, waist circumference has been used to identify health risks for obesity in place of BMI. A waist circumference ≥35 inches in women and ≥40 inches in men is associated with higher cardiovascular disease risk. One practical question you probably have is, how is waist circumference measured? Hold the tape snugly right around your belly button. It is that easy. Go ahead—measure yourself when you're ready. I encourage my students to track their waist circumference every two months after they start their HIIT workouts to see what changes are occurring here.

15. **What can I do to prevent myself from getting cardiovascular disease?** This is the perfect question to finish this health section. If I could get everyone to follow the following guidelines, we would be celebrating a magnificent reduction in cardiovascular disease throughout the world. Here are the top ten evidence-based strategies to prevent cardiovascular disease.

   a. Do not smoke. If you don't smoke, don't start. Those who smoke have a sevenfold increase in risk.

   b. Stay active, and keep it brisk. The evidence is crystal clear that physically active people have a lower risk of heart disease. But it's important to challenge yourself, too! Be sure that whatever activity you do gets progressively more challenging. The better your cardiovascular health, the lower your disease risk. Remember, for every thirty minutes of sitting, get your three minutes (or more) of movement.

   c. Check your weight regularly. Being overweight increases the risk of being obese. And, obesity increases the risk for cardiovascular disease. Use the weight management strategies in this book to put yourself on the road to optimal health, fitness, and quality of life.

   d. Keep your blood pressure under control. High blood pressure intensifies the risk of a heart attack more in women than it does in men, but it is vitally important for men to have healthy blood pressure too. Ideally, you want a systolic blood pressure under 120mmHg and diastolic under 80mmHg. Following a heart healthy diet and exercise plan is the best way to manage blood pressure.

   e. Go heart-healthy. The American Heart Association encourages you to eat fatty fish two to three times a week to get those very healthy omega-3 fats. If you eat meat, just select smaller portion sizes. Eat plenty of fruits, nuts, beans, vegetables, and whole grains. Definitely choose unsaturated fats, which come from foods like avocado, seeds, nuts, and vegetable oils. Avoid and/or minimize sugary foods and refined carbohydrates. Reduce your intake of processed foods that have those undesirable hydrogenated oils and trans fats.

   f. Keep sodium consumption down. Watch out for the big three here: processed food, restaurant meals, and fast-food. See if you can cut back on one, two, or all three.

   g. If you drink, drink moderately. Moderate drinking is not more than two drinks a day for men and one drink a day for women. That is doable.

   h. Manage your stress. Chronic stress can be enormously disruptive psychologically and physiologically. If you need help, go get it!

   i. Monitor your cholesterol. Have your health practitioner check your LDL (bad) cholesterol and HDL (good) cholesterol regularly. This information gives you some useful knowledge when it comes to knowing how well your body's cardioprotection is shielding you from cardiovascular events.

   j. Have your blood sugar checked. Men and women with moderately elevated blood sugar—what we call prediabetes—are at a higher risk of cardiovascular disease. At yearly health checkups, where you get to monitor your cholesterol, be sure to also have your blood sugar measured and checked.

One final thought on heart disease. It is always helpful to be aware of any family history of heart disease, since it is a disease that runs in families. Discovering that it's part of your family history may make you more aggressive in following the preventative strategies I described above. You are in control!

Questions on Nutrition

16. **Is it OK if I drink smoothies?** Several franchises now sell many types of smoothies, or "functional beverages," as we academic types like to call them. Most of these smoothies are made from fruit, juice, milk, yogurt, sorbet, and special "boosts" of herbs, vitamins, fiber, protein, and other substances. Some of the claims made by these businesses are pretty outlandish, suggesting the drink can control stress, improve mood, and increase energy. However, smoothies made from melons, carrots, berries, and other produce truly do have healthy minerals, vitamins, fiber, and phytochemicals. Phytochemicals are quite beneficial for human health and in preventing diseases. Some of the phytochemicals from plant foods can neutralize those unsafe free radicals that we talked about earlier in the book. The downside of some of these smoothies is that they pack a lot of calories; some have 500 to 700 calories per smoothie, which may very well contribute to weight gain. So, although healthful for the most part, they may not be the best for a weight management program.

17. **Why are foods with hydrogenated oils bad for me?** The problem with hydrogenated oils is they contain trans fats, which raise the bad LDL cholesterol and lower the good HDL cholesterol. In the hydrogenation process, hydrogen atoms are added to a vegetable oil's available bonds. Unfortunately, as the level of hydrogenation increases, the level of saturated fat also increases. I encourage you to read food labels. If the ingredient list contains the words "hydrogenated" or "partially hydrogenated," the food contains trans fats, and you should steer clear. Foods that often contain trans fats include fried fast-foods, cakes, cookies (particularly with frosting), pies, doughnuts, baked goods, frozen biscuits, breakfast sandwiches, crackers, microwave popcorn, frozen pizza, and some margarines. As you may know, the process of hydrogenation extends the shelf life of a product, thus saving money for the company that produces it. Good for them, perhaps, but not good for you.

18. **Do vitamins give me extra energy?** This is a very popular question that I get all of the time. Unlike carbohydrates, fats, and proteins, vitamins do not provide usable energy. I tell my students that vitamins are the worker bees in metabolism, because they assist enzymes in releasing energy from carbohydrates, fats, and proteins. However, vitamins are almost entirely calorie free.

19. **What are the best foods to eat after one of my challenging workouts?** First and foremost, focus on replenishing lost water after your workout. So, start by hydrating. Next, select a food rich in complex carbohydrates (starches, not sugars) and some protein. For instance, you could have a peanut butter and banana sandwich, or hummus and tomato on pita bread, or half a turkey wrap with veggies.

20. **What is dietary fiber?** Dietary fiber is basically a type of complex carbohydrate made up of plant material that cannot be digested by the human body. Refining and processing foods removes almost all of its natural fiber. The main sources of dietary fiber are whole-grain cereals and breads, fruits, and vegetables. Optimal amounts of fiber in the diet increase gastric movement and therefore may reduce the incidence of diverticulitis (bulging sacs or small blisters that appear in the lining of your large intestine), colon and rectal cancer, and obesity.

21. **Are natural vitamins better for me than manufactured vitamins?** No. For the most part your body can't distinguish the difference between vitamins manufactured in a laboratory and natural vitamins extracted from food. So if you get a cold, go ahead and eat oranges and other vitamin-C rich fruits and get plenty of supplemental vitamin C.

22. **What is the difference between brown rice and white rice?** Brown rice has slightly more vitamin E, magnesium, and some other minerals. The nutty flavor and chewy texture of brown rice is due to retention of the grain's bran. Brown rice also has more grams of fiber than white rice.

23. **What's the final scoop: butter or margarine?** Good question. According to the Mayo Clinic, margarine usually tops butter. Butter is made from animal fat, so it contains more saturated fat. However, stick margarines contain trans fats to keep them solid. As I've mentioned, trans fats can increase your risk of heart disease. The best advice is to look for a soft tub margarine that doesn't have trans fats and has the least amount of saturated fat. Another option would be to spread your bread with olive oil. Olive oil is a monounsaturated fatty acid, which is considered a healthy fat. Try it and see if you like it. I use it all the time!

24. **What is the most common nutritional deficiency in the United States?** Iron deficiency. Despite iron's abundance on earth, iron deficiency is surprisingly common in humans and is the prevailing cause of anemia throughout the world. It affects some eight million women of childbearing age and upward of seven hundred thousand toddlers. Iron deficiency anemia happens when your body doesn't have enough iron to make hemoglobin. Hemoglobin is the part of red blood cells that gives blood its red color and helps the red blood cells carry oxygen throughout your body. Examples of iron-rich foods include leafy green vegetables, iron-fortified foods, meat, and eggs.

25. **Are phytonutrients the same as phytochemicals? Tell me more about them.** Yes, phytonutrients are phytochemicals. These unique nutrients are concentrated in the skins of many vegetables and fruits, and are responsible for their color, scent, and flavor. Phytochemicals are not vitamins or minerals, however, they are plant nutrients that offer great health benefits. They have been shown to protect against heart disease, cancer, diabetes, osteoporosis, and other medical conditions. The only way to get phytochemicals is to eat or drink them in fruits, vegetables, juices, nuts, and whole grain products. Foods that are rich in phytochemicals include grapes, red cabbages, sweet potatoes, broccoli, kale, tomatoes, red onions, green tea, parsley, spinach, blueberries, raspberries, blackberries, and melons. The best-known phytochemicals are flavonoids, carotenoids, polyphenols, indoles, lignans, and isoflavones. Do you recognize any of these names?

26. **Can vegetarians get enough protein?** Yes, vegetarians who eat a wide variety of foods each day will absorb a full complement of essential amino acids. Essential amino acids are the protein building blocks your body is unable to synthesize on its own, so we get these from the foods we eat. Nuts, seeds, legumes, and many grains are good sources of amino acids.

27. **Why are whole grains better than refined grains?** Refined grains include white bread, white rice, regular white pasta, and other foods that have been made with white flour. Many cookies, cakes, breakfast cereals, crackers, and snack foods are also made of refined grains. Whole grains consist of the entire grain. They still contain the bran and germ, which are rich in dietary fiber and micronutrients. Whole grains are associated with a lower risk of cardiovascular disease, cancer, and all causes of mortality. Go with whole grains!

28. **What suggestions do you have for choosing veggie burgers?** Buyers beware. Even though veggie burgers are made of veggies, the amount of processing these ingredients go through may zap most of the essential nutrients from them. Start by checking the sodium level. Some veggie burgers have 500 (or more) milligrams of sodium, which is a third of your day's recommended total. Try to choose a veggie burger that has 350 milligrams or less. Next, check the protein in the veggie burger. In a 3-ounce beef burger you will get about 20 grams of protein. The protein in veggie burgers ranges from 5 to 20 grams, so shoot for one that has at least 10 grams of protein. The good news is most veggie burgers are made with soybean oil, corn oil, or canola oil, all of which have more polyunsaturated fat, the good fat. Stay away from veggie burgers with quorn. The main ingredient in quorn is mycoprotein, which is a processed mold that can lead to very unhealthy reactions for some people. Alas, taste is the last decision. That is completely up to you.

29. **As I start working out harder, would it be beneficial to have a pre-exercise snack?** A pre-exercise snack may be helpful if you feel like you don't have energy to complete your workouts. However, pre-exercise snacks have calories, and thus may thwart some of your weight management goals. Nevertheless, here's the scoop on pre-exercise snacks: muscle glycogen (the stored form of glucose, or sugar) is the principal fuel used by the body during exercise, followed by fat. This is primarily because we break down carbohydrates about thirty to forty times faster than we break down fat for energy, and during exercise we need energy rapidly to keep up with a challenging workout. Low muscle glycogen stores may result in muscle fatigue and the body's inability to complete your workouts, particularly as you do the more challenging workouts. So, the demand for carbohydrates is relatively high for all types of challenging exercise. A carbohydrate and protein snack or drink prior to aerobic exercise has been shown to increase performance during challenging workouts. If you feel you need more energy for your workouts, try this approach: Choose a carbohydrate to protein supplement drink or snack that has 3–4 units of carbohydrate to 1 unit of protein. We call this a 3/1 carbohydrate to protein ratio or a 4/1 carbohydrate to protein ratio; many health food stores have sports drinks and snacks you can try with these ratios. I recommend you have your drink or snack within thirty minutes of exercise. See if this helps give you the energy to sustain your workouts.

30. **I am thinking of snacking on nutrition bars between some of my regular meals. What do I need to know to choose the right one?** Nutrition bars are also called energy bars. They offer wonderful convenience and variety and can be a snack, protein booster, nutritional supplement, or even a meal replacement. They also travel well on trips. Before choosing a nutrition bar, though, consider that they contain an average of 150–300 calories. For a person on a weight-loss program, that is a lot! If you are on a weight management program, seek a lower-calorie bar. Also, even though they have the word "nutrition" on the label, many of these bars are packed with sugar, including high fructose corn syrup, honey, molasses, cane sugar, and more. Sugar is sugar, which means there really isn't any nutritional value to any of these sugars, just extra calories. Try to avoid nutrition bars with processed sugars such as fructose, sucrose, and dextrose. Cranberries, dates, figs, apricots, and raisins, and other dried fruits are healthier sweeteners in nutrition bars. When it comes to protein, many nutrition bars have 10–15 grams of protein, often from whey protein, which is a dairy source. Some bars get their protein from seeds, legumes, and nuts. You probably don't need that much protein, but protein does promote satiety, so you will feel full for a longer period of time. Steer away from soy protein isolate, which may act as a hormone disruptor in the body. In regard to fat, check to see if the bar has the favorable unsaturated

fats, including canola oil, sunflower oil, nuts, and seeds. Steer away from nutrition bars that have saturated fats such as palm oil, coconut oil, and cocoa butter. In addition, most nutrition bars have 3–5 grams of fiber, which is healthful. Many nutrition bars have about 100 to 150 milligrams of sodium, which is fine for this kind of a snack. Moreover, many nutrition bars have an array of added nutrients such as vitamin E, vitamin C, beta-carotene, folic acid, copper, and magnesium. That said, if you are eating a healthy diet you may not need any more of these nutrients. Now that you know how to recognize a healthy nutrition bar, the last step is making sure you find a brand and flavor that tastes good to you. It's best to buy different bars separately, as opposed to in a box, so you can try them out first. Some health food stores also let you buy a sampler box of different bars to better make your final choices. Healthy snacking!

31. **I am thinking of switching to non-dairy milk. What should I look for when I buy it?** Many Americans have made the switch from cow's milk to "milks" made from cashews, almonds, flax, hemp oats, rice, soy, and other plants. As a result, the non-dairy milk market is booming. Here are some tips in making your selection for non-dairy milk. In regard to protein, cow's milk has 8 grams of protein per cup of milk. Most of your plant options are much lower, coming in closer to 1 gram per cup. However, soy milk delivers protein levels similar to cow's milk. Make sure you check the label if protein is one of the macronutrients you are seeking. Cow's milk has plenty of calcium, potassium, vitamin D, and vitamin B-12. Check for these nutrients in the non-dairy options. Please don't be fooled by the big calcium claims in some of these non-dairy milks. The calcium "Recommended Dietary Allowance" for adults is 1,000 milligrams per day, and 1,200 milligrams for women over fifty and men over seventy. Too much calcium, however, puts you at risk for hip fractures and kidney stones. More calcium is not better! Also watch out for the sugar in non-dairy options. Cow's milk has 12 grams of natural sugar (called lactose), which is about 3 teaspoons. Try the unsweetened non-dairy milk options or some of the "original" non-dairy milk options such as original soy or almond milk. An ingredient in some non-dairy milk to avoid is carrageenan, which has been shown to cause long-lasting digestive problems. Guar gum and xanthan gum are two other substances often found in non-dairy milks that you should avoid; they have been linked to digestive problems and weight gain. Lastly, most non-dairy milks are low in saturated (bad) fat.

32. **Please clarify: it is now OK to eat eggs?** That is correct. The Dietary Guidelines Advisory committee has concluded that cholesterol in foods such as eggs is NOT the main cause of unhealthy blood cholesterol levels. Now, this isn't a green light to eat as many eggs as you want. But, having a couple of eggs every other day is fine. However, please use moderation if you have bacon, sausage, and/or ham with your eggs, as those processed meats are highly linked to cancer and heart disease.

Questions on Weight Management

33. **What's a good substitute for those high-fat potato chip snacks?** Try pretzels. They're almost fat free. If you are intent on buying chips, look for the chips that are baked, not fried, and avoid chips made in hydrogenated oil. Remember to check the total fat content and serving size, too.

34. **Are there any foods that will make me more satisfied and less likely to binge?** Yes. Some of the most filling foods include boiled potatoes, steamed fish, oatmeal, oranges, apples, whole wheat pasta, grilled lean beef, baked beans, grapes, and whole grain bread.

35. What is grazing? Grazing is an eating plan some people have adopted where they eat frequent small meals (up to six) spaced throughout the day. Some people find that this helps control appetite, and they actually consume fewer calories than if they had eaten three square meals. The one downside of this eating plan is the time it takes to plan, prepare, and then eat the smaller meals.

36. Is it true that when you eat out, you usually eat more calories than at home? Yes. Large portion sizes and high-calorie entrees carry most of this responsibility. Be aware that when you go out you are almost always less likely to eat nutritious food. Also remember that appetizers (which means "small dishes") have calories too. Alas, most Americans neglect fruits and vegetables when eating out.

37. Are liquid meal replacements OK to take on a regular basis? Many of these liquid meals provide sufficient calories as well as a number of minerals and vitamins, but they do not provide the health promoting fiber and phytochemicals that are in fruits and vegetables. So, I don't mean to discourage their consumption, but make sure you balance them with real meals, fruits, and vegetables.

38. I like orange juice with pulp. Does it have more fiber than juice without pulp? There is no significant difference in the fiber content between juice with pulp and juice without it. The pulp is composed of specialized cells that help store the juice.

39. Can I reduce the number of fat cells in my body? No, you can reduce the size of the fat cells, but not their number. Woefully, you can certainly increase the number of fat cells. Continual weight gain will lead to the expansion of existing fat cells and the creation of more cells. Once created, these new fat cells will not go away!

40. What is the intuitive eating diet? Intuitive eating is a dietary strategy that encourages you to listen and respond to your body's hunger signals for food choices. The view of this non-diet approach is to encourage normal, healthy, and conscious eating. Intuitive eating has an empowering philosophy to be more mindful at meal times. This enables people to trust themselves in what they eat and how much they eat. Study results indicate that intuitive eating promotes heightened awareness and responses to body signals that result in healthy, long-term behavior change. Try this—it works for many people.

41. Why does the mirror show my change of shape before the scale? Great observation. Muscle is denser than fat. A pound of fat bulges out 18 percent more than a pound of muscle. Because you are adding muscle to your body as you shape up, you will often notice a loss of inches before a loss of weight.

42. What role does genetics play when it comes to weight management? It is now well established that overweight and obesity are conditions that tend to concentrate within a family. The risk for obesity is two to eight times higher for a person with a family history of obesity, as opposed to a person with no family history of obesity. However, genes do not always predict the future. A person's susceptibility for obesity derives from a lifestyle of abundant food intake in combination with little exercise. Obesity is definitely preventable.

43. Will eating spicy foods help me burn more calories? Spicy foods such as red or green chili peppers contain capsaicin, a chemical compound that can mildly boost your metabolism. Some studies suggest the effect only lasts about half an hour, however. Therefore, in the long run, eating lots of spicy food is not an effective weight management strategy.

44. **What can I do to avoid eating too much junk food?** One of the first steps to avoiding junk food is to not get too hungry between meals. There are so many irresistible food cues from fast-food enticing you to eat it when you are hungry. Make a list of healthy snacks that you can enjoy if you get hungry between meals, and choose these first. For some people, daily stressors sometimes prompt the consumption of junk food. Be aware of this and have some healthy stress-relief solutions at the ready. As well, laser focus on always eating the healthiest foods for your body, and make sure you have healthy snacks readily available when you are experiencing cravings.

45. **I realize cutting sugar-sweetened beverages is important for weight control. Please explain why these drinks have become such a problem.** The consumption of soft drinks, sodas, and sugar-sweetened beverages has been increasing in almost every country in the world. This is an alarming trend, given how strong the evidence linking drinking sugary drinks and weight gain is, particularly when it comes to children. Accordingly, limiting the consumption of sugar-sweetened beverages has a particularly central role in weight management. A typical 20-ounce soda has fifteen to eighteen teaspoons of sugar and over 240 calories. A 64-ounce fountain soda drink could have up to 700 calories. Why are people drinking these? Research studies suggest people who drink sugar-sweetened drinks do not feel as full as they would have if they had eaten the same number of calories from solid food. Therefore, they do not compensate by eating less food. Fundamentally, these sugar-sweetened sodas deliver a pack of calories with sugar dissolved in water, which our bodies do not compensate for by eating less of other foods. And, regrettably, these sugar-sweetened drinks have little to no nutritional value. The best advice is to start substituting water for sugary sodas. Start slowly, remembering your goal (the same one that applies to all of the changes proposed in this book): inch by inch, it's a cinch.

46. **Is there any research suggesting alternative-day fasting is a viable option to try for weight loss?** Alternate-day fasting is a new approach for weight loss. It's meant to address the reality that many people just do not like to reduce their calories on a daily basis. With the alternate-day fasting approach, participants restrict calories every other day. This strategy involves a "fast" day where you consume 25 percent of your usual intake, approximately 500 kcal. The "fast" day alternates with a "feast day" where you are permitted to consume food at your pleasure—whatever you feel. There are several published books on this approach and a few two- to three-month studies that show impressive 3–7 percent drops in body weight among people who used this strategy. These short-term studies also show improvements in blood pressure, blood fats, and the body's ability to use glucose for fuel. A 2017 study published in *JAMA Internal Medicine* compared alternate-day fasting to a traditional caloric restriction diet for a one-year period with one hundred men and women eighteen to sixty-five years of age. At six months both groups had lost approximately 7 percent body weight and at twelve months both groups pretty much maintained their loss in body weight. Also, by twelve months there were no differences between the two groups when it came to changes in blood pressure, blood fats, and glucose metabolism. The researchers concluded that alternate-day fasting was equivalent to daily caloric restriction for weight loss, weight maintenance, and cardioprotection. So, alternate-day fasting appears to be an effective weight management approach that may be of interest to you.

47. **Is there evidence to support the claim that a gluten-free diet is good for weight loss?** Gluten-free diets are one of the newer weight loss crazes endorsed by celebrities and supported by a surge of internet articles and books. To understand more about these diets, let's start by exploring celiac disease. According to the Celiac Disease Foundation, celiac disease is an autoimmune disorder where the ingestion of gluten leads to damage in the small intestine. This hereditary disease is estimated to impact one in one hundred people worldwide. When a person with celiac disease eats gluten, a protein found in

wheat, rye, and barley, their body's immune system attacks the lining of the small intestine. This causes pain, bloating, cramps, diarrhea, and eventual vitamin deficiencies. Gluten acts like glue that holds food together, and thus can be found in many types of foods. People on a gluten-free diet must avoid foods with any trace of wheat, rye, or barley. Wheat is found in breads, soups, baked goods, pasta, cereals, salad dressing, and sauces. Barley is found in food coloring, soups, beer, malt, and brewer's yeast. Rye is found in rye bread, pumpernickel bread, and some cereals. Fortunately for people with celiac disease, there is an ever-increasing market of gluten-free products that can help them enjoy a satisfying lifestyle. But, the question many people have is, will a gluten-free lifestyle melt down the pounds? A rigorous search for randomized control studies (the most effective investigations) focusing on gluten-free eating and weight loss don't exist at this time. Nevertheless, whenever anyone goes on a restrictive diet, she/he typically eats less, which may explain why some people have lost weight on a gluten-free diet. Yet, be forewarned, many gluten-free products on the market have higher portions of fats and proteins. So, if you go gluten-free, keep an eye on your calorie intake.

48. **I know I need to cut down on salt, but how do I do this?** Most Americans eat more than the recommended 2,300 milligrams of daily sodium. Sodium has a fundamental role in the function of muscles and nerves to work efficiently. If you are able to eat less salt by choosing low-sodium foods, this will likely lower your blood pressure if elevated, or better manage your current blood pressure. It is important to note that high blood pressure is associated with heart disease, stroke, congestive heart failure, and kidney disease. You get a whopping 80 percent of your dietary salt from eating at restaurants or pre-prepared, processed meals. So, be aware of this. Also, there are many spice substitutes you can try instead of salt. For meats, poultry, soups, and sauces try spicing things up with cayenne pepper, allspice, chili powder, cilantro, or paprika. For salads and vegetables try parsley, sage, thyme, and cinnamon. Enjoy!

49. **I see a number of advertisements for "fat burner" products. Do any of them work?** Dietary supplement manufacturers often use the term "fat burner" to describe supplements or products that supposedly speed up your body's metabolism of fat and calories. The manufacturers of these products claim the unique combination of substances in their special pill/powder/etc. provides a weight loss effect on your body. Some of the most popular "fat burners" include the following ingredients: carnitine, caffeine, conjugated linoleic acid, green tea, forskolin, chromium, kelp, and fucoxanthin. All of these products have little rigorous scientific proof to their claims. The scientist in me would like to discuss all of these ingredients with you, but, the practitioner in me will get straight to the bottom line: Please save your money on these advertised fat burner products for now. Although a few products show some promise, more research is needed before you can get too enthusiastic about using them. A much better—and rigorously tested—solution is to start moving more every day, do your HIIT workouts, and find a healthy dietary strategy that works for you!

50. **Will I burn more calories from fat if I exercise first thing in the morning on an empty stomach?** No. This question has been a big controversy in the fitness industry for decades. Some fitness "gurus" have been proclaiming that to lose more fat people should exercise in the morning in a fasted state. The research, however, clearly refutes this claim. Indeed, if you want to burn more calories you should eat a light breakfast or snack prior to your morning workout. In fact, the research shows that when you have a light breakfast prior to your workout, you actually burn more fat and more total calories over the twenty-four hours after the workout. WOW! Try this approach: Have a light breakfast of some fruits, whole grain cereal, an energy bar, or even a sports drink at least twenty to thirty minutes and up to one hour before your morning workout. Doing this before your morning workout will help you get some fuel in your tank for burning more calories and burning more fat.

51. **I do aerobics and resistance training in the same workout. Which sequence is better—aerobics first or resistance training first?** Good news, science suggests that doing either of these types of exercise first has a different physiological advantage. One investigation has clearly shown that aerobic exercise using the same muscles that will be trained in the resistance exercise can lessen (not by much) the amount of work completed during the resistance exercise. So, if you cycle before you do a leg workout, this may slightly impair your leg workout. However, cycling before upper body exercises will not impair your workout. Yet another recent study shows that doing aerobics prior to resistance training will elicit a slightly greater post-workout caloric expenditure—you may burn a few more calories using this sequence. Best advice—vary your sequence.

52. **There seems to be a lot of debate as to whether pre-workout stretching has any effect on reducing injuries. What is the best recommendation?** This answer is still being debated. Importantly, a good warm-up is probably more imperative than stretching for the prevention of injuries in most exercises and sports. Let's face it, a good warm-up increases blood flow to muscles, enhances oxygen and food-stuffs to the working muscle while it simultaneously removes waste products. And it improves blood viscosity within muscle. Animal studies suggest a good warm-up increases muscle elasticity, which decreases the likelihood of muscle injures. Focus on a thorough warm-up before your workout and complete your stretching for muscle elongation after your workout.

53. **I'm confused! After reading all of the harmful effects of obesity, I now see articles that say you can be Fit and Fat! Where is the line here?** People who are slightly or moderately overweight but NOT OBESE can be fit if they exercise regularly and eat a healthy diet. If a person has borderline to high blood pressure, elevated blood sugar, or abnormal cholesterol levels, then one of the helpful health suggestions is to lose some weight. For most people, a little overweight is not a health problem, except that it often leads to gradual weight gain.

54. **I understand there is new research on lactic acid or the "burn" during exercise. What is it?** During intense exercise the development of the "burn" in muscle, referred to as acidosis, has been traditionally explained as an increase in the body's production of lactic acid. This "lactic acid" cause of acidosis is taught in many physiology, biochemistry, and exercise physiology courses throughout the world. The most recent research shows that lactate production is ACTUALLY A CONSEQUENCE of cellular acidosis and NOT the cause of the acidosis. More blatantly, lactate production actually RETARDS ACIDOSIS. Lactate is a temporary 'neutralizer' or 'buffer' to the cells elevated accumulation of protons during high-intensity exercise. Lactate production is therefore considered good and not bad for contracting muscle. Lactate is not a bad molecule, and it has been given a bad rap by being falsely blamed for the cause of the burn.

55. **Should you exercise on hot, humid days?** Keep it light. Sweat will not evaporate well (to cool you off) in the humidity, and you may overheat.

56. **Are those so-called "sports drinks" beneficial during exercise?** The composition of these drinks is basically water, electrolytes (minerals capable of carrying an electrical charge), and glucose. Sweat consists mostly of water and electrolytes. In prolonged endurance events, glucose (carbohydrate) replacement may be beneficial. Also, endurance exercise in heat contributes to heavy losses of water and electrolytes, which need to be replenished.

57. **Is it OK to drink water while exercising?** Yes, your body's circulation system must get food and nutrients to the working cells to carry out their chemical reactions. Sweating during exercise depletes your body's water supply, which may lead to dehydration. Do not depend on your thirst to tell you to drink water. Try to drink at least 8 ounces of cool water for every 30 minutes of vigorous exercise. Use that water bottle!

58. **Should additional salt be taken after exercise?** There's plenty of salt from the food we eat and what we sprinkle on it. Excess salt can irritate the stomach, dry out body tissue, and raise blood pressure.

59. **Will I get more out of my workout by speeding up the exercises?** No. Smooth, controlled movements, properly executed through the full range of motion at an even tempo, are more important than speed.

60. **Do all exercise programs give the same benefits?** No, but everyone needs sustained, full-body, moderately paced aerobic activity.

61. **What training effects happen to your body with aerobic exercise?** (1) Your lungs will be able to process more oxygen. (2) The heart becomes a stronger muscle and pumps out more blood with each beat (stroke volume), which in turn allows you to increase oxygen delivery. (3) The blood vessels offer less resistance to blood flow, reducing the work of the heart. (4) The working muscles become more efficient at utilizing oxygen and nutrients for energy (ATP).

62. **How long does it take to realize the benefits of a regular exercise program?** It takes about four to 12 weeks for benefits to appear and up to six months for you to get "hooked" on exercise.

63. **How many days of exercise can you miss before beginning to lose what you've gained?** No more than three days in a row.

64. **How long can you completely lay off exercise before you lose it all?** From five to eight weeks.

65. **What is muscle soreness and how do you get rid of it?** Muscle soreness or delayed onset muscle soreness (DOMS) is soreness and swelling that becomes evident 8 to 10 hours after exercise and peaks between 24 and 48 hours. One hypothesis of soreness is the connective tissue theory, which suggests there is trauma and strain to the connective tissues within muscle. Still, most recently, a newer theory explains that strenuous or unaccustomed exercise may cause the release of too many calcium ions from the sarcoplasmic reticulum. This ion accumulation may lead to micro damage of muscle proteins. Performing the same exercise (at a lesser intensity) that caused the muscle soreness will help to relieve it.

66. **What is that pain in the side sometimes felt in aerobics?** That sharp pain below the rib cage, often called a "stitch in the side," is usually caused by poor circulation in the muscles of the diaphragm or rib cage. Slow down your pace to allow the proper dilation of the affected blood capillaries, and the pain will go away.

67. **What is cross-training?** Cross-training is a method of integrating different fitness activities with the purpose of gaining or maintaining total-body fitness while reducing injuries. Each person must find the best mix of aerobics, resistance training, swimming, cycling, racquet sports, walking, and recreational sports. It is a very safe, effective, and balanced approach to fitness. Cross-training is extremely effective in a weight-loss program, as total work and hence caloric expenditure can be increased without increasing the risk of overuse injuries.

68. **Explain what steady state and lactate threshold mean?** Steady state in aerobic exercise represents a balance between the oxygen needs of the working muscles and their oxygen supply. As exercise intensity increases, the oxygen supply to the working muscles cannot meet all the oxygen needs of the muscles, and therefore, anaerobic energy systems will contribute more to the total energy production of the working muscles. The eventual transition of predominantly aerobic, oxidative energy production to include more anaerobic energy production during increasing exercise intensity is referred to as the lactate threshold, or onset of blood lactate.

69. **Why do you perspire more after you stop working out?** During exercise, your muscles need most of the blood to get oxygen for the activity. Upon the cessation of exercise, more blood is diverted to the skin to cool the body by means of sweat production. Also, during most modes of exercise, you are moving a lot, which helps sweat evaporate more efficiently during the activity.

70. **I only have time right before bed to exercise and am worried that it will impair my evening sleep patterns.** Interestingly enough, recent research has shown that vigorous exercise ending 30 minutes before bedtime failed to disrupt sleep.

71. **What causes muscle cramps?** New research on exercise-associated muscle cramping suggests the cramp occurs as a result of abnormal nerve activity from the spine, probably related to fatigue. Although not well understood, it is believed that tired muscles going through repeated shortening contractions are more vulnerable to cramping. Avoid overfatiguing workouts and incorporate regular stretching to best ward off muscle cramps.

72. **What does the term "MET" mean?** This term is used to describe energy expenditure of an activity. One MET is equivalent to the energy expenditure of a person at rest. It is expressed in terms of oxygen uptake (i.e., 3.5 ml O_2/kg/min). It is very much like a shorthand method of describing energy requirements. For instance, running 6 miles per hour is about 10 METs, whereas walking 3 miles per hour is about 3.3 METs.

73. **What are the limiting factors of flexibility?** With the muscles relaxed, and reflex mechanisms minimally involved, researchers have found the relative contributions of soft tissue to joint stiffness to be the following: joint capsule, including ligaments (47%), muscles and their fascial sheaths (41%), tendons (10%), and the skin (2%).

Disease and Chronic Health Issues

74. **What is the difference in atherosclerosis and arteriosclerosis?** Arteriosclerosis means hardening and thickening of the arteries. This occurs in most individuals as they age. Atherosclerosis is a type of arteriosclerosis. 'Athero' means paste, which refers to the buildup of plaque in arteries. Plaque, the clogging substance in arteries, is a mixture of cholesterol, fats, calcium, blood-clotting material, and cellular debris.

75. **What is angina pectoris?** This is chest pain caused by too little oxygen reaching the heart. It often occurs during some type of physical exertion or elevated emotional excitement.

76. **Please explain what is happening with a heart attack.** A heart attack is referred to as a myocardial infarction. In this life-threatening situation, one of the arteries that supply blood to the heart muscle gets blocked. If a clot gets stuck in the artery, the lack of oxygen leads to heart tissue death.

77. **Does heart disease affect women?** Heart disease kills more women than any other disease, including cancer. A woman who has a heart attack is twice as likely as a man to die from it within the first few weeks.

78. **Besides heart disease and diabetes, is obesity linked to any other diseases?** Absolutely. It appears that obesity is associated with postmenopausal breast cancer, colorectal cancer, endometrial cancer, esophageal cancer, and kidney cancer. Obesity also increases the risk of stroke, hypertension, reflux disease, gallstones, and osteoarthritis. Remember, if overweight, a 5 to 10 percent decrease in starting weight can significantly improve many of these diseases.

79. **Who is affected most by osteoporosis and how can I prevent it?** Women are most affected, but it does occur in men, too. Presently, 10 million Americans have osteoporosis. Another 34 million citizens have osteopenia—this is a bone density that is below normal. To prevent this from occurring, do at least 30 minutes of "bone loading" exercise daily. Examples of this are walking, jogging, and elliptical cross training. People between 19 and 50 years of age need to get at least 1,000 mg of calcium a day (1,200 for those individuals over 50 years). Try to also get at least 400 international units of Vitamin D daily. Lastly, eat plenty of fruits and vegetables, which are wonderful sources of potassium.

80. **What is the difference between Type 1 and Type 2 diabetes?** With Type 1 diabetes, the body's immune system destroys its own insulin-producing cells. Without insulin, blood sugar can't enter the cells where it is used for energy. In Type 2 diabetes, the cells become resistant to insulin. So, insulin shows up to the cell, but the cell is not working properly to allow insulin to do its job. When a fat or muscle cell becomes resistant to insulin, the sugar won't be driven into the cell and your blood glucose levels rise abnormally. Other consequences of this insulin resistance are high blood pressure, high blood fats, and inflammation to the blood vessels.

81. **How do age and gender affect coronary heart disease risk?** Generally, the older you are, the greater your risk for heart attack. Between the ages of 35 and 44, coronary heart disease is less frequent in women than men, probably due to the production of the female hormone estrogen. Heart attacks appear to even out with older age.

82. **What are the four most important coronary heart disease risk factors?** Cigarette smoking, high blood pressure, abnormal levels of cholesterol, and physical inactivity.

83. **Is there any evidence that exercise can reduce heart disease?** Yes, a scientific study of over 16,000 Harvard alumni suggests that people who expend 2,000 calories per week in brisk exercise reduce death rates from heart disease by 25 to 33 percent, compared to those who do not exercise. Death rates decreased with increased weekly calorie expenditure (up to 3,500 calories) after which there was no advantage to those who did more exercise.

84. **What are free radicals and antioxidants?** Free radicals, also called reactive oxygen species, are unstable molecules produced by chemical reactions utilizing oxygen in the body's cells. A variety of external factors can promote free radical formation including smoking, drinking alcohol, and pollution. Antioxidants (vitamin C, E, and beta carotene—a precursor to vitamin A) protect the cells from free radicals by neutralizing the process of molecular oxidation that leads to their formation.

85. **What are the leading causes of death in the United States?** According to the National Center for Health Statistics, they are heart disease, cancers, strokes, injuries, chronic lung diseases, pneumonia, diabetes, suicide, AIDS, and homicide.

86. **What is cholesterol?** Cholesterol is a fatlike substance used to help build cell membranes, make some hormones, synthesize vitamin D, and form bile secretions that aid in digestion. Because fat can't mix with water, which is the main ingredient of blood, cholesterol's most important job is to help carry fat through your blood vessels. Before cholesterol can enter the bloodstream it is coated with a protein, referred to as a lipoprotein. Lipoproteins are transport vehicles in the circulation plasma that are composed of various lipids such as cholesterol, phospholipids, triglycerides, and proteins known as apoproteins. The major classes of lipoproteins are chylomicrons, very low-density lipoprotein cholesterol, low-density lipoprotein cholesterol, and high-density lipoprotein cholesterol.

87. **Which is the "bad" and "good" cholesterol?** The low-density lipoprotein cholesterol (LDL-C) is the primary transport carrier of cholesterol in the circulation. It is referred to as the "bad" cholesterol because too much cholesterol, from eating foods high in saturated fat, often leads to LDL-C pieces adhering to the inner walls of the blood vessels, narrowing the blood passages. On the other hand, the high-density lipoprotein (or helpful) cholesterol's (HDL-C) primary function is to transport cholesterol from the tissues and blood to the liver for excretion or recycling. It is referred to as the good cholesterol.

88. **What are triglycerides?** Triglycerides (TG) are fats that circulate in the bloodstream that provide energy for the body. It is uncertain whether high TG levels are associated with coronary heart disease. However, high TG levels are associated with diabetes, kidney diseases, and obesity. Steps to lower TG levels include cutting down on saturated fat, losing weight, exercise, and quitting smoking.

89. **I've heard recent reports that eating an egg or more a day isn't that bad for your heart after all.** More controlled research is needed. The American Heart Association and U.S. Department of Agriculture suggest no more than 300 milligrams a day of cholesterol intake. One egg has 215 milligrams of cholesterol, which leaves you only 85 milligrams for any other foods.

90. **Is it unhealthy to skip breakfast?** Some people think skipping breakfast will help you lose weight. That's incorrect. Not eating breakfast actually may lead to weight gain, as your body goes into a starvation mode to retain stored fuel sources. Eating a light breakfast is more associated with successful weight loss and improved nutrition intake.

91. **What dietary substances are needed to prevent osteoporosis besides calcium and vitamin D?** Two other substances of importance are magnesium and potassium, which are both found in fruits, vegetables, milk, and whole grains.

92. **I read a recent study that said high-fiber diets don't cut colon cancer.** Even if the study was well-conducted research, it is still only one study. Decades of research suggest that high-fiber foods are a protection against colon cancer. Remember, stay away from those sugary sweets that are consistently associated with colorectal cancer.

93. **How can I, as a young man, protect against prostate cancer?** Very wise preventative measure. Prostate cancer is the second leading cause of cancer in American men. Research confirms that diets high in fat, calories, and animal products are strongly associated with this deadly disease. Diets high in grains, cereals, soybeans, nuts, and fish, on the other hand, appear to have protective effects.

94. **What are the most common types of arthritis?** There are actually more than 100 different forms. Osteoarthritis is a wearing and tearing form that affects the fingers and weight-bearing joints (knees, back, hips). Rheumatoid arthritis causes irritating joint stiffness and swelling. Fibromyalgia leads to pain at different points of the body as well as insomnia, morning stiffness, and constant fatigue. Gout is caused when uric acid accumulates in the joints, specifically the big toe, knees, and wrists. Lupus can damage the kidneys, heart, skin, lungs, and joints.

95. **What does "prediabetes" mean?** The American Diabetics Association and the U.S. Department of Health and Human Services now use the term prediabetes to describe blood sugar levels that are higher than normal. Left untreated, many individuals will develop diabetes within 10 years. Losing 5 to 10 percent of body weight and doing at least 30 minutes of aerobic exercise daily will return blood sugar to normal.

96. **Is it true that eating big meals is associated with heart attacks?** Yes, a meal high in calories may quadruple the risk of a heart attack in those at risk to coronary heart disease. Researchers theorize that the large meals may temporarily elevate blood pressure, which could break loose some atherosclerotic plaque in an artery. This free-floating plaque in the bloodstream could lead to a blood clot in a coronary artery. Enjoy your meals, but eating in moderation is good for heart health as well as weight control.

97. **I thought all I had to be concerned with for heart disease is checking my cholesterol and triglyceride levels. What's this new protein associated with heart disease?** There's a new clue in understanding heart disease. It involves how the body's immune system works. The development of atherosclerotic plaque (hardening of the arteries) triggers the body to begin an inflammatory process to try to heal the artery wall. With some people, this inflammation process leads to ruptures of the atherosclerotic plaque. This could break off a piece of plaque into the bloodstream and be a precursor to heart attacks (if the clot goes to the heart) or a stroke (if the clot goes to the brain). The best blood predictor for this inflammation process, which is very easy and inexpensive to measure, is called hs-CRP for high sensitivity C-reactive protein.

If you have high levels of hs-CRP you can reduce the risk of heart disease by eating a diet low in saturated fat and cholesterol, lose weight if you are overweight, do regular aerobic exercise, stop smoking if you smoke, and control your blood pressure.

98. **What is heartburn?** Heartburn occurs when gastric fluids, which are very acidic to better digest food in the stomach, enter the esophagus. If this happens frequently, the esophagus may develop scar tissue and be more susceptible to developing cancer.

99. **What are the top 5 diseases in the world?** According to the World Health Organization the top 5 are as follows: heart disease, stroke, COPD, lower respiratory infections, and alzheimers disease (and other dementias).

100. **What is the closest thing to a 'super pill' for a long-lasting, quality life?** Regular aerobic exercise and resistance training.

Thirteen Exercise Myths

1. **If you are thin, you're fit.** Sorry, but being thin is no indication of how efficient your heart, lungs, and muscles are. Body composition testing has demonstrated that many thin people actually have more than the recommended percentage of body fat. You've got to exercise!

2. **Sit-ups get rid of stomach fat.** Wouldn't that be nice! This myth is based on spot reducing. Research clearly shows that exercises for specific body areas firm the muscles, but fat reduction comes from aerobic exercise and a decrease in caloric intake. Fat is reduced proportionally throughout the body.

3. **Sweat loss means weight loss.** You do lose weight temporarily when you sweat, but this is mostly water loss, not fat loss, and is regained as you quench your thirst. Similarly, "sauna sweat suits" induce a temporary water loss and can be dangerous if you get too dehydrated.

4. **Aerobic exercise and jogging cause a woman's breasts to sag.** There is no evidence documenting this claim. However, a good supportive bra is recommended for comfort.

5. **Go for the burn.** Listen to your body. Any type of pain is a warning signal. None of the physiological mechanisms associated with "the burn" have been demonstrated to have beneficial results for you.

6. **Lifting weights gives women bulky muscles.** Women do not produce enough male hormones to allow for large muscle growth. And women don't have as much muscle fiber or mass as a man. Lifting weights will help a woman develop a better figure.

7. **A low resting heart rate means you're fit.** Exercise can lower your resting heart rate. However, this alone does not indicate a person's fitness level.

8. **Electrical stimulation can reduce fat, increase tone, and build strength.** Wow, all those results for just sitting there with electrodes attached to you. How appealing! Though electrical stimulation devices are used by physical therapists for rehabilitation purposes, they are quite ineffective as an effortless exercise alternative.

9. **Muscles turn to fat when you stop exercising.** There are many retired athletes who seem to prove this. However, fat cannot change to muscle (or vice versa). When you stop exercising, your muscles start to waste away and lose their firmness. If you continue to eat a substantial diet (as many of these athletes do), the overconsumption of food will result in larger fat cells.

10. **Cellulite is a unique type of fat.** Cellulite is excess fat bulging between connective tissues under the skin giving that "orange peel" appearance. Rubbing creams don't work. Lessen the appearance of cellulite through aerobic conditioning, body firming exercises, and a proper diet.

11. **There is major physiological deterioration as we age.** Although there is a slight tendency toward reduced performance with age, in general, people continuing their aerobic exercise maintain much of their aerobic efficiency and exercise capacity.

12. **Free weights are better than machines.** Not so fast. There are advantages of both modes of resistance training.

   ○ **Machines:** Machines ensure that you go through a standardized movement pattern, while targeting specific muscles. The newer exercise devices also have built-in safety features for the user. Several machine designs provide an effective variable resistance through the movement range to make exercises more challenging. Lastly, the exerciser doesn't have to balance the weight when training with machines.

   ○ **Free Weights:** For many trainers, having to balance the weight, as is the case with free weights, is an advantage because this involves more stabilizing muscles. Free weights offer much more versatility in their use from the way you hold the weight, as well as your position using the weight. The inexpensive cost of free weights is a major advantage. Finally, free weights allow the user to go through different planes of motion than machines, which have fairly fixed planes of motion (although some companies have now developed this feature with some machines).

13. **Weight gain is inevitable as you get older.** Actually, this is more related to a reduction in physical activity as opposed to age. With inactivity a person loses muscle mass, which reduces the metabolic rate at which they expend calories. At the same time, this inactivity leads to a gradual accumulation of body fat. The best way to prevent this is to include aerobic exercise and resistance training into your daily life.

Fitness Trivia Quiz

Try this trivia quiz to learn some additional fitness facts!

1. True or False: The average foot walks more than a thousand miles a year.
2. Is it training **affect** or training **effect**?
3. True or False: Muscles waste away if they are not used.
4. What percent of your body weight is water? 40%, 60%, 80%.
5. True or False: There are over 600 muscles in the human body.
6. What unique dynamic ability do muscles possess?
7. Which is the single most important source of fuel for your body? Fats, carbohydrates, proteins.
8. What is the junction of two bones called?
9. What is the term for enlargement of muscles?
10. True or False: It only takes 23 seconds for blood to circulate through your entire body.
11. One pound of fat equals how many calories?
12. The average heart beats how many times a minute? 62, 72, 82.
13. Name four of the six classifications of nutrients you need to eat.
14. True or False: Vitamins contain calories.

15. True or False: Vitamins are named as alphabet letters because, when they were discovered, scientists did not know their chemical structure and could not give them "proper" names.

16. Lack of what mineral is associated with "tired blood"?

17. True or False: Your appetite increases in cold weather.

18. Fast-twitch muscle fiber, known for its explosive characteristics, is referred to as _____muscle fiber. (red or white)

19. What is the longest muscle in the body?

20. What is the largest tendon in your body?

21. Your skeleton comprises what percent of your body weight? 15%, 25%, 35%.

22. How many years does it take for the cell structure of your skeleton to completely rejuvenate itself? 5 years, 7 years, 10 years.

23. True or False: Two-thirds of exercise-induced injuries are caused by overuse.

24. Which is the only joint in the body with 360 degrees of rotation?

25. True or False: Sweat is your body's way of cooling off.

26. What is the single most preventable cause of death?

27. True or False: Women live approximately eight years longer than men.

28. True or False: Current estimates in the United States indicate that over 65 percent of all adults have a weight problem.

29. How many glasses of water should you drink each day?

30. True or False: Drinking cool water during exercise is beneficial because it reduces internal body heat.

Answers on page 194.

Health Trivia Quiz

Try this trivia quiz to learn some additional health facts.

1. What is the least favorite day of the workweek?

2. A specific fear associated with a place, thing, or person is called a _____.

3. True or False: In the United States more women smoke than men.

4. True or False: Studies show that 85% of teenagers who occasionally smoke two to three cigarettes (a day) go on to become nicotine dependent.

5. Women can reduce infant mortality by _____% if they stopped smoking. 10%, 20%, 30%.

6. True or False: Drinking alcohol helps a person attain restful sleep.

7. True or False: Alcohol increases one's creativity.

8. If someone is addicted to alcohol, what is the best way to change this addiction?

9. True or False: Pathological gamblers are not intelligent people.

10. True or False: Shopaholics often make unnecessary purchases because the process of buying is often more important that what is bought.

11. True or False: Workaholics are driven perfectionists who would rather work than play.

12. True or False: If you consume a lot of protein you also need to increase your water intake.

13. True or False: Eating foods with fiber helps you manage your weight better.

14. True or False: If you eat too much sugar you will get diabetes.

15. Which is more nutritious: fruit juices or fruit drinks?

16. What constitutes a low-in-sodium food?

17. What is a processed food?

18. What neurotransmitter in the brain is associated with well-being and depression?

19. What cycle determines your body's blood pressure, temperature, hormone output, cell division, and sleep/wake cycles?

20. Is it better to try to go to bed at the same time nightly or wake up at the same time every morning?

21. What is the leading cause of nonfatal injuries in the United States and second-leading cause of death from injury?

22. What age group is prone to getting bored?

23. The causes of 90 percent of high blood pressure are uncertain and referred to as _____.

24. Heart attacks occur most frequently on what day?

25. The heart's built-in heartbeat comes from where?

26. Is heart disease reversible?

27. What type of tumor contains tissues not typically found where they originate?

28. What is it called when unwanted cells in the body spread like seeds to other parts of the body?

29. What is a fake solution or fake cure to a health problem called?

30. What is the single most important thing you can do to prevent the transmission of infectious organisms?

Answers on page 195.

Answers to Fitness Trivia Quiz

1. True
2. Training effect
3. True
4. 60%
5. True
6. They contract
7. Carbohydrates
8. A joint
9. Hypertrophy
10. True
11. 3500 calories
12. 72
13. Carbohydrates, fats, proteins, water, vitamins, minerals
14. False—vitamins do not contain calories
15. True
16. Iron
17. True
18. White
19. Sartorius on the thigh
20. Achilles tendon
21. 15%
22. 10 years
23. True
24. Shoulder
25. True
26. Cigarette smoking
27. True—One of the primary reasons for this is the higher incidence of heart attack deaths among men before the age of 55.
28. True
29. 8 to 10 eight-ounce glasses
30. True

Answers to Health Trivia Quiz

1. Monday
2. Phobia
3. False—Actually, more men (31%) smoke than women (26%). However, women who do smoke are heavier smokers and usually start at younger ages.
4. True
5. 10%
6. False—Alcohol interferes with normal sleep rhythms.
7. Although drinking alcohol may reduce one's inhibitions, it does nothing to improve your productivity or creativity.
8. The majority of alcoholism practitioners agree that giving up drinking entirely is the best solution.
9. False—They often have superior intelligence.
10. True
11. True—Workaholics are obsessed with their career and making a living.
12. True—Protein requires seven times more water than carbohydrate and fat for metabolism.
13. True—Foods high in fiber are low in fat and have a bulking effect in your stomach that aids in the feeling of fullness.
14. False—Diabetes results from two problems: an increased insensitivity of the body's cells in the presence of insulin and an insufficient production of insulin by the pancreas.
15. Fruit juice, which will be low in sodium and high in potassium.
16. 140 mg of sodium or less per serving.
17. Food that has been cooked, mixed with additives, or altered in texture.
18. Serotonin
19. Your circadian rhythm
20. Most experts recommend trying to get up at the same time of morning.
21. Falls
22. Late teens and early 20s. Boredom is the opposite of anxiety. Anxiety arises when one has low levels of skills and high levels of challenge.
23. Primary (or essential) hypertension.
24. Mondays between 8 a.m. and 9 a.m.
25. The pacemaker known as the sinoatrial node.
26. Yes, through stress-relieving techniques, a heart-healthy diet, and exercise.
27. Malignant tumor
28. Metastasize
29. Quackery
30. Wash your hands often.

Online Health, Fitness, and Wellness Resources

Brand new to *Anybody's Guide to Total Fitness* is this all-inclusive list of internet sources on fitness, health, wellness, aging, disease, sleep, supplements, medical, drugs, organizations, and much more.

These resources can be found at: https://www.unm.edu/~lkravitz/Miscellaneous%20/onlinehealth.html

GLOSSARY

cardiovascular disease A group of diseases of the heart and circulatory system.

cartilage The resilient covering of the weight-bearing surface of bones. The cartilage absorbs shock and prevents direct wear on the bones.

cellulite A label given to lumpy deposits of fat commonly appearing on the back of the legs and buttocks of some individuals.

cholesterol A fatlike substance that plays an important role as a building block for cells and hormones. It is obtained from eating foods of animal origin and also produced by the body. Elevated levels are associated with increased risk of heart disease.

circuit training Exercises performed in sequence from station to station. Usually done at a rapid pace.

contraindication A sign or symptom suggesting that a certain activity should be avoided.

cool-down An "aerobic cool-down" refers to a gradual decrease of vigorous aerobic conditioning. A "workout cool-down" refers to the stretching and relaxation phase at the end of a training session.

coronary heart disease The impairment of the coronary arteries of the heart associated with a buildup of cholesterol and fatty substances on the inner artery wall.

creatine phospate Molecule that rapidly helps to resynthesize ATP.

cross-training Selection and participation in more than one physical activity on a consistent basis.

D

dehydration The condition that results from excessive loss of water.

depression Prolonged emotional sadness that persists beyond a reasonable length of time. Often occurs with symptoms such as insomnia, headaches, exhaustion, irritability, loss of interest, impaired concentration, and feelings that life is not worth living.

diabetes mellitus A metabolic disorder in which the body is unable to regulate the level of glucose in the blood.

E

energy The capacity or ability to perform work.

exercise heart rate The heart rate during aerobic exercise that will result in cardiorespiratory benefits. Also referred to as "training heart rate."

F

fat A food substance used as an energy source. It is stored when excess fat, carbohydrate, or protein is ingested.

fiber The indigestible polysaccharides found in the leaves and stems of plants.

flexibility The range of motion of a joint or group of joints.

frequency Refers to the number of workouts needed per week to establish a training effect.

G

glucose Energy source (in the form of sugar) transported in the blood.

glycogen The form in which glucose is stored in the body (primarily in the muscles and liver).

glycolysis The metabolic breakdown of glucose.

gynoid obesity Female pattern of fat deposition in the thighs and gluteal areas that does not carry the same risk as upper body obesity.

H

heart attack Death of a part of the heart muscle caused by a lack of blood flow.

heart rate The number of times the heart beats per minute.

homeostasis The tendency of the body to maintain internal equilibrium and regulation of bodily processes.

hypoglycemia Low blood sugar.

hypertension High blood pressure.

hypertrophy An increase of mass in a muscle from resistive exercise.

hyperglycemia An elevation of blood sugar.

I

insoluble fiber Cellulose, lignin, and hemicellulose that add bulk to the contents of the intestine, accelerating the passage of food remnants through the digestive tract. Insoluble fiber may help to reduce colon cancer of the digestive tract.

intensity The level of physiological stress on the body during exercise.

isokinetic contraction A contraction in which the tension is constant throughout the range of motion.

isometric (static) contraction A contraction in which tension is developed but there is no change in the length of the muscle.

isotonic contraction A dynamic contraction in which the muscles generate force against a constant resistance.

L

lactate Lactate is the product of a side reaction in glycolysis.

lactate threshold The point during exercise when blood lactate begins to increase considerably. It is a good indicator of the highest sustainable work rate.

lordosis An abnormal curvature of the low back.

M

maximum heart rate The highest your heart will beat during aerobic exercise.

maximum oxygen consumption The maximal rate at which the muscles can consume oxygen in one minute.

metabolism The sum total of all physical and chemical processes occurring in the body.

mitochondria Organelles within the cells that utilize oxygen to produce ATP.

mitochondrial respiration metabolic reactions that take place in the mitochondria of cells to produce ATP for energy.

minerals Inorganic substances of the body including sodium, potassium, chloride, calcium, phosphorous, magnesium, sulfur, and at least 14 trace minerals that perform several necessary roles in the body.

monosaccharide Simple sugars such as table sugar and honey.

muscular endurance The ability to exert force (not necessarily maximal) over an extended period of time.

N

nutrients The basic substances of the body obtained by eating foods.

O

obesity An above-average amount of fat in the body. In males 25 percent or greater and in females 32 percent or greater is considered obese.

osteoporosis The thinning and weakening of the bones that is seen predominantly in postmenopausal women.

overload To exercise a muscle or group of muscles with resistance greater than normally encountered.

overtraining A condition from too much exercise characterized by a lack of energy, a decrease in performance, and bodily aches and pains.

overweight Excess weight for one's height regardless of body composition.

P

perceived exertion A subjective rating of the intensity of a particular exercise activity.

polysaccharide The joining of three or more simple sugars to form a starch.

protein A food substance that sustains basic structural properties of the cells and serves as a source for hormones and enzymes in the body.

R

recovery heart rate The gradually declining heart rate following the cessation of aerobic exercise.

repetition A repetition represents each time an exercise movement is completed.

resting heart rate The average heart rate prior to initiating any physical activity.

S

saturated fat Animal fat and fat found in dairy products and eggs that contribute to atherosclerosis.

set Group(s) of repetitions. One set might consist of 10 repetitions.

skinfold A pinch of skin and subcutaneous fat from which total body fat may be estimated.

spot reducing A myth that fat can be specifically reduced from one body area through exercise.

static stretch A stretch that is held.

strength The capacity of a muscle to exert near maximal force against a resistance.

stress It is a nonspecific response of the body to pleasurable and painful demands made on it.

stretch reflex A reflexive contraction of a muscle that is being stretched.

stroke volume The amount of blood pumped by the left ventricle of the heart per beat.

T

testosterone A sex hormone appearing in much higher concentrations in males than females.

triglyceride A compound consisting of three molecules of fatty acid and glycerol. It is the main type of lipid found in the body.

U

unsaturated fat The molecules of a fat that have one or more double bonds and are thus capable of absorbing more hydrogen. These fats are usually of vegetable origin.

V

valsalva maneuver Condition occurring when a person lifts heavy weights while holding the breath. The glottis closes and intrathoracic pressure increases, hindering blood flow to the heart.

vitamins Nutrients required in microamounts that are essential to numerous bodily functions.

W

warm-up The first portion of a workout, designed to prepare the body for the vigorous exercise to follow.

NEW
PHYSICAL ACTIVITY GUIDELINES
RELEASED

Fitness pros throughout the world extol the benefits of regular exercise to clients, educating them on why starting and staying with an exercise program is the right journey for life. In November 2018, the U.S. Department of Health and Human Services released the first update of their original 2008 physical activity report with the Physical Activity Guidelines Advisory Committee Scientific Report. Over a period of twenty months, a seventeen-member expert committee and consultants conducted an extensive scientific review of research, focusing particularly on articles published in the ten years since the publication of the 2008 report. Overarching messages and details are presented in this section.

Current State of Physical Activity: We Are Still an Inactive Society

The minimal physical activity recommendations for physical activity encourage adults to get at least 150 (and up to 300) minutes of moderate-to-vigorous aerobic activity each week, with muscle strengthening activities on two days during the week to stay healthy. Youth, ages six through seventeen should do sixty minutes of moderate-to-vigorous physical activity each day. However, according to a press release from the U.S. Department of Health and Human Services, only 19 percent of women, 26 percent of men, and 20 percent of adolescents meet these recommendations. According to the new report, the consequences of physical inactivity currently result in approximately $117 billion in annual healthcare costs, with 10 percent of all premature mortality due to a physically inactive lifestyle. The evidence suggests that more time spent in sedentary behavior is associated with the incidence of type 2 diabetes, all-cause mortality, CVD mortality, and the incidence of colon, endometrial, and lung cancer.

Highlighted Findings from the New Physical Activity Guidelines Report

There are several key findings from the new report that warrant the attention of fitness pros, who may wish to share with clients.

Exercise is a boost in brain health: With every single exercise bout a person does, acute improvements in executive function occur. Executive function involves the processes of the brain that help a person manage their daily activities and plan for upcoming future events. Other aspects of executive function include handling behaviors, starting new tasks, and controlling emotions. Physical activity has been shown to be a boost for also improving cognition (the process of acquiring knowledge), memory, attention, and academic performance.

Exercise helps people manage depression: Consistent physical activity reduces depressive symptoms (or the severity of symptoms), and has been shown to be effective in reducing the risk of clinical depression. In addition, women doing moderate-to-vigorous physical activity are less likely to develop postpartum depression than their less active counterparts. As well, pregnant women with anxiety or depression can promote a healthy pregnancy, for both mother and fetus, even if they do low doses of physical activity.

Exercise helps improve the quality of sleep: There is impressive evidence that regular moderate-to-vigorous physical activity improves a person's quality of sleep. The research indicates that exercise lessens the length of time it takes to go to sleep as well as cuts the time a person is awake after going to sleep. Consistent exercise has also been shown to increase deep sleep while lowering daytime sleepiness. Most interestingly, the research also highlights that, in general, the time frame before bedtime at which the physical activity is completed does not matter. The health benefits of exercise are equivalent for bouts of physical activity performed more than eight hours before bedtime, three to eight hours before, and less than three hours before bedtime.

Every bout of exercise, no matter how long, improves quality of life: A most encouraging finding in the new report is there are immediate health benefits from a single bout of activity, such as reduced anxiety, improved blood pressure, better quality of sleep, and improved insulin sensitivity. The 2008 guidelines stated that a minimum of ten-minute bouts of physical activity was necessary to improve markers of health. This previous requirement has been removed, because activity, of any length of time, generates a positive impact on a person's quality of life.

Exercise is important for weight management: A stinging point for many fitness pros has been how various media and professional outlets have minimized the important role of exercise in a weight management program. The report summarizes that there is a strong correlation between greater amounts of physical activity and decreased weight gain in adults. The evidence indicates a positive influence on exercise in weight gain prevention occurs when doses are ≥150 minutes per week at a moderate-to-vigorous level of intensity.

Walking step counts still make a difference. The new document states that step counts are quite easy to understand by most people and support the public health message to move more in a person's daily life. Walking steps can be at light-, moderate-, and vigorous-intensity levels, providing a broad range of exertion choice to promote walking for levels of fitness and at all ages. However, because of this range of intensities, and the potential for varied outcomes, the new physical activity guides does not support a specific number, such as 10,000 steps per day.

Higher intensity exercise is better for cardiovascular health. The new Physical Activity Guidelines clarifies that exercising at higher intensity brings greater gains in cardiorespiratory fitness than steady-state exercise, but also has a greater risk of injury, especially if one is unaccustomed to vigorous physical activity. The report adds the caveat that the long-term sustainability of HIIT training regimens is currently not fully known. Alas, even with these impressive benefits of higher intensity exercise, the 2018 report recommends frequency and duration of aerobic activity should be increased before intensity, reaching these guidelines first.

Spread out the exercise through the entire week. Persons who accumulate all or almost all of their weekly moderate-to-vigorous physical activity on one or two days per week do NOT experience reductions in all-cause and cardiovascular mortality equivalent to those persons who accumulate an equivalent total volume on three or more days per week. Aim to spread out the exercise frequency on three or more days of the week.

Children benefit from regular exercise too: For the first time, the new report indicates there is research now showing that even three- to five-year-olds also benefit from consistent physical activity. Importantly, the evidence conveys that higher amounts of physical activity are correlated with a reduced risk of excessive increases in body weight and adiposity, improved cardiovascular risk factor status, fewer symptoms of depression, and favorable indicators of bone health in children ages three to seventeen years. The type of physical activity associated with bone health is hopping, skipping, jumping, tumbling, and other forms of high-impact, dynamic, short duration exercise. Children should aim to accrue up to sixty minutes per day of moderate-to-vigorous physical activity.

Exercise is a must as we grow older: With persons ≥65 years of age, considerable evidence has emerged showing the benefits of various modes or combinations of physical activity (e.g., progressive resistance training, multicomponent exercise, dual-task training, tai chi, yoga, dance) for specific physical function outcomes (e.g., activities of daily living, gait speed, strength, and balance). The term "multicomponent" describes physical activity interventions that include more than one type of physical activity, with common types being aerobic, muscle-strengthening, and balance training. Dual-task interventions combine cognitive intervention (such as counting backward) with a physical activity intervention. A target range of 150 to 300 minutes per week of moderate relative intensity activities is an appropriate target for older adults. Also, older adults expend more energy than younger adults for the same task, such as walking, so progress at a relative intensity based on their fitness level.

Summary Message of New Physical Activity Guidelines

The 2018 Physical Activity Guidelines report highlights that regular moderate-to-vigorous physical activity may reduce the risk of type 2 diabetes, gestational diabetes, hypertension, heart disease, stroke, excessive weight gain, dementia, anxiety, depression, postpartum depression, and falls with injuries among the elderly. Additionally, breast, colon, endometrial, esophageal, kidney, stomach, and lung cancer are all less common among individuals who are or become more physically active. If quality of life and improved physical function is a person's goal, regular exercise is the only way to go. Keep moving . . . briskly!

Source: 2018 Physical Activity Guidelines Advisory Committee. 2018 Physical Activity Guidelines Advisory Committee Scientific Report. Washington, DC: U.S. Department of Health and Human Services, 2018. HHS Press Release: HHS Releases Physical Activity Guidelines for Americans, 2nd ed. Retrieved from: https://www.hhs.gov/about/news/2018/11/12/hhs-releases-physical-activity-guidelines-americans-2nd-edition.html

Proper Steps to Follow for Accurate Blood Pressure Measurement

In the new blood pressure guidelines, the following steps are suggested for accurate blood pressure measurement.

KEY STEPS FOR BP MEASUREMENT	INSTRUCTIONS TO FOLLOW
A. Student Preparation	1. After having student empty his/her bladder, have student sit restfully (without speaking) for >5 min with both feet on floor and back supported. 2. Make sure student has avoided exercise, caffeine, and smoking for at least 30 minutes before measurement. 3. Remove clothing covering the location of the blood pressure cuff placement.
B. Proper BP measurement technique	1. Use a valid, appropriately sized and correctly calibrated BP measurement device. 2. Comfortably support student's arm at a level to the midpoint of the sternum.
C. Measurement protocol	1. For the initial measurement, assess BP in both arms and use the higher reading if they differ. 2. Repeat measurement after 1–2 minutes. 3. If using an auscultatory technique, record systolic blood pressure as the first Korotkoff sound. Record diastolic blood pressure as the disappearance of all Korotkoff sounds. 4. If the student is on blood pressure measurements, make a note when the medication was last taken. 5. Use an average of ≥2 readings obtained on ≥2 occasions to estimate a person's blood pressure measurements. 6. Provide student with his/her blood pressure readings both verbally and in writing. 7. For students using blood pressure devices, make sure the tool has been validated by some internationally accepted protocol with published data supporting its accuracy.

THE MUSCLE SYSTEM

Muscle and Exercise Chart

This chart lists the major muscle groups and specific exercises presented in this book, as well as the opposing groups.

Deltoids
Push-up Variations
Dips
Side Lateral Raises
Chest Press
Shoulder Press

Pectorals
Chest Press
Wide-arm Push-ups
Flys

Trapezius
Power Rows

Latissimus Dorsi
Standing Rows

Biceps
Bicep Curls

Triceps
Tricep Extensions
Dips
Pike Push-ups
Chest Press

Abdominals
Crunch Variations

Obliques
Twisting Crunches
All-Around Crunches
Rope Pull Crunches

Erector Spinae
Back Extensions
Horizontal Side Bridge
Rolling Side Bridge
Bird-Dog Exercise

Gluteus Maximus
Squats
Lunges
Prone Leg Lifts
Power Exercises
Back Thigh Lifts

Rectus Femoris, Vastus Lateralis, Vastus Medialis
Squats
Lunge Variations

Biceps Femoris, Semitendinosus, Semimembranosus
Squats
Lunge Variations

Gracilis, Adductor Longus
Inner Thigh Variations
Hip Adduction
Wide Squats

Tensor Fasciae Latee, Gluteus Medius
Hip Abduction

Gastrocnemius and Soleus
Heel Raises

Examples of Opposing Muscle Groups

Biceps vs. Triceps
Deltoids vs. Latissimus Dorsi
Pectorals vs. Rhomboids and Trapezius
Quadriceps vs. Hamstrings
Abdominals vs. Spinal Extensors
Thigh Abductors vs. Thigh Adductors

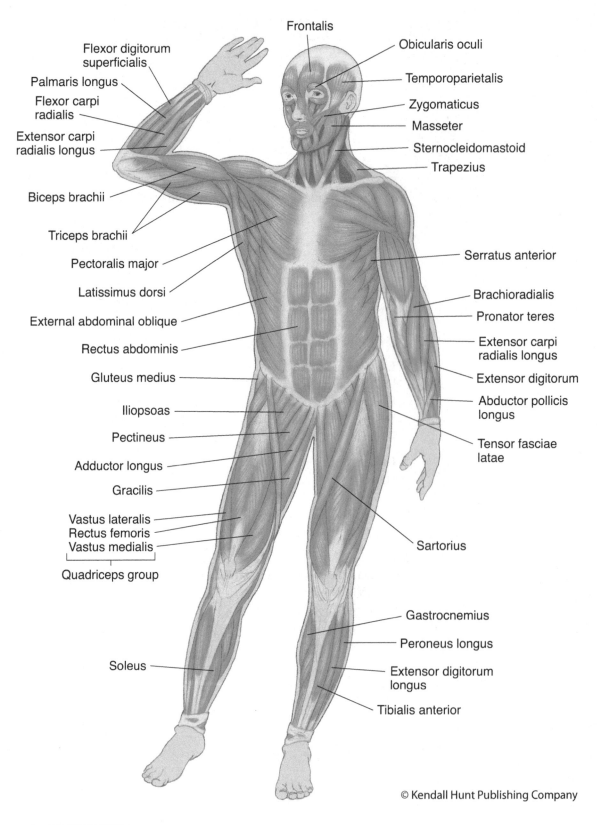

Frontalis

Obicularis oculi

Temporoparietalis

Zygomaticus

Masseter

Sternocleidomastoid

Trapezius

Serratus anterior

Brachioradialis

Pronator teres

Extensor carpi radialis longus

Extensor digitorum

Abductor pollicis longus

Tensor fasciae latae

Sartorius

Gastrocnemius

Peroneus longus

Extensor digitorum longus

Tibialis anterior

Flexor digitorum superficialis

Palmaris longus

Flexor carpi radialis

Extensor carpi radialis longus

Biceps brachii

Triceps brachii

Pectoralis major

Latissimus dorsi

External abdominal oblique

Rectus abdominis

Gluteus medius

Iliopsoas

Pectineus

Adductor longus

Gracilis

Vastus lateralis
Rectus femoris
Vastus medialis

Quadriceps group

Soleus

© Kendall Hunt Publishing Company

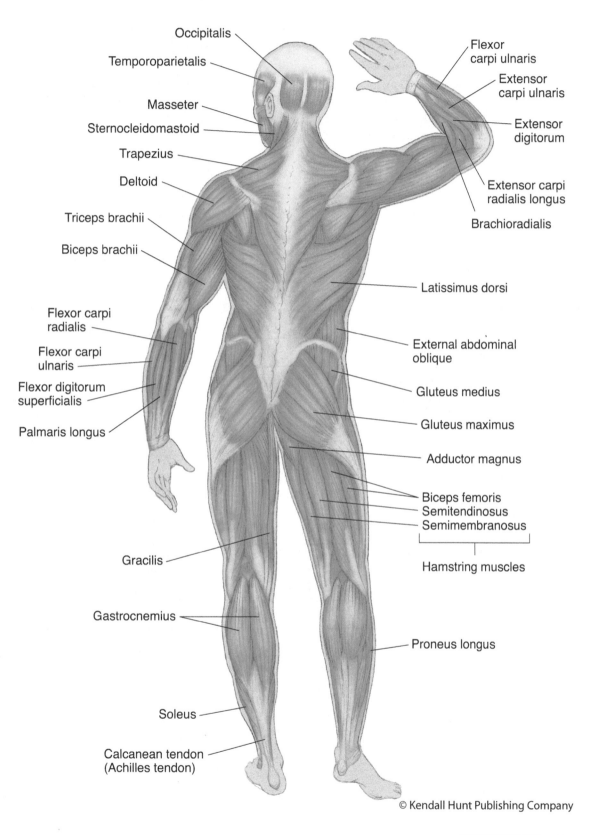

Occipitalis

Temporoparietalis

Masseter

Sternocleidomastoid

Trapezius

Deltoid

Triceps brachii

Biceps brachii

Flexor carpi
radialis

Flexor carpi
ulnaris

Flexor digitorum
superficialis

Palmaris longus

Gracilis

Gastrocnemius

Soleus

Calcanean tendon
(Achilles tendon)

Flexor
carpi ulnaris

Extensor
carpi ulnaris

Extensor
digitorum

Extensor carpi
radialis longus

Brachioradialis

Latissimus dorsi

External abdominal
oblique

Gluteus medius

Gluteus maximus

Adductor magnus

Biceps femoris
Semitendinosus
Semimembranosus

Hamstring muscles

Proneus longus

© Kendall Hunt Publishing Company

ACSM Publishes Updated Position Stand on the Quantity and Quality of Exercise

The new American College of Sports Medicine quantity and quality Position Stand paper is an update that cites over 400 publications from scientific reviews, epidemiological studies, clinical studies, meta-analyses, consensus statements, and evidence-based guidelines. The purpose of this ACSM Position Stand paper is to present evidence-based direction to health and fitness enthusiasts and professionals for the development of individualized exercise training programs for apparently healthy adults of all ages.

CARDIORESPIRATORY FITNESS RECOMMENDATIONS	
Variable	Evidence-Based Recommendation
Frequency	≥5 day/wk moderate* intensity or ≥3 days/wk vigorous** or a combination of both on ≥3–5 days/wk
Intensity	Moderate and/or vigorous is recommended for apparently healthy adults
Time	30–60 minutes at a moderate intensity or 20–60 minutes at a vigorous intensity or a combination of both
Type	Purposeful, continuous, rhythmic exercise involving the major muscle groups of the body
Pattern	Exercise may be performed in one continuous session per day or in multiple sessions of ≥10 min to accumulate the desired duration
Progression	Progress intensity, duration, and frequency gradually until desired goal is attained

*Moderate intensity includes exercise that is fairly light to somewhat hard, or a rating of perceived exertion (RPE) of 12–13.

**Vigorous exercise includes exercise that is somewhat hard to very hard, or a RPE of 14–17.

***The exercise program should be modified according to an individual's habitual physical activity, physical function, health status, exercise responses, and stated goals.

NEUROMOTOR EXERCISE RECOMMENDATIONS	
Variable	Evidence-Based Recommendation
Frequency	≥2–3 days/week
Intensity	Not determined at this time
Time	≥20–30 min/day may be needed
Type	Exercises that improve balance, agility, coordination and gait, particularly for older adults to improve/maintain physical function and to prevent falls
Volume	The optimal volume of repetitions and sets is currently unknown

RESISTANCE EXERCISE RECOMMENDATIONS

Variable	Evidence-Based Recommendation
Frequency	Major muscle groups should be trained 2–3 days/week with a 48-hour rest between sessions for muscle groups
Intensity (Strength)	40–50% of 1RM or very light to light load for beginning older persons and for beginning sedentary persons 60–70% of 1RM or moderate to hard load for novice to intermediate adult exercisers ≥80% of 1RM or hard to very hard load for experienced weight lifters
Intensity (Endurance)	<50% of 1RM or light to moderate load
Intensity (Power)	20–50% of 1RM or very (very) light to light load in older adults
Repetitions	10–15 repetitions to improve strength in beginning, middle aged, and older persons 8–12 repetitions to improve strength and power in most adults 15–20 repetitions to improve muscular endurance in most adults
Sets	Single set training for novice and older adults 2–4 sets are recommended for strength and power of most adults ≤2 sets for muscular endurance
Rest	2–3 minutes of rest between multiple set training

FLEXIBILITY EXERCISE RECOMMENDATIONS

Variable	Evidence-Based Recommendation
Frequency	≥2–3 days/week of stretching the major muscles groups; greater gains will be attained if done daily
Intensity	Stretch to the point of slight discomfort or feeling of tightness in muscle
Time	30–60 seconds of static stretching holds for older persons 10–30 seconds of static stretching holds for most adults
PNF Stretches	3–6 seconds of a muscle contraction at 20–75% of maximum intensity followed by 10–30 seconds of an assisted stretch
Pattern	2–4 repetitions of each stretch is advocated
Volume	Provide a total of 60 seconds of stretching time per target muscle group for any stretching method utilized

Adapted from: Garber, C.E., Blissmer, B., Deschenes, M.R., Franklin, B.A., et al. (2011). Quantity and quality of exercise for developing and maintaining cardiorespiratory, musculoskeletal, and neuromotor fitness in apparently healthy adults: Guidance for prescribing exercise. *Medicine & Science in Sports & Exercise*, 43 (7), 1334–1349.

Do You Know Your Important Risk Factor 'Numbers'?

All exercise enthusiasts need to be aware of their clinical 'numbers' for well being. This section serves as an informative resource for identifying the many 'numbers' involved in clinical and health parameters that are not covered in other sections of the text.

Cholesterol, Triglycerides, and C-Reactive Protein

Cholesterol, which is vital to the body, is used to assemble cell membranes, produce sex hormones, and form bile acids, which are required for the digestion of fats. When certain blood cholesterol levels are elevated, some of the excess is deposited in the arterial walls, thus the risk for heart disease is increased (See Table 1 for levels). Elevated blood triglycerides (fats) are also an inde-pendent risk factor for coronary heart disease, meaning that some particles of fat can collect on arterial walls and lead to atherosclerotic plaque.

Current research additionally suggests that inflammation plays a role in the formation of atherosclerosis. C-reactive protein (CRP), a substance the body produces in response to inflammation and infection serves as a very good marker for heart disease risk. The blood vessel test for inflammation is called the high-sensitivity CRP or hs-CRP.

TABLE 1. CHOLESTEROL, TRIGLYCERIDE AND HS-CRP LEVELS	
Total Cholesterol	
Desirable	Less than <200 mg/dL
Borderline high	200–239 mg/dL
High	>240 mg/dL
LDL ("Bad") Cholesterol	
Optimal	<100 mg/dL
Near optimal	100–129 mg/dL
Borderline high	130–159 mg/dL
High	160–189 mg/dL
Very high	>190 mg/dL
HDL ("Good") Cholesterol	
Low	<40 mg/dL
High	≥60 mg/dL
Triglycerides (Fats in the Blood)	
Normal	<150 mg/dL
Borderline-high	150–199 mg/dL
High	200–499 mg/dL
Very high	≥500 mg/dL
C-Reactive Protein (hs-CRP)	
Low CVD risk	<1.0 mg/dL
Average CVD risk	1.0–3.0 mg/dL
High CVD risk	>3.0 mg/dL
Data from American Medical Association, 2001 and American Heart Association, 2010	

Body Mass Index

Body mass index (BMI) is an alternative screening tool to percent fat measurement that can be used to categorize individuals as underweight, overweight, or obese, and to observe changes in body weight that may be associated with health problems (See Table 2).

Example Calculations:

With the metric system, the formula for BMI is weight in kilograms divided by height in meters squared.

Weight = 120 kg, Height = 193 cm (1.93 m)

Calculation: $120 \div (1.93)^2 = 32.2$

The BMI formula for weight in lbs and height in inches is weight (lb) divided by height $(in)^2 \times 703$

Weight =150 lbs, Height = 65 inches

$(150 \div \{65\}^2) \times 703 = 24.96$

TABLE 2. INTERNATIONAL CLASSIFICATION OF BMI RANGES FOR ADULTS	
BMI Value	Classification
<16.00	Severe thinness
16–16.99	Moderate thinness
17–18.49	Mild thinness
18.5–24.99	Normal Range
25.0–29.9	Overweight (Pre-Obese)
	Obesity
30.0–34.9	Class I
35.0–39.9	Class II
≥40	Class III
Adapted from World Health Organization, 2010	

© Jill Pankey

Other Laboratory Tests

Exercise enthusiasts often receive their medical reports from their primary physician. Table 3 describes selected blood variables usually tested.

TABLE 3. OTHER SELECTED BLOOD VARIABLES OF CLINICAL IMPORTANCE		
Selected Blood Variable	**Normal Value**	**Description of Variable**
Hematocrit	40-52% (men) 36-48% (women)	The percent volume of red blood cells in whole blood.
Hemoglobin	13.5–17.5 g/dL (men) 11.5–15.5 g/dL (women)	Protein molecule within red blood cells that carries oxygen and gives blood its red color
Potassium	3.5–5.5 meq/dL	Electrolyte and a mineral. It helps keep the water (the amount of fluid inside and outside the body's cells) and electrolyte balance of the body. Potassium is also important in how nerves and muscles work.
Blood Urea Nitrogen	4–24 mg/dL	Measure of the amount of nitrogen in the blood in the form of urea, and a measurement of renal function.
Creatinine	0.3–1.4 mg/dL	Reliable indicator of kidney function. Also a waste product of muscles from exercise.
Iron	40–190m/dL (men) 35–180μm/dL (women)	Mineral needed for production of hemoglobin, the main protein in red blood cells that carries oxygen.
Calcium	8.5–10.5mg/dL	Builds and repairs bones and teeth, helps nerves work, assists in muscle contraction, helps blood clot, and facilitates heart function.
Data from Heyward, V.H. (2006). Advanced Fitness Assessment and Exercise Prescription, (5th edition), *Human Kinetics*		

Be Proactive with Your 'Numbers'

The exercise enthusiast now has these clinical values at his/her fingertips to promote actions steps for well-being improvement. Take a proactive approach as you strive for optimal health.

Caloric Expenditure Chart

You can easily estimate the number of calories you expend during aerobic exercise activities. To determine the number of calories expended, multiply the total number of minutes of activity times the calories per minute. For example, a 110-pound woman doing 20 minutes of continuous aerobic dance would expend approximately 172 Calories ($8.6 \times 20 = 172$).

CALORIC EXPENDITURE CHART FOR SELECTED AEROBIC ACTIVITIES	
(Aerobic dance, cycling, brisk walking, rope skipping, rowing on a machine, running, skating, and swimming.)	
Your weight in pounds	Calories Expended per minute
95–104	8
105–114	8.6
115–124	9.0
125–134	9.7
135–144	10.3
145–154	11
155–164	11.5
165–174	12
175–184	12.7
185–194	13.3
195–204	13.7
205–214	14.2
215–224	14.7
225–234	15.2
235–244	15.7
245–254	16.2
255–264	16.7
265–274	17.2
275–284	17.7
Values may vary from individual to individual.	

Total number of minutes of aerobic exercise _____

Calories expended per minute according to your weight _____

Your estimated caloric expenditure _____

Estimating Your Caloric Needs

You can estimate the breakdown of your daily intake of carbohydrates, proteins, and fats. Follow the steps below.

To estimate your daily caloric needs, first multiply your weight by 16 (if you are moderately active) or 12 (if you are relatively sedentary).

1 gram of carbohydrate	=	4 calories
1 gram of protein	=	4 calories
1 gram of fat	=	9 calories

Daily Nutritional Needs

Carbohydrates	=	58% of your daily calories
Proteins	=	12% of your daily calories
Fats	=	30% of your daily calories

Weight (lbs): _____ × 16 or 12 = _____ (Estimate of daily caloric needs)

Carbohydrates

Carbohydrate Calories per Day

Estimate of calories per day: _____ × 0.58 (58%) = _____ calories/day

Carbohydrate Grams per Day

Divide the above product by 4: _____ ÷ 4 = _____ grams/day

Proteins

Protein Calories per Day

Estimate of calories per day: _____ × 0.12 (12%) = _____ calories/day

Protein Grams per Day

Divide the above product by 4: _____ ÷ 4 = _____ grams/day

Fats

Fat Calories per Day

Estimate of calories per day: _____ × 0.30 (30%) = _____ calories/day

Fat Grams per Day

Divide the above product by 9: _____ ÷ 9 = _____ grams/day

SUGGESTED READINGS

Section 1

Booth, F. W., Roberts, C. K., & Laye, M. L. (2012). Lack of exercise is a major cause of chronic diseases. *Comprehensive Physiology*, 2:1143–1211.

Cardiovascular Diseases (CVDs). (2017). World Health Organization. Retrieved from https://www.who.int/news-room/fact-sheets/detail/cardiovascular-diseases-(cvds)

MacAuley, D., Bauman, A., & Frémont, P. (2016). Exercise: Not a miracle cure, just good medicine. *British Journal of Sports Medicine*, 50(18), 1107–1108.

Morton, G. A, & Kravitz, L. (2016). 35 Ailments, One Prescription, *IDEA Fitness Journal*, 13(2), 30–40.

Whelton, P. K., Carey, R. M., Anonow, W. S., et al. (2018). Guideline for the Prevention, Detection, Evaluation, and Management of High Blood Pressure in Adults: A Report of the American College of Cardiology/American Heart Association Task Force on Clinical Practice Guidelines. *Journal of the American College of Cardiology*, 71:e127–e248.

Section 2

Chambers, A., & Kravitz, L. (2009). Nutrient timing: The new frontier in fitness performance. *AKWA: The Official Publication of the Aquatic Exercise Association,* 22(4), 4–6.

Graham, D. (2013). Prevention and care of athletic injuries. *Food 'n' Sport Press.*

Kravitz, L. (2008). Water: The science of nature's most important nutrient. *IDEA Fitness Journal,* 5(10), 42–49.

Section 4

Dempsey, P. C., Larsen, R. N., Sethi, P., et al. (2016). Benefits for type 2 diabetes of interrupting prolonged sitting with brief bouts of light walking or simple resistance activities. *Diabetes Care*, 39(6), 964–972.

Gibala, M. J., Heisz, J. J., and Nelson, A. J. (2018). Interval training for cardiometabolic and brain health. *ACSM's Health and Fitness Journal*, 22(6), 30–34.

Hamilton, M. T., Healy, G. N., Dunstan, D. W., et al. (2008). Too little exercise and too much sitting: Inactivity physiology and the need for new recommendations on sedentary behavior. *Current Cardiovascular Risk Reports*, 2, 292–298.

Katzmarzyk, P. T., Church, T. S., Craig, C. L., et al. (2009). Sitting time and mortality from all causes, cardiovascular disease, and cancer. *Medicine & Science in Sports & Exercise*, 41(5), 998–1005.

Morris, J. N., & Crawford, M. D. (1958). Coronary heart disease and physical activity of work. *British Medical Journal*, 2(5111), 1485–1496.

Owen, N., Bauman, A., & Brown, W. (2009). Too much sitting: A novel and important predictor of chronic disease risk? *British Journal of Sports Medicine*, 43(2), 81–83.

Piras, A., Persiani, M., Damiani, N., et al. (2015). Peripheral heart action (PHA) training as a valid substitute to high intensity interval training to improve resting cardiovascular changes and autonomic adaptation. *European Journal of Applied Physiology*, 115, 763–773.

Section 5

Adult obesity facts. (2018). *Centers for Disease Control and Prevention*. Retrieved from https://www.cdc.gov/obesity/data/adult.html

Albuquerque, D., Stice, D., Rodriguez-Lopez. R., et al. (2015). Current review of genetics of human obesity: From molecular mechanisms to an evolutionary perspective. *Molecular Genetics and Genomics*, 290(4), 1191–1221.

Bjorntorp, P. (2001). Do stress reactions cause abdominal obesity and comorbidities? *Obesity Reviews*, 2(2), 73–86.

Dornas, W. C., de Lima, W. G., Pedrosa, M. L., et al. (2015). Health implications of high-fructose intake and current research. *Advanced Nutrition*, 6, 729–737.

Fabricatore, A. N., & Wadden, T. A. (2003). Treatment of obesity. An Overview. *Clinical Diabetes*, 21(2), 67–72.

Fothergill, E., Guo, J., Howard, L., et al. (2016). Persistent metabolic adaptation 6 years after "The Biggest Loser" competition. *Obesity*, 24(8), 1612–1619.

Hall, K. D., Heymsfield, S. B., Kemnitz, J. W., et al. (2012). Energy balance and its components: Implications for body weight regulation. *The American Journal of Clinical Nutrition*, 95(4), 989–994.

Hill, J. O. (2009). Can a small-changes approach help address the obesity epidemic? A report of the Joint Task Force on the American Society for Nutrition, Institute of Food Technologists, and International Food Information Council, *The American Journal of Clinical Nutrition*, 89(2), 477–484.

Imamura, F., O'Connor, L., Ye, Z. et al. (2015). Consumption of sugar sweetened beverages, artificially sweetened beverages, and fruit juice and incidence of type 2 diabetes: Systematic review, meta-analysis, and estimation of population attributable fraction. *British Medical Journal*, 2015. doi:10.1136/bmj.h576

McGuire, M. T., Wing, R. R., Klem, M. L., et al. (1999). What predicts weight regain in a group of successful weight losers? *Journal of Consulting and Clinical Psychology*, 67(2), 177–185.

Montes, M. V., & Kravitz, L. (2011). Unraveling the stress-eating-obesity knot. *IDEA Fitness Journal*, 8(2), 45–50.

NWCR. (2017). NWCR Facts. National Weight Control Registry. Retrieved from http://www.nwcr.ws/

Overweight and Obesity. (2017). World Health Organization. Retrieved from http://www.who.int/mediacentre/factsheets/fs311/en/

Pasquali, R. (2012). The hypothalamic-pituitary-adrenal axis and sex hormones in chronic stress and obesity: Pathophysiological and clinical aspects. *Annals of the New York Academy of Sciences,* 1264(1), 20–35.

Pietilainen, K. H., Saarni, S. E., Kaprio, J., et al. (2012). Does dieting make you fat? A twin study. *International Journal of Obesity*, 36, 456–464.

Schmidt, L. A. (2014). New unsweetened truths about sugar. *JAMA Internal Medicine*, 174(4), 525–526.

Sifferlin, A. (2017). This diet may help you lose weight. *TIME*, June 5, 50–55.

Te Morenga, L. A., Howatson, A. J., Jones, R. M., et al. (2014). Dietary sugars and cardiometabolic risk: Systematic review and meta-analyses of randomized controlled trials of the effects on blood pressure and lipids. *American Journal of Clinical Nutrition*, 100:65–79.

Wang, Z., Heshka, S., Gallagher, D., et al. (2000). Resting energy expenditure-fat-free mass relationship: New insights provided by body composition modeling. *American Journal of Physiology-Endocrinology and Metabolism*, 279(3), E539–E545.

Wing, R. R., & Phelan, S. (2005). Long-term weight loss maintenance. *American Journal of Clinical Nutrition*, 82 (suppl), 222S–225S.

Yang, Q., Zhang, Z., Gregg, E. W., et al. (2014). Added sugar intake and cardiovascular diseases mortality among U.S. Adults. *JAMA Internal Medicine*, 174(4):516–524.

Section 6

Armbruster, C.K., Evans, E.M., Laughlin, C.M. (2018) *Fitness and Wellness: A Way of Life.* Human Kinetics.

Fahey, T., Insel, P.M., Roth, W.T., and Insel, C.A.E. (2017). *Fit and Well: Core Concepts and Labs in Physical Fitness and Wellness* 12th Edition. McGraw-Hill College.

Section 7

Attie, A. D., & Scherer, P. E. (2009). Adipocyte metabolism and obesity. *Journal of Lipid Research*, 50, S395–S399.

Bacon, L., Stern, J. S., Van Loan, M. D., et al. (2005). Size acceptance and intuitive eating improve health for obese, female chronic dieters. *Journal of the American Dietetic Association,* 105(6): 929–936.

Bangalore, S., Fayyad, R., Laskey, R., et al. (2017). Body-weight fluctuations and outcomes in coronary disease. *The New England Journal of Medicine*, 376, 1332–1340.

Bao, Y., Han, J., & Hu, F. B. (2013). Association of nut consumption with total and cause-specific mortality. *The New England Journal of Medicine*, 369, 2001–2011.

Berkeley Wellness. (2017). 13 heart-healthy steps for women (and men, too). University of California, *Berkeley Wellness Letter*, May, 5.

Berkeley Wellness. (2017). What's in your nutrition bar? University of California, *Berkeley Wellness Letter*, May, 4.

Bjorntorp, P. (2001). Do stress reactions cause abdominal obesity and comorbidities? *Obesity Reviews,* 2(2), 73–86.

Calton, J. B. (2010). Prevalence of micronutrient deficiency in popular diet plans. *Journal of the International Society of Sports Nutrition.* https://doi.org/10.1186/1550-2783-7-24

Celiac Disease Foundation. (2017). What is celiac disease? Retrieved from https://celiac.org/celiac-disease/understanding-celiac-disease-2/what-is-celiac-disease/

Despres, J-P. (2015). Obesity and cardiovascular disease: Weight loss is not the only target. *Canadian Journal of Cardiology,* 31(2), 216–222.

Fabricatore, A. N., & Wadden, T. A. (2003). Treatment of obesity. *Clinical Diabetes*, 21, 2, 67–72.

Fothergill, E., Guo, J, Howard, L., et al. (2016). Persistent Metabolic Adaptation 6 Years After "The Biggest Loser" Competition. *Obesity.* https://doi.org/10.1002/oby.21538

Hall, K. D., Heymsfield, S. B., Kemnitz, J. W., et al. (2012). Energy balance and its components: Implications for body weight. *American Journal of Clinical Nutrition*, 95, 989–994.

Healthy Lifestyle. (2017). Caffeine: How much is too much? Mayo Clinic. Retrieved from http://www.mayoclinic.org/healthy-lifestyle/nutrition-and-healthy-eating/in-depth/caffeine/art-20045678

Hill, J. O. (2009). Can a small-changes approach help address the obesity epidemic? A report of the Joint Task Force on the American Society for Nutrition, Institute of Food Technologists, and International Food Information Council. *American Journal of Clinical Nutrition*, 89, 477–484.

Hurley, J., & Liebman, B. (2015). Not milk? *Nutrition Action Healthletter*, 42(1), 13–15.

Jeukendrup, A. E., & Randell, R. (2011). Fat burners: Nutrition supplements that increase fat metabolism. *Obesity Reviews*, 12(10), 841–851.

Knize, M. G., & Felton, J. S. (2005). Formation and human risk of carcinogenic heterocyclic amines formed from natural precursors in meat. *Nutrition Reviews*, 63(5), 158–165.

Kyro, C., & Tjonneland, A. (2016). Whole grains and public health, *BMJ*, 2016, 353:i3046

Liebman, B. (2015). Are multivitamins a waste of money? Nutrition Action.com. Retrieved from https://www.nutritionaction.com/daily/dietary-supplements/are-multivitamins-a-waste-of-money/

Liebman, B. (2015). Bye bye beef? *Nutrition Action Healthletter*, 42(8), 3–7.

Liebman, B. (2017). What makes us eat too much. *Nutrition Action Healthletter*, 44(3), 3–6.

McGuire, M. T., Wing, R. R., Klem, M. L., Lang, W., & Hill, J. O. (1999). What predicts weight regain in a group of successful weight losers? *Journal of Consulting and Clinical Psychology*, 67(2), 177–185.

Miller, J. L. (2013). Iron deficiency anemia: A common and curable disease. Cold Spring Harbor Perspectives in Medicine. https://doi.org/10.1101/cshperspect.a011866

Montes, M. V., & Kravitz, L. (2011). Unraveling the stress-eating-obesity knot. *IDEA Fitness Journal*, 8(2), 45–50.

Ness-Abramof, R., & Apovian, C. M. (2008). Waist circumference measurement in clinical practice. *Nutrition in Clinical Practice*, 23(4), 397–404.

NIH, National Cancer Institute. Retrieved from https://www.cancer.gov

NWCR. (2017). NWCR Facts. National Weight Control Registry. Retrieved from http://www.nwcr.ws/

Overweight and Obesity. (2016). World Health Organization. Retrieved from http://www.who.int/mediacentre/factsheets/fs311/en/

Paoli, A., Marcolin, G., Zonin, F., et al. (2011). Exercising fasting or fed to enhance fat loss? Influence of food intake on respiratory ratio and excess postexercise oxygen consumption after a bout of endurance training. *International Journal of Sport Nutrition and Exercise Metabolism*, 21(1), 48–54.

Pasquali, R. (2012). The hypothalamic-pituitary-adrenal axis and sex hormones in chronic stress and obesity: Pathophysiological and clinical aspects. *Annals of the New York Academy of Sciences,* 1264(1), 20–35.s

Pietilainen, K. H., Saarni, S. E., Kaprio, J., et al. (2012). Does dieting make you fat? A twin study. *International Journal of Obesity*, 36, 456–464. https://doi.org/10.1038/ijo.2011.160

Romieu, I., Dossus, L, Barquera, S., et al. (2017). Energy balance and obesity: What are the main drivers? *Cancer Causes Control*, 28(3), 247–258.

Schmidt, L. A. (2014). New unsweetened truths about sugar. *JAMA Internal Medicine*, 174(4), 525–526.

Sifferlin, A. (2017). This diet may help you lose weight. *TIME*, June 5, 50–55.

Te Morenga, L. A., Howatson, A. J., Jones, R. M., et al. (2014). Dietary sugars and cardiometabolic risk: Systematic review and meta-analyses of randomized controlled trials of the effects on blood pressure and lipids. *American Journal of Clinical Nutrition*, 100:65–79.

Thom, E., Wadstein, J., & Gudmundsen, O. (2001). Conjugated linoleic acid reduces body fat in healthy exercising humans. *Journal of International Medical Research*, 29(5), 392–396.

Trepanowski, J. F., Kroeger, C. M., Barnosky, A., et al. (2017). Effect of alternate-day fasting on weight loss, weight maintenance, and cardioprotection among metabolically healthy obese adults: A randomized clinical trial. *JAMA Internal Medicine*, 177(7), 930–938.

U.S. Department of Health and Human Services and U.S. Department of Agriculture. 2015–2020 Dietary Guidelines for Americans, 8th ed., December 2015. Retrieved from http://health.gov/dietaryguidelines/2015/

Wang, Z., Heshka, S., Gallagher, D., et al. (2000). Resting energy expenditure-fat-free mass relationship: New insights provided by body composition modeling. *American Journal of Physiology. Endocrinology and Metabolism*, 279, E539–E545.

Weaver, A. M., & Kravitz, L. (2014). Understanding iron-deficiency anemia & sports anemia. *IDEA Fitness Journal*, 11(8), 16–19.

Wing, R. R., & Phelan, S. (2005). Long-term weight loss maintenance. *American Journal of Clinical Nutrition*, 82 (suppl), 222S–225S.

Yang, Q., Zhang, Z., Gregg, E. W., et al. (2014). Added sugar intake and cardiovascular diseases mortality among U.S. Adults. *JAMA Internal Medicine*, 174(4):516–524.

Zeratsky, K. (2015). Which spread is better for my heart—butter or margarine? Mayo Clinic. Retrievedfromhttp://www.mayoclinic.org/healthy-lifestyle/nutrition-and-healthy-eating/expert-answers/butter-vs-margarine/faq-20058152

INDEX

1.5 mile run test, 14

A

Abdomen, as skinfold site, 21
Abdominals, 116, 207
Abdominals, and chest stretches, 124
Abdominal strength and endurance test, 17
Abductors, 116
Absolute strength, 27
Accelerated biological aging, exercise and, 3
Achilles stretch and calf-stretch, 126
Active listening, 167
Active start, 72
Activity energy expenditure (AEE), 71, 135
Adductor Longus, 207
Adductors, 116
Adenosine triphosphate (ATP), 69–70
Adrenal cortex, 148
Adrenocorticotrophic hormone or ACTH, 148
Aerobic conditioning, 7, 190
Aerobic efficiency, 75, 190
Aerobic exercise, 75–80, 184
    energy and, 165
    injury and, 45
    jabs, 78
    jogging in place, 76
    jumping jacks, 79
    jump kicks, 80
    jump rope hops, 77
    lunge claps, 79
    metabolic syndrome and, 10
    power runs, 78
    reminders, 75
    side leg slides, 77
    step kicks, 76
    step knee hops, 76
    stride runs, 80
    training effects and, 185
    type 2 diabetes and, 12
Aerobic fitness, 24–26
    F.I.T. formula, 24
    heart rate, 24–25
    perceived exertion, 26
    talk test, 26
Aerobic kickboxing, 81
    safety guidelines, 81
Aerobic metabolism, 69
Aging and exercise, 205
Agonist, 30
Alcohol, 158–159, 173
    reasons for drinking, 158
    responsible drinking, 159
    women and drinking, 159
Alcohol continuum, 158–159
All-around crunch, 95
Alternative-day fasting, 182
American College of Sports Medicine (ACSM)
    cardiorespiratory fitness recommendations, 210
    flexibility exercise recommendations, 211
    neuromotor exercise recommendations, 210
    position on quantity and quality of exercise, 210–211
    resistance exercise recommendations, 211
American Heart Association logo and food, 173
Anabolic phase, 53
Anaerobic exercise, 69
Anaerobic metabolism, 69
Anatomic alignment mindful exercise program component, 128
Anatomical skinfold site, 21
Angina pectoris, 186
Ankle sprain, 45
Antagonist, 30
Anterior tibialis, 116
Antioxidants, 187
Anxiety, exercise and, 3
Aquatics, 82
Arm reaches, warm up, 74
Arteriosclerosis, 186
Ashtanga yoga, 128
Atherosclerosis, 186
Arthritis, 189

B

motivation for starting plan, 139
physical activity, 138–139
regaining weight, 139
strategies for successful weight loss maintenance, 138
Natural vitamins *vs.* manufactured, 178
Neck extensions and 360-degree head rolls, 41
alternative to, 41
Neck stretch, 122
Nicotine, 160
Nonalcoholic fatty liver disease, exercise and, 3
Non-dairy milk, 180
Nutrient, 52, 53, 142, 143, 144, 145
Nutrition, 53
nutrient timing, 53
Nutritional deficiency in U.S., 178
Nutrition bar, 179–180
Nutrition questions, 177–180
Nuts, 175

O

Obesity, 71, 133. *see also* Weight loss
disease and, 187
exercise and, 3
stress and, 147–148
Obliques, 207
Occupational wellness, 157
Opiates, 161
Opposing muscle groups, 31
Orange juice, 181
Osteoarthritis, exercise and, 3
Osteoporosis, 187, 188
exercise and, 3
Overfat *vs.* overweight, 174
Overload, 22
Overtraining, 42
Overweight, 153, 168, 174, 213

P

Pace of exercise, 185
Pain
avoiding, 31
exercise and, 3
Pain relief, and back, 48
Pectorals, 116, 207
Pelvic tilt, 48
Perceived exertion, 26

Peripheral artery disease, exercise and, 3
Peripheral heart action (PHA) training, 108–111
biomotor functional power exercises, 112–115
biomotor functional power workout, 116
vs. HIIT, 108–109
workouts, 110–111
Perspiration, 186
Physical activity and weight loss, ACSM position on, 153
Physical Activity Guidelines Advisory Committee Scientific Report 2018, 203
findings from, 203–205
summary, 205
Physical wellness, 157
Physiology, of workout, 69–70
Phytochemical, 178
Phytonutrient, 178
Pike push-ups, 93
Pilates, 129
Pituitary gland, 148
Plaque, 67, 173, 186, 189
The plow, 39
alternative to, 39
Polycystic ovary syndrome, exercise and, 3
Polyunsaturated fats, 10
Poor exercise technique, 42
Positive energy balance, 71
Posture
good *vs.* poor, 51
test for, 51
Power deltoid, 121
Power hamstring, 120
Power knee, 110, 111, 120, 121
Power lunges, 107, 120
Power row, 121
Power runs, 78, 120
Power side, 120
Power yoga, 128
Prediabetes, 189
Pre-exercise snack, 179
Prehydration, 50
Premature death, exercise and, 3
Pretzels, 180
Pre-workout stretching, 184
Problem solving, 166
Progression, 22
Prone prop, 50
variation of, 50